The Aesthetics of
Dedalus and Bloom

The Aesthetics
of Dedalus and Bloom

Marguerite Harkness

Lewisburg
Bucknell University Press
London and Toronto: Associated University Presses

© 1984 by Associated University Presses, Inc.

Associated University Presses
440 Forsgate Drive
Cranbury, N. J. 08512

Associated University Presses
25 Sicilian Avenue
London WC1A 2QH, England

Associated University Presses
2133 Royal Windsor Drive
Unit 1
Mississauga, Ontario
Canada L5J 1K5

Library of Congress Cataloging in Publication Data

Harkness, Marguerite.
 The aesthetics of Dedalus and Bloom.

  Bibliography: p.
  Includes index.
  1. Joyce, James, 1882–1941—Aesthetics. 2. Joyce,
James, 1882–1941—Characters. 3. Aesthetics in
literature. 4. Aestheticism (Literature) 5. Naturalism
in literature. I. Title.
PR6019.09Z575 1983   823′.912   82-45564
ISBN 0-8387-5050-8

Printed in the United States of America

For the Ironman:
"All must work, have to, together."

Contents

Acknowledgments

This book, like most, involves debts. For intellectual, psychic, and collegial support, I'd like to thank Mark Booth, Christine Gallant, Bryant Mangum, and Richard Priebe, all of Virginia Commonwealth University. My former chairman, M. Thomas Inge (now of Clemson University), encouraged me over the long haul to continue. Long over-due thanks go to the faculty of the English Department at SUNY Binghamton, especially John Hagan, John V. Hagopian, Robert Kroetsch, and Patricia Speyser—all early and important readers of my work.

One of the remarkable facts about established Joyceans is that many of them actively aid younger readers and writers. Zack Bowen (University of Delaware), Bernard Benstock (Tulsa University), and the reader for Bucknell University Press particularly lent not just encouragement but advice and help. Professor Bowen, in fact, saw the original work for this book in a dissertation years ago and has managed to sustain his interest and support. I owe him much.

During 1977–78, I participated in a Seminar for College Teachers sponsored by the National Endowment for the Humanities at the University of Pennsylvania, where I did some of the research for this book. To the National Endowment go thanks for financial support. But I also owe a debt of a more intellectual variety to David DeLaura, who directed the seminar, and to my fellow seminarians.

Finally, I wish to thank my husband, Boyd M. Berry, for copy editing, skeptical readings from a Miltonist, and necessary urgings not to despair of finishing.

Despite all this help, remaining errors of fact or judgment are purely my own.

The author gratefully acknowledges permission to reprint the following material.

From *Letters of James Joyce*. Volume I edited by Stuart Gilbert, copyright © 1957 by The Viking Press, Inc. Volumes II and III edited by Richard Ellmann, copyright © 1966 by F. Lionel Monro as Administrator of the Estate of James Joyce. Reprinted by permission of Viking Penguin, Inc. and Faber and Faber Ltd.

From *A Portrait of the Artist as a Young Man* by James Joyce, copyright © 1916 by B. W. Huebsch, renewed 1944 by Nora Joyce. Copyright © 1964 by the Estate of James Joyce. Reprinted by permission of Viking Penguin, Inc. and The Society of Authors (for the Estate of James Joyce).

From *Ulysses* by James Joyce, copyright © 1934 by the Modern Library, Inc., renewed 1946 by Nora Joseph Joyce. Reprinted by permission of The Bodley Head, Random House, Inc., and The Society of Authors (for the Estate of James Joyce).

From *Autobiography* by W. B. Yeats, copyright © 1916, 1935 by Macmillan Publishing Co., Inc., renewed 1944, 1963 by Bertha Georgie Yeats. Reprinted by permission of Macmillan Publishing Co., Inc. and Anne and Michael Yeats.

From *Collected Poems* by W. B. Yeats, copyright © 1924 by Macmillan Publishing Co., Inc., renewed 1952 by Bertha Georgie Yeats. Reprinted by permission of Macmillan Publishing Co., Inc. and Michael and Anne Yeats.

From *Essays and Introductions* by W. B. Yeats, copyright © Mrs. W. B. Yeats, 1961. Reprinted by permission of Macmillan Publishing Co., Inc. and Anne and Michael Yeats.

From *Mythologies* by W. B. Yeats, copyright © Mrs. W. B. Yeats, 1959. Reprinted by permission of Macmillan Publishing Co., Inc. and Anne and Michael Yeats.

From *Uncollected Prose of W. B. Yeats*. Volume I edited by John P. Frayne, copyright © 1970 by John P. Frayne and Michael Yeats. Volume II edited by John P. Frayne and Colton Johnson, copyright © 1975 by John P. Frayne, Colton Johnson, and Michael Yeats. Reprinted by permission of Macmillan, Ltd. of London and Basingstoke and Columbia University Press.

Abbreviations

P	*A Portrait of the Artist as a Young Man* (Joyce)
U	*Ulysses* (Joyce)
Letters	*Letters of James Joyce* (Joyce)
FW	*Finnegans Wake* (Joyce)
Autobiography	*Autobiography* (Yeats)
E&I	*Essays and Introductions* (Yeats)
Mythologies	*Mythologies* (Yeats)
MBK	*My Brother's Keeper* (Stanislaus Joyce)
DG	*The Picture of Dorian Gray* (Wilde)
M	*Marius the Epicurean* (Pater)
CW	*Critical Writings of James Joyce*

Introduction

A would-be Aesthete could, in the words of a Gilbert and Sullivan song, walk down Picadilly with a lily in his hand. More serious writers, faced with crumbling or changing institutions—religious, political, educational, familial—tried in the last half of the nineteenth century to justify their art, analyzing and asserting the values of literature. What forces or concerns prompted these justifications are too numerous to enter into here: one obvious cause was that Victorian culture exalted tangible progress and success so much that it seemed its society increasingly denigrated art as useless. These defenses or credos, however, differed from one artist to the next; in general, we can group the different and contradictory philosophies about art prominent in 1900 into two categories.

The young William Butler Yeats found alchemy attractive because it seemed to promise the "universal transmutation of all things into some divine and imperishable substance," an analogue to the "transmutation of life into art."[1] Oscar Wilde looked for art to provide a "momentary perfection" since it ignored the realistic tediousness and squalor of life.[2] These people, and many others with similar views, we have called "Aesthetes." A second group argued that art was important for its ability to improve the human condition. Émile Zola urged men to write experimental novels, novels that would help humanity "master certain phenomena of an intellectual and personal order." Novelists, in his view, would be "experimental moralists," working in a laboratory.[3] Closer to home, G. B. Shaw felt himself obliged to write plays that "should refine our sense of character and conduct, of justice and sympathy . . . making us intolerant of baseness, cruelty, injustice, and intellectual superficiality or vulgarity."[4] These people, and others with similar views, we have called "realists" or "naturalists." The debate implicit even when not direct between these groups formed part of the cultural milieu for an artist in 1900.

In 1900, James Joyce was eighteen years old; D. H. Lawrence was fifteen; Virginia Woolf was eighteen; Yeats was, in contrast, an ancient thirty-five. To come of age, as Joyce and many modernist writers did, during such a debate forced an artist to choose rather more consciously than earlier artists a mode and a purpose for art. Joyce's early aesthetic

11

notebooks, for example, indicated he felt that necessity. Possibly, Joyce was never entirely able to make an unambiguous choice, but he certainly deliberated. This is a study of how Joyce responded to those aesthetic alternatives particularly as those responses dramatically enter his work.

In simplest terms, most of this study is about Aestheticism and the attractions and limitations of Aestheticism as they were perceived by this one major modernist. It is almost a truism that Stephen Dedalus in *Portrait* sounds like the early Yeats, or like Walter Pater, or like a Pre-Raphaelite at times; it is also almost a critical truism that Joyce was affected by Aesthetes and symbolists. While Joyceans have long assumed, even pointed to particular passages as demonstrations of, Stephen's indebtedness to Aestheticism, no one has yet investigated in detail the extent of that indebtedness, Joyce's rebellion against it, or its coherence with the rest of the characterization of Stephen Dedalus. Critics such as Archie Loss, George Geckle, Robert M. Scotto, K. E. Robinson, and Harold I. Shapiro have pointed to specific passages and specific connections they see between Joyce's work and the Pre-Raphaelites, Yeats, Pater, the symbolists, or John Ruskin,[5] but the pervasiveness of these connections is, I believe, more crucial to our understanding of Joyce and his works than are specific echoes and references. That is, it is the *pattern* of connections that interests me here. To interpret that pattern, to suggest its significance more particularly and more broadly than, for instance, Richard Ellmann could in *Eminent Domain: Yeats among Wilde, Joyce, Pound, Eliot, and Auden*[6] is to discover not just biographical connections between Joyce and various aestheticians but Joyce's complex and ambiguous relationships to the aesthetic concerns prominently current in 1900. The significance of Aestheticism to Joyce lies not simply in the many references that stand as testimonials to his interest in it, but in the repeated set of images and words that are coherent, both with each other and with the rest of the character of Stephen Dedalus; these images and words and this character manifest particular and definable attitudes about art and life that Joyce associated with Aestheticism. Again, my point is not entirely new. Hélène Cixous and Dorothy Van Ghent have, for instance, discussed Stephen's penchant for ordering his world through images and words,[7] a tendency that we can associate with Aestheticism if we study it closely; neither critic, except in passing, connects that personality trait with the Aesthetes. Yet these connections can be shown to be pervasive, and, particularly when they become part of the authorial point of view as well, allow us to understand Joyce and his novels as he dramatized or gave "human form" to intellectual tendencies. That is, such a study places Joyce and his works firmly within his cultural context and demonstrates the human values Joyce associated with aesthetic theories.

Joyce used Aestheticism to characterize Stephen Dedalus. He used Stephen Dedalus to comment upon Aestheticism. To use Aestheticism to characterize Stephen, Joyce employed the words, images, and themes found in the writing of artists we call "Aesthete" or "symbolist" to describe Stephen, or placed those words in Stephen's mind to show how he tries to understand himself. Thus, for instance, when Stephen expresses his frustration over E. C.'s relationship to Father Moran, he thinks that she "would unveil her soul's shy nakedness" to the peasant priest rather than to him, "a priest of eternal imagination."[8] That phrase, that way of thinking about or denoting the artist, was, in 1900, associated with and prevalent in the thinking of Aesthetes such as Yeats, Wilde, and Swinburne. Joyce might assume that, while he was not directly quoting any particular writer, his audience would associate Stephen with a kind of artistry and with certain kinds of broadly held notions about the function of art. Even if that assumption proved untrue, the pervasiveness of the images marks an association in Joyce's mind.

At the same time, if Stephen Dedalus is, from Joyce's point of view, an Aesthete, then the kind of character he is suggests what Joyce thought about Aestheticism; Stephen's characterization gives us clues to Joyce's own attitudes about artistic method and to his own aesthetic allegiances. Even more important, Stephen's character dramatized the connections that Joyce saw between daily behavior and artistic theories. For Aestheticism is not the only means Joyce used to characterize Stephen; the novel is not simply one of ideas or simply about art. We know Stephen through many other fictional techniques: dialogue, plot, setting, etc. We know Stephen because he thinks of things other than art. For Joyce artistic choices are choices that cohere with other, nonaesthetic choices. Whatever it is that shapes a man or woman's behavior—in family, in politics, in society—also shapes his mode of behavior as an artist. Behavior as poet is part of and consonant with modes of behavior as a social being and an individual. Those nonartistic modes of behavior in Stephen Dedalus provide, of course, part of his characterization. Those aspects of his character, seemingly discrete from his artistry, comment upon his art. Thus, as a brief example, Stephen's inability to perceive women except as examples of certain stereotypes is coherent with the kind of art he espouses. If Stephen is represented as an Aesthete and if he sees women as stereotypes, Aestheticism was, in Joyce's view, similarly limited. This kind of coherence dramatizes Joyce's commentary upon art, making *Portrait* more than a novel of ideas.

Joyce presented his analysis of Aestheticism and naturalism in his novels through the words and images of his prose. This study, then, of necessity focuses on the words, images, and symbols used in the works of Joyce and others because it is through words, and words alone, that we learn or intuit Joyce's own attitudes. Because I am dealing with ideas implicit in the words used by Joyce and his contemporaries rather than just with the extractable ideas those words represent, much of my study is one of words which were crucial to Aestheticism; I follow the lead of Ruth Zabriskie Temple, who argued that symbolists may be most clearly identified by their choice of words.[9] To understand Joyce and his characters, it is essential to know as precisely as possible what terms such as *priest*, or *beauty*, or *transmutation* meant and suggested, and the contexts within which they commonly occurred at the beginning of the twentieth century.

Joyce dramatized the opposing artistic tendency, the tendency toward realism and naturalism, in the character of Leopold Bloom. Here again we understand that character largely through Bloom's and Joyce's use of certain groups of words, words that indicate particular modes of perception and particular values. While Aesthetes labeled artists as priests, naturalists used other terms. Zola thought of himself as a medical man, a doctor or scientist[10]; similarly, H. G. Wells valued the role of the scientist.[11] Shaw thought of himself as a scribe, a man charged with the responsibility of recording the life of his people, and he used that post to help save himself from the war madness of World War I.[12] Shaw's sermons were not priestly homilies; they were didactic analyses of his world. These people stressed the edifying nature of literature, the improving nature of it, its use as a way to solve the problems of life. So, too, does Bloom, the adman. Naturalistic terms and attitudes are comfortable to Bloom, who thinks about his world in scientific or pseudoscientific ways. While Stephen does not think that art should move the viewer to do anything (art that does, he tells Lynch in *Portrait*, is improper art), the advertiser and the naturalist—like Bloom—hoped their art would move men; thus, it is no accident that Bloom values art for its kinetic effect in *Ulysses* while Stephen espouses artistic stasis.

For Joyce, naturalism, like Aestheticism, is an artistic mode that coheres with other behavior, attitudes, and ideas. Bloom's attraction to socialism, his analysis of Ireland's political and economic plight, his perception of women are as different from Stephen's political philosophy and analyses and his views of women as naturalism is from Aestheticism. In the coherence between Bloom's nonartistic attitudes and his taste in art, Joyce dramatizes his response to another major artistic mode of his day.

Joyce is more precise and careful in his analysis of Aestheticism than of naturalism or realism because it is, for him, simultaneously the more attractive and more dangerous tendency. I suspect, but cannot prove in this study, that Aestheticism was, for most people we now call "the moderns," the more attractive tendency. Richard Ellmann tells us that "as Wilde prepared his own fall, he read . . . Yeats's story, 'The

Crucifixion of the Outcast,'" a story about the martyrdom of an artist
at the hands of monks.[13] When Joyce denied in a letter to his brother
any desire to be a martyr for his art, he at the same time revealed how
deeply he had internalized the views of the Aesthetes, who personally
and in their art saw the artist as martyr. Joyce's attraction, however, is
balanced by a sense of its limits—limits dramatically represented in the
fictional life of his characters. For Joyce, a kind of exorcism was necessary and part of that exorcism occurred as he created Stephen Dedalus,
called in *Ulysses* that "morbidminded esthete."[14]

Joyce's attraction to Aestheticism, and, I suspect, that of most of
the high moderns, is clear; it is not something that he simply "out-
grew." The passage of time and Joyce's own development did change
that attraction; the fact that he labeled his Aesthete artist a "young man"
in itself comments on the immaturity, from Joyce's point of view, of
such notions about art. In Joyce's canon, however, there is no parallel
portrait of the artist as a young man who is a realist or a naturalist. Nor
is there, ultimately, a serious artist who is a naturalist. Those facts
reflecting Joyce's ambivalent attraction to (and repulsion from) Aestheticism dictated the proportions of my book. While I want to investigate Joyce's response to realism and naturalism as well as his response to
Aestheticism, the latter response is stronger, more complex, and more
pervasive in Joyce's writing and life. Thus the reader will find that all
but two chapters in this study focus largely upon Aestheticism.

Notes

1. William Butler Yeats, *"Rosa Alchemica," Mythologies* (New York: The Macmillan Co.,
Collier Books, 1969), p. 267. Hereafter this collection will be cited parenthetically.

2. Oscar Wilde, "The Critic as Artist," *The Complete Works*, 12 vols. (Garden City, N.Y.:
Doubleday, Page & Co., 1923), 5:113. Hereafter Wilde will be cited parenthetically.

3. Émile Zola, *The Experimental Novel and Other Essays*, trans. Belle M. Sherman (New
York: Haskell House, 1964), p. 25.

4. George Bernard Shaw, "The Sanity of Art," in *Major Critical Essays* (London: Constable
and Co., 1932), p. 315.

5. Archie Loss, "The Pre-Raphaelite Woman, the Symbolist *Femme-Enfant*, and the Girl
with the Flowing Hair in the Earlier Work of James Joyce," *Journal of Modern Literature* 3
(1973): 3–23; George L. Geckle, "Stephen Dedalus and W. B. Yeats: The Making of the Villanelle," *Modern Fiction Studies* 15 (1969): 87–96; Robert M. Scotto, "'Visions' and 'Epiphanies':
Fictional Technique in Pater's *Marius* and Joyce's *Portrait*," *James Joyce Quarterly* 11 (1973): 41–
50; K. E. Robinson, "The Stream of Consciousness Technique and the Structure of Joyce's
Portrait," *James Joyce Quarterly* 9 (1971): 63–84; Harold I. Shapiro, "Ruskin and Joyce's *Portrait*," *James Joyce Quarterly* 14 (1977): 92–93.

6. Richard Ellmann, *Eminent Domain: Yeats among Wilde, Joyce, Pound, Eliot, and Auden*
(New York: Oxford University Press, 1965).

7. Hélène Cixous, *The Exile of James Joyce*, trans. Sally A. J. Purcell (New York: David
Lewis, 1972); Dorothy Van Ghent, *The English Novel* (New York: Rhinehart, 1953).

8. James Joyce, *A Portrait of the Artist as a Young Man* (New York: Viking Critical Edition,
1968), p. 221. Hereafter cited parenthetically *(P)*.

9. Ruth Zabriskie Temple, *The Critics Alchemy: A Study of the Introduction of French Symbolism into England* (New York: Twayne, 1953). See especially p. 14.

10. Zola, *The Experimental Novel.* Zola explores and uses this metaphor repeatedly.

11. Wells's concern for science is demonstrated repeatedly: his science fiction, the persona of *Tono-Bungay,* his correspondence with Henry James, and his desire to write of "problems of adjustment . . . dislocation . . . adjustment" (H. G. Wells, *Experiment in Autobiography: Discoveries and Conclusions of a Very Ordinary Brain [Since 1866]* [New York: The Macmillan Co., 1934], p. 410), all attest to this interest.

12. George Bernard Shaw, *Heartbreak House,* in *Collected Plays with their Prefaces* (London: The Bodley Head Ltd., 1972), 5:22–23.

13. Ellmann, *Eminent Domain,* pp. 3–4.

14. James Joyce, *Ulysses* (New York: Random House, 1961), p. 420. Hereafter cited parenthetically *(U).*

The Aesthetics
of Dedalus and Bloom

1

The Artist as a Young Man

"Once upon a time and a very good time it was there was a moocow." (*A Portrait*, 8)

"Old father, old artificer, stand me now and ever in good stead." (*A Portrait*, 253)

"The wisest, at least among 'the children of this world,' [spend their life] in art and song." (Pater, "Conclusion" to *The Renaissance*)

"Lying, the telling of beautiful untrue things, is the proper aim of Art." (Wilde, "The Decay of Lying")

A Portrait of the Artist is a novel about lying.

Perhaps, to put it more genteelly, it is novel about the ways in which we create fictions and the motives for our fictions. Lying or making fictions is, according to Vivian in Oscar Wilde's "The Decay of Lying," "the telling of beautiful untrue things, . . . the proper aim of Art." Life, which the realists find "crude" and leave "raw" is not attractive or congenial to human beings (5: 17). The artist must not work from nature at all, in his view, but rather cultivate and learn the fine art of lying, of making beautiful things. "The object of Art," asserts Vivian, "is not simple truth but complex beauty" (5: 28). In Wilde's sense of the word *lying*, then, *A Portrait* is about the cultivation of the faculty in a young man—that is, it is about Stephen's attempts to lie. His lies mark him as an artist.

In another sense, lying marks Stephen as simply human, for the making of lies is a part of the process by which we all shape our lives into sense. Structure and pattern, at least from the extreme point of view of Walter Pater and various philosophers contemporary to Joyce, exist only in the mind. Pater even claimed that "that clear, perpetual outline of face and limb [which we see] is but an image of ours, under which we group" our impressions and that "when reflexion begins to play upon those [external] objects they are dissipated under its influence."[1] Again Vivian in "The Decay of Lying" makes much the same point: "If . . . we regard Nature as the collection of phenomena external to man, people

19

only discover in her what they bring to her. She has no suggestions of her own." As an example, he asserts that Wordsworth "found in stones the sermons he had already hidden there" (5: 26). As Pater and Wilde indicate, we as well as the artist attribute to random and perhaps meaningless events and impressions the meanings we crave or that we have produced previously or internally. These meanings, thus, are fictions, or artifice, or art. As Stephen Dedalus creates his fictions and makes his lies, Joyce demonstrates the limits of their value. The process here is indebted to Aestheticism while Joyce presents it to demonstrate some of the limits of the thinking and belief of Aesthetes.

I wish to take two rather commonly held points about *A Portrait*—that the narrative point of view is Stephen's and that the structure of the novel centers on Stephen's adopting and rejecting of various ways of ordering, or attributing sense to, his world—and demonstrate what these common perceptions have to do with Aestheticism. When juxtaposed to the statements, beliefs, and practices of Walter Pater and Oscar Wilde, these fictional techniques place Joyce in a particular moment in literary history and with a particular group of writers, the Aesthetes.

The fact that *A Portrait* is narrated through the perceptions of Stephen Dedalus, a critical commonplace, locates Joyce's narrative technique in its historical context and indicates Joyce's indebtedness to Aestheticism. In 1868 Pater had written that "experience, already reduced to a group of impressions, is ringed round for each one of us by the thick wall of personality through which no real voice has ever pierced on its way to us, or from us to that which we can only conjecture to be without. Every one of those impressions is the impression of the individual in his isolation, each mind keeping as a solitary prisoner in its own dream of a world" (p. 237). This kind of awareness of relative or unique perception led writers to adopt specialized narrative points of view—or windows on the world, as Henry James had called them. True, Pater's belief was not limited to literary artists—but such a view was clearly aligned with or essential to the Aesthetes' theories of art. The speakers in Wilde's dialogues claimed that to see an individual soul's activities was, finally, the fascination of literature; indeed, Wilde's decision to write dialogues in which we cannot with certainty identify his personal attitudes indicates how seriously and intuitively he took Pater's assertions. If there is no discernible truth out there, then the impressions of the individuals in the dialogues are, simultaneously and irrelevantly, both true and false; a dialogue generically allows the author to avoid asserting unambiguously any particular idea. Wilde's choice of genre was influenced or affected not just by his particular personality, not just by Pater's assertions, but also by a commonly held emotional and intellectual attitude that we know only specific impressions of specific minds.

Pater claimed that we see through a ring of personality in which each of us is imprisoned. Because each individual is isolated, we know people only through the impressions we "read" of their characters; by extension, a fictional character, like a human being, knows the world only through his unique impressions. To know anyone best is to understand the impressions he or she receives from the world. So, for Joyce to adopt a narrative point of view that is filtered through the mind of a character, as he does in some of the stories of *Dubliners* and in *A Portrait*, was to recognize and act upon the insight of Pater's and James's and Wilde's assertions and behavior. I am not concerned here with "proving" that Joyce consciously chose such a fictional technique because of the writing of these men; I am concerned that the choice was conditioned by a particular cultural moment. Joyce, by moving the narration into Stephen's head, by excluding what Stephen cannot or does not know, makes artistic form out of one major assumption of Aestheticism and of modernism. To describe a young artist who would come to maturity at the beginning of the modernist period—and in the middle of explicit and implicit critical debate about literature—that narrative point of view is appropriate, particularly if that artist is to be an Aesthete.

One of the crucial documents that influenced the English Aesthetes was Pater's "Conclusion" to *The Renaissance,* the text from which I have been quoting. Pater moves there from a consideration of contemporary science that has portrayed the external world as just a group of impressions affected and distorted by personality and constantly in flux (or so he saw the result of scientific discoveries), to the image of a whirlpool and the flame of life (images that are destructive), to the isolation of the individual, to his own solution, which, like Stephen's, is to turn to art: "the wisest, at least among 'the children of this world' [spend their brief interval or life] in art and song" (p. 238). Stephen moves, in *A Portrait*, from secure innocence to knowledge, and that knowledge, like the knowledge of scientific discoveries, creates a sense of confusion, isolation, and terror. Art provides, from Stephen's point of view, a way of alleviating his unhappiness. That is, Joyce presents a human version with emotional, intellectual, and material motivations of that intellectualized movement from terror and isolation to art which Pater had presented. And Joyce presents it in a narrative point of view that affirms as well as casts doubt upon Pater's solution.

Although we can cite many passages from *A Portrait* that indicate Stephen's particular and limited point of view, I want here to discuss only two well-recognized ones of that type,[2] both occurring at the end of chapter 4. There Stephen determines that he is destined to be an artist and he sees a girl who seems to confirm that vocation. In these passages the narrative point of view is most clearly allied to Aestheticism. Although my interpretations are not new, I must digress into well-ploughed critical fields before I can return to set this analysis in its proper cultural context.

The lyrical impulses of these passages at the end of chapter 4 initially obscure what is happening because the emotion-laden scene contains Stephen's impressions of and responses to the world. It is Stephen, not Joyce, who verbally transmutes one rather skinny girl into an angel, the envoy from the gates of life.

> A girl stood before him in midstream, alone and still, gazing out to sea. She *seemed* like one whom magic had changed into the likeness of a strange and beautiful seabird. Her long slender bare legs were delicate as a crane's and pure save where an emerald trail of seaweed had fashioned itself as a sign upon the flesh. Her thighs, fuller and softhued as ivory, were bared almost to the hips. . . . Her bosom was as a bird's soft and slight, slight and soft as the breast of some darkplumaged dove. [*P*, 171, italics mine]

This girl, who seemed changed by magic in the first perception, and who is slightly skinny with crane's legs (an image that reverberates negatively), becomes for Stephen, a conscious temptress:

> *Her eyes had called him and his soul had leaped at the call.* To live, to *err*, to *fall*, to triumph. . . . A wild angel had appeared to him . . . to throw open . . . the gates of all the ways of error and glory. [*P*, 172, italics mine]

Stephen sees in this girl a woman that he wishes to see and that his mind has already "created." When he writes his villanelle, ostensibly addressed to E.C., in chapter 5, he transfers the image that he "saw" on the beach to E.C., the temptress of his villanelle. In that poem, E.C. "hold[s] our longing gaze/With languorous look and lavish limb!" (*P*, 223). That is, the poem echoes the description of the beach girl. This girl on the beach who holds his gaze "long, long" has "thighs, fuller and softhued as ivory." But Stephen's perception is at least suspect even as we read the end of chapter 4. The narration reveals that she is a young girl, not an angel, and she does not call to him with her eyes. Just before Stephen responds to her as though to a temptress, he describes her eyes: "Her eyes turned to him in quiet sufferance of his gaze. . . . Long, long she suffered his gaze and then quietly withdrew her eyes from his" (*P*, 171). In less than one page of text she has been changed from a creature who "suffers" his gaze and withdraws her eyes to one whose "eyes had called him and his soul had leaped at the call" (*P*, 172). Even here, at the climactic moment of Stephen's young life, his vision and perception are inaccurate—or "artistic"; they are "beautiful untrue things." He changes or alters the quality and the facts of his experience so that the girl confirms his notion of his destiny to be the artificer, the Daedalus. So much is critical commonplace.

Pater might say at least two different things about such a passage. First, as he had argued in the "Conclusion," impressions are "unstable, flickering, inconsistent" and "extinguished with our consciousness of them"; the girl does not exist separate from Stephen's impressions; that since impressions are constantly created and dissolved as they are in this passage, Stephen's final impression is the only truth he can know. Second, we have here two different impressions of the world at work— Joyce's and Stephen's—or perhaps three impressions—Joyce's and Stephen's and the reader's. Or perhaps more: perhaps we have Stephen's immediate and then revised impressions. While the narrative accurately records a dramatic example of Pater's analysis of the human mind, it also undercuts that analysis by allowing the reader to perceive the inaccuracies of Stephen's vision. He saw first a girl, then a magical figure, then an angel of life—and that is what the narrative records. Vivian would say that Stephen discovers this "temptress" because he has brought her to the beach. Joyce presents a young girl standing in the water and a young man transmuting her, through his shifting impressions, into the "wild angel" who calls to him. This discrepancy provides part of our understanding of Stephen and a clue to Joyce's relationship to Aestheticism.

In the same scene, we are given another example of the limited and artistic perception of an individual. Just before Stephen sees the girl, he believes that his soul has taken flight; he verbally transforms himself into the Daedalian figure of the artist and art object: "a hawklike man flying sunward . . . , a prophecy of the end he had been born to serve . . . , a symbol of the artist forging anew in his workshop" (*P*, 169). In counterpoint to his perception, however, some of his friends yell:

> —One! Two! . . . Look out!
> —O, cripes, I'm drownded!
> . . . .
> —Stephaneforos! [*P*, 169]

Stephen's mind, and hence the narrative of the novel, make no response to the yells. Yet, as Hugh Kenner pointed out, the boys' yells are ironically appropriate and recall the less triumphant aspects of the myth of Daedalus.[3] Icarus, the son, drowns himself because he has flown, out of pride, too close to the sun. Stephen does not attribute any significance to the boys' yells, yet by juxtaposition and because we know more than he does, we see the ironic detachment of Joyce from Stephen in the passage. We receive an impression that is not quite the same as the impression that Stephen receives. The question "Is Stephen a Daedalus or an Icarus?" appears again at the end of the novel when Stephen calls upon Daedalus as "old father" (*P*, 253). Stephen's mind, a "solitary prisoner in its own dream of a world," in Pater's words, selects the events and provides the images or impressions, the explicit interpretations and the explicit moral judgments of the events and individuals in the novel. He thus fulfills Pater's implied prophecy; art has become the idiosyncratic ordering and perceiving of the external world. "No real voice . . . pierced through" to Stephen, or as he says in chapter 2, "Nothing moved him or spoke to him from the real world unless he heard in it an echo of the infuriated cries within him" (*P*, 92). Stephen becomes an artist, a maker of lies, in part because he does not hear any "real voice" from the "real world." Yet Joyce uses this Aesthetic sense of individual perception in part to indicate its limits; we are presented with a reality external to Stephen that is meaningful.

Stephen becomes an artist in response to a series of threatening events and experiences that he cannot control. As the external factors of his life increasingly threaten to drown him—the family's poverty, the terrors of the Church, the voices that would destroy his youth and freedom—Stephen increasingly turns to art, the artificial shaping of life, to escape the terrors and to live more fully as Pater had urged his readers to do. In chapter 2, prayer and the insistent rhythms of telegraph poles quiet an alarm he feels on a train going to Cork; in the same chapter Shelley's "To the Moon" with its alternation of moods alleviates his grieving; in chapter 4 the vision of the girl helps to move him to artistry—becoming the controlling God of an art work.

That comment brings me to my second point. Almost all critics see Stephen moving from one way of structuring the world—with its rules and values—to another as *A Portrait* moves from one chapter to the next. Stephen moves to art and artistry in response to threat, most obviously the threats of disorder and chaos, the same threats that inspired Pater. Lies, fictional or real, are ways of ordering the universe, constructing the world in which we live, or controlling the chaos we perceive in the world. We each wish to live in a beautiful one; we each think that we want to create our own. Stephen adopts and rejects a series of lies, or fictional constructs of the world, as he moves toward his vocation. The first lie or order is created by his family and comes to him prefabricated—that is, he does not participate in the construction; to a large extent, that world is given to him by the liar—the storytelling father—whose words open the novel. The order is relatively simple: to be good he must believe in Parnell and Irish nationalism, he must be a good Catholic, he must "never . . . peach on a fellow," never "speak with the rough boys in the college" (*P*, 9). At school, he needs to pay attention to the bells, lessons, and prayers that order and shape experience into a beautiful, stable lie. Stephen begins to participate in the shaping as he controls the noise of the dining hall by closing and opening the flaps of his ears to lessen an attack of disease, that is, as he attempts to make his "lie" more beautiful, because more his own. He mentally orders the boys by their different ways of walking (*P*, 13).

Stephen orders his world through systems of hierarchy as he does in his geography book:

> *Stephen Dedalus*
> *Class of Elements*
> *Clongowes Wood College*
> *Sallins*
> *County Kildare*
> *Ireland*
> *Europe*
> *The World*
> *The Universe*
>
> [*P*, 15]

But the ordering process is really rather simple; whether he creates this original order or others do, there is little conflict. The hierarchy, artificial as it may be, is a satisfying lie: it places Stephen at the head of the universe, it makes sense out of the various scholastic and civil authorities that he is aware of.

But the lie, the pattern of order, is threatened by Parnell's disgrace and adultery, which drive a wedge between two of the certainties of Stephen's early life: Irish nationalism and Irish Catholicism. When, over Christmas dinner, that conflict becomes overt, the child's world of security and peace is disrupted; the cause is political and religious; Stephen's rejection of politics in the last chapter of the novel has its roots in this disruption. He thinks: "Who was right then?" (*P*, 35) and raises his "terrorstricken face" to see "that his father's eyes were full of tears" (*P*, 39). Faced with the failure of one apparently secure world to remain secure, Stephen turns to his school for an ordered universe.

Father Conmee is the pinnacle of the structure of Clongowes. When Stephen is unfairly punished, he appeals to Conmee, who sits with a "skull on the desk and a strange solemn smell in the room" (*P*, 56), dispensing justice and mercy, a lie that satisfies and may even be relatively true. And Stephen gets justice. Yet Stephen's sense of order is destroyed in chapter 2 when he discovers that Father Conmee has made a joke of his appeal (*P*, 72); furthermore, the family order, recently disrupted by a forced move, is not available to Stephen: "These changes in what he had deemed unchangeable were so many slight shocks to his boyish conception of the world" (*P*, 64). The disorder of the world surrounding him intensifies the insecurities and anxieties felt by most young boys; through knowledge, Stephen comes to confusion. He internalizes the problems and looks for a solution through transfiguration:

> He wanted to meet in the real world the unsubstantial image which his soul so constantly beheld. . . . They would meet quietly. . . . and in that

moment of supreme tenderness he would be transfigured. He would fade
into something impalpable under her eyes and then in a moment, he
would be transfigured. [*P*, 65]

Stephen begins, in response to external and internal conflicts, to use the
words and metaphors that were associated with the Aesthetes-
symbolists: "In a moment, he would be transfigured." Stephen wishes
to meet the female his soul imagines, to undergo a mystical experience,
and to emerge a new being, as he thinks he does in chapter 4. There the
vision approves and confirms the creation of Stephen's new soul adum-
brated in chapter 2.

In this early chapter, as Stephen attempts to find a new and more
appropriate order for his world, he accompanies his father to Cork to
auction the family's remaining property. During that trip, he meditates
upon "his monstrous way of life," which removes him "beyond the
limits of reality," and makes him incapable of responding to "earthly or
human appeal" (*P*, 92). That inability involves a real loss of identity and
separation from the father. In an attempt to reestablish himself he repeats:

  —I am Stephen Dedalus. I am walking beside my father whose name
  is Simon Dedalus. We are in Cork, in Ireland. Cork is a city. [*P*, 92]

Stephen attempts frantically to reestablish the order of reality that
unified him with his family. He uses his prize money to "build a break-
water of order and elegance against the sordid tide of life without him,"
by lending money to the family and establishing a common bank, but he
is doomed to failure: it is "useless" (*P*, 98).

Similarly, Stephen seeks order in romantic literature only to discover that Mercedes cannot satisfy "the wasting fires of lust" (*P*, 99). A
whore can. The initial visit to the whore reflects Stephen's images of the
soul going out for a mystical experience. "He was in another world,"
with "yellow gasflames . . . burning as if before an altar" and people are,
there, "arrayed as for some rite" (*P*, 100). The whore becomes part of
his idealized figure of the woman; her room reflects, almost artistically,
her profession: life as Stephen perceives it is shaped as rite. "Her room
was warm and lightsome. A huge doll sat with her legs apart in the
copious easychair beside the bed" (*P*, 100).

The whore does provide one of Stephen's necessities: release from
sexual frustration. The orgasmic ecstasy of sex is confused by Stephen
with the expected transfiguration. But the ordering or shaping Stephen
enacts through this visit and subsequent ones doesn't create for him the
satisfying whole that was lost when he lost the once perfect security in
family and school. The result of succumbing to the appetites, and allowing his appetites to shape his experience, is clear immediately in the next

chapter. Stephen's soul appears to him to have become as bestial as his mind and body, and that bestiality causes Stephen to reject this means of structuring the world. Instead of his mind determining his actions, his body does: "He felt his belly crave for its food. . . . Stuff it into you, his belly counselled him" (*P*, 102). The images of the stew with its "fat mutton pieces to be ladled out in thick peppered flourfattened sauce" (*P*, 102) adumbrate Stephen's vision of his soul; in the "greasestrewn plates" he sees his soul "fattening and congealing into a gross grease, plunging ever deeper in its dull fear into a sombre threatening dusk" (*P*, 111) like the dusk of the first paragraph of the chapter. "From the evil seed of lust all other deadly sins had sprung forth" (*P*, 106). Stephen is ready for a retreat. He judges himself with his choice of words; he recognizes one of his prior mental constructs as a lie. Thus the ordering of experience and the world according to the demands of the appetites gives way to the ordering of the world through the rites and rituals of the Church, as Stephen moves to, or adopts, another possible order, another potential life. He is, again, transposed into "Another life!" (*P*, 146).

But, again in chapter 4, as in chapters 2 and 3, events destroy the pattern of order Stephen has created for his life. He develops a static, sterile, mercantile image of a "great cash register" recording the value of his prayers and acts of piety in heaven; that image adumbrates the mirthless, inhuman qualities of the director and the Jesuit order, the qualities that cause Stephen to reject the order. We see the signals of rejection in the Church's inability to produce what Pater had called passion. The "love and hate pronounced solemnly on the stage and in the pulpit" mean nothing to him (*P*, 149). "A brief iniquitous lust" is the only love he feels; indifference the only hate. Order, and an apparently artistic order, prevails: "He saw the whole world forming one vast symmetrical expression of God's power and love" (*P*, 149). Yet the Church's order doesn't "merge his life in the common tide of other lives" (*P*, 151); neither the unity with family and school lost in chapter 2 nor the physical unity with a woman lost in chapter 3 is replaced.

In rejecting the priesthood Stephen recognizes the limitations of the order he has adopted, and immediately he asserts that he will fall. Each time that he has accepted an order of his own making, he has "seen" a woman; thus, Stephen has accepted the whore as the vision of his soul's transfiguration; he has then accepted his own fiction of Emma and later the Virgin Mary or the Virgin of the canticles as interceding in heaven for him. In each case, Stephen has been convinced that he has discovered his destiny. The rejection of the appeal to the priesthood is, then, a rejection of another false vision of his soul. The parental ordering of the universe had failed to explain satisfactorily the political and moral controversy that impinged upon him; the school's ordering had denied him justice; the appetites' ordering had denied his brain and spirit. Finally, the Church's ordering denies something that Stephen cannot or will not reject. None of these lies is beautiful; none produces genuine passion. As he walks out of the office of the director, he hears music, smiles and looks at the priest's face, "seeing in it a mirthless reflection of the sunken day" and against the "grave and ordered and passionless life" (*P*, 160) offered, "some instinct . . . armed him against acquiescence" (*P*, 161). His pride, his uniqueness, and even his humanity deny the call.

Thus it is that having rejected family, politics, the appetites, and religion as ways of ordering his world, Stephen comes to art. Art, he believes, allows him to use and create whatever in his life is important and to owe no allegiance to anyone or anything; it will fill his life with genuine passion. The vision of his soul that he believes will remove doubt, timidity, and insecurity appears to him on the beach. He begins to embrace art and aesthetics as the ordering principles of his life. The religious images through which Stephen has "seen" life and found meaning in his life do not disappear; the images remain but their meanings are no longer specifically or exclusively religious. The images acquire artistic import. Because Stephen's "thick wall of personality," that prison within which Pater believed we all live, perceives through those windows, the images remain even though their meanings alter radically. Each chapter of his development suggests that Stephen has achieved his "final solution"; each shows that he hasn't. Therefore each chapter presents us with information that foreshadows and makes inevitable Stephen's ultimate decision to become the creator-artist-manipulator-God. Stephen is reborn at the end of chapter 4 just as he was at the end of chapter 3; he enters a new world of life as he did at the end of chapter 2; he feels triumph over his enemies as he felt at the end of chapter 1. All the prior signals of change and triumph are repeated; that the signals remain constant forms an ironic commentary on his notion of destiny. Just as Stephen had, literally and rigidly, codified his religious life, so in chapter 5 his personality demands that art be rationalized, explained, codified—a process that spawns his esthetic discussions in chapter 5 and leads to his exile.

This way of seeing the structure of *A Portrait* is not new. My point here is that that structure, too, has its analogues in Aestheticism. Oscar Wilde claimed that art was the telling of beautiful untrue things that made life better; Pater's clear implication in the "Conclusion" to *The Renaissance* was that all our orderings of the world are but our impressions of the world—that they originate within us, not with some external truth. The plot of *A Portrait* parallels and dramatizes the argument of Pater's "Conclusion." Stephen's lying, his constructing of order within which to live, is thus part of the Aesthetic tradition that interests me in this study.

That the narrative point of view, the structure, and the themes of the novel simultaneously suggest and deny the relativity of truth and the ideas and behavior of Pater, Wilde, the young Yeats, Symons—the Aesthetes and their progenitors—becomes obvious only when we look in detail at the word choice and metaphors in the novel and at the similarities between this novel and other tales of young artists available to Joyce. Joyce traces the steps through which Stephen constructs the mythic figure of the artist; he details Stephen's creation of symbols from words and images. Imitating his artistic task, Stephen and Joyce transmute their lives into art—the novel—but they show us rudimentary, then increasingly sophisticated acts of transmutation within the novel. Eventually, Stephen uses art to change, even usurp life. Stephen's esthetic theory forms his own rationale for the novel. At each stage, in each of these areas, Joyce uses material from earlier writers as one means of characterizing Stephen and his ideas. At each stage, in each of these areas, Joyce dramatizes the human motives that underlie apparently artistic choice, commenting indirectly on intellectual discussions of art and artists.

Notes

1. Walter Pater, "Conclusion," *Studies in the History of the Renaissance* (London: Macmillan and Co., 1910), p. 236. Hereafter cited parenthetically.

2. See James Naremore's "Style as Meaning in *A Portrait of the Artist*," *James Joyce Quarterly* 4 (1967): 331–42, for a discussion of the double vision of the narrative and its significance.

3. Hugh Kenner, *Dublin's Joyce* (Bloomington, Ind.: Indiana University Press, 1956), pp. 31–32.

2

Priest of Eternal Imagination

Joyce constructs a figure of the artist in *A Portrait* that typifies the Aesthetic artist of the late nineteenth century. Early in the novel Stephen announces his allegiances, although these may not be immediately clear. Stephen remembers a traumatic conversation that centered on writers. He was asked "who is the greatest writer," and replied that Newman was the greatest prose writer and "Byron, of course," the best poet (*P*, 80–81). Just as revealing is Stephen's response to the name Tennyson, that symbol of high Victorian poetry and morality. "— Tennyson a poet! Why, he's only a rhymester!" (*P*, 80). Whatever a reader today might think of Tennyson, here, too, Stephen reveals his aesthetic heritage. By 1900, Tennyson's reputation was beginning to decline, especially among critics who allied themselves with symbolism and decadence. For instance, Yeats quietly demonstrates one objection to the laureate in "The Symbolism of Poetry":

> If people were to accept the theory that poetry moves us because of its symbolism, what change should one look for in the manner of our poetry? A return to the way of our fathers, a casting out of descriptions of nature for the sake of nature, of the moral law for the sake of the moral law, a casting out of all anecdotes and of that brooding over scientific opinion that so often extinguished the central flame in Tennyson.[1]

Just as critical is the term Stephen uses to describe Tennyson, for those who still defended the poet were, more and more, defending him as a craftsman and not defending his insight into the emotional truths and mysteries of people and life. Those who attacked Tennyson for making compromises with mid-Victorian prosperity, and with his audience, and with his position as the official court poet still granted him technical competence (a "rhymester"), but refused him the accolades of the poet.

Catherine Stevenson has suggested that the most obvious reference to Tennyson's poems in *A Portrait* occurs while Stephen, in the infirmary at Clongowes, dreams or hallucinates about Parnell's death. "Morte d'Arthur" and "The Passing of Arthur" from the *Idylls,* like

Stephen's description of the death of Parnell, depict the passing of an age in the person of a beloved hero. Stephen's and Simon's "uncrowned king" and Bedivere's crowned king "perish by this people" which they "made" ("Morte d'Arthur," 1. 73).[2] Betrayed by the people they wished to serve, both kings die and with them passes the ideal world that might have been. For Stephen, the betrayal and passing of Parnell lead directly to the violent argument at Christmas dinner that disrupts his own secure world.[3] The atmosphere, the mournful female, the funeral barge, the failure of an ideal social order, the death of the "proper" king: all these elements link Stephen's dream vision with the visionary experience of Tennyson's poem. One point to notice is that Tennyson's poetry is referred to only before Stephen finds it necessary to break with his nation and his family's politics. In this dream, he reconstructs a national and family unity already shattered: Dante, who has already rejected Parnell (*P,* 16), is reconverted to his service and walks mournfully clad in his color as well as Michael Davitt's. Tennyson and Arthur stand at a pivotal point in Stephen's development—at the last point of security within the ordered world bequeathed to him by his culture. Tennyson, the Victorian poet, thus is rejected because, in part, Stephen finds his world, like Arthur's and Parnell's, impossible.

In miniature, this reference does what most of the references to nineteenth-century aesthetics do: Stephen rejects Tennyson, just as the Aesthetes and symbolists do, but Joyce gives us personal and hence human motivations for his doing so. Stephen rejects Tennyson because he stands for a world that is crumbling and impossible and yet hypocritically pretending that nothing has changed. Modernists rejected all things Victorian for much the same motives.

Byron, in contrast, is Stephen's nominee for best poet precisely because Byron represents the isolated, rejected poet. He fits the archetype of the exiled poet, hounded and misunderstood by the philistines with whom Tennyson had compromised. Byron and the myth of Byron attracted Aesthetes who felt rejected by the society they scorned; he was seen as a precursor. Joyce's own favorite poet, at a parallel age, was Shelley, according to Stanislaus Joyce.[4] Joyce selects and changes his own experience here, substituting a poet less acceptable to Victorian morality—hence, more heroic, less conventional, more "immoral." Stephen's other favorite, Newman, is similarly indicative of his values. Although Newman was a safe and approved choice for a Catholic schoolboy, he also had an association with writers now coupled with Aestheticism.[5] Newman was not favored by the symbolists and Aesthetes as much as Pater was; yet as a stylist, not as a theologian, Newman was respected by symbolists and decadents, and received from that unwilling ally of the movement, Arnold, the praise Stephen accords him. Newman's "Ilative sense" parallels the individualistic and relativistic theories of perception crucial to the poets of the 1890s.

Thus, early in the book and early in Stephen's development, Joyce places Stephen with a particular variety of artists, even though he does it so briefly and indirectly that we may not notice. Later in the novel, Stephen moves more forcefully toward the concepts of the artist that were current in symbolist and decadent aesthetics.

Stephen sees the artist as priest; he belongs to what Beckson has called the "religion of art."[6] To be consistent, therefore, Stephen must fashion his perception of the artist just as Yeats, Arnold, Symons, and the Pre-Raphaelites had done, almost equating the artist with the priest. Other concerns or elements of the artist present in the tradition appeal to Stephen too, most of which are corollaries of the priesthood of art. For instance, Stephen's concern for words is analogous to the ceremonies of the priesthood in which the precise words create Christ on the altar. Similarly, the division Stephen and his predecessors make between this world—mundane and realistic—and the world of art—beautiful, full of essences and truths—derives from concepts of the priesthood and religion, in which the devotee relinquishes the temporal world for a finer world, a heaven of beauty, essence, truth, salvation. The devaluation of the temporal world occurs in both the religious symbol system and in the artistic symbol system. Hence Stephen is derivative in two senses: first, his concepts of the artist derive from those present in the culture around 1900 and, second, those concepts themselves derive from a Victorian perception of medieval priesthood.

Like the priest, the artist must feel that his destiny is to be a chosen representative of an eternal form, he must undergo a process of recognition and conversion to his vocation, and he must withdraw from the pettiness of earthly pursuits into the palace or temple of art. Beyond those analogous patterns, Stephen's artist, like the dedicated priest, must forswear all that is desirable in this world and run the risk of martyrdom. In return, the artist earns the right to create and to express himself. Just as the priest accepts a new family as he joins the order—in the Catholic Church he may even reckon his age by entry date—so Stephen in constructing his artist figure accepts or fashions a new father figure, analogous perhaps to God; even the Daedalus-father, thus, is a derivative or corollary of the metaphor of the priest.

Stephen's metaphor of the artist-priest comes from a long tradition, a tradition intensified and given respectability in England by Matthew Arnold. For Arnold, the deterioration of the Christian faith left man without a pattern of belief and stability; for him, poetry and the poet were the only available substitutes for religion and priest.[7] For a Stephen Dedalus, however, this idea would probably come from compatriots, W. B. Yeats and Oscar Wilde, as well as from Arthur Symons, the prophet of symbolism. Oscar Wilde, for instance, used a cliché when he spoke of Keats as "a Priest of Beauty slain before his time."[8] Similarly, Symons spoke of Mallarmé as a "priest," and in the introduction to *The*

Symbolist Movement, he is as clear about the analogy as Yeats is. Literature—symbolism—"becomes itself a kind of religion, with all the duties and responsibilities of the sacred ritual."⁹ Yeats, in several essays, stresses this new role for the artist. In "The Symbolism of Poetry," he asks if literature can create the "new sacred book" and hold men's heartstrings again, "without becoming the garment of religion as in old times?" (*E & I,* 162–63). In "The Happiest of Poets," he commends William Morris as a priest: "He knew clearly what he was doing towards the end, for he lived at a time when poets and artists have begun again to carry the burdens that priests and theologians took from them angrily some few hundred years ago" (*E & I,* 64). He reiterates the message in "The Autumn of the Body": "The arts are, I believe, about to take upon their shoulders the burdens that have fallen from the shoulders of priests, and to lead us back upon our journey by filling our thoughts with the essences of things" (*E & I,* 193). In "The Theatre," Yeats claims that artists will become "this priesthood" spreading "their religion everywhere" (*E & I,* 168). In short, Yeats shared Stephen's amalgamation of the artist's and priest's roles and ultimately saw the artist's role as more sacred.

The combination of Stephen's humility, "to try slowly and humbly and constantly to express . . . an image of the beauty" (*P,* 207), and his arrogance, his refusal to serve and his equation of himself with Christ, is the same paradoxical pattern that Yeats advocated for the Irish artist in Ireland during Stephen's youth: "We who care deeply about the arts find ourselves the priesthood of an almost forgotten faith, and we must, I think, if we would win the people again, take upon ourselves the method and the fervour of a priesthood. We must be half humble and half proud" ("Ireland and the Arts," *E & I,* 203). It is this tradition of the artist, then, that Stephen by virtue of his historic-geographic location finds as he is shaping his life. Stephen's exaggeration of this tradition appears most vividly when his vision of his own priesthood focuses on a "church without worshippers" (*P,* 159). While Arnold and Yeats sought through the analogy to establish a relationship between readers and poets, even if that relationship is feudal and unequal, Stephen uses the analogy to produce more distance and no relationship. At times, indeed, Yeats had also only wanted a small circle of readers; but Stephen comes close to wanting none at all.

In order to be a priest, as most schoolboys knew, one must first sense a destiny, experience a sense of having been chosen by God for some divine purpose. Just as a young man might sense his vocation through prayer or the ritual of the Church, Stephen senses his destiny through words, the medium of his chosen vocation. In chapter 2 the words of his older male relatives reveal "glimpses of the real world about him," and he senses that "the hour when he too would take part in the life of that world seemed drawing near and in secret he began to make ready for the great part which he felt awaited him the nature of which he only dimly apprehended" (*P*, 62). That destiny is what will *make* Stephen significant, and he envisions its confirmation as a tryst:

> He wanted to meet in the real world the unsubstantial image which his soul so constantly beheld. He did not know where to seek it or how: but a premonition which led him on told him that this image would, without any overt act of his, encounter him. They would meet quietly as if they had known each other and had made their tryst, perhaps at one of the gates or in some more secret place. They would be alone, surrounded by darkness and silence: and in that moment of supreme tenderness he would be transfigured. He would fade into something impalpable under her eyes and then in a moment, he would be transfigured. Weakness and timidity and inexperience would fall from him in that magic moment. [*P*, 65]

Stephen feels he will confirm his vocation in the vision of a woman—both a muse and an intercessor. Even this early in the novel, Joyce indicates Stephen's ultimate vocation through a veiled analogy to one of Yeats's essays. In "Poetry and Tradition," Yeats describes a "trysting-place of mortal and immortal" where one finds the rose, a symbol of art and of the imagination. Yeats's essay even suggests when the vision will occur, for it must follow an understanding of the self and an understanding of words (*E & I*, 255–56).

But before Stephen can realize his true priestly vocation, he is tempted by his "anti-Christ," the director of students. The temptation involves the lure of power:

> —To receive that call . . . is the greatest honour that the Almighty God can bestow upon a man. No king or emperor on this earth has the power of the priest of God. No angel or archangel in heaven, no saint, not even the Blessed Virgin herself has the power of a priest of God: the power of the keys, the power to bind and to loose from sin, the power of exorcism, the power to cast out from the creatures of God the evil spirits that have power over them, the power, the authority, to make the great God of Heaven come down upon the altar and take the form of bread and wine. What an awful power, Stephen! [*P*, 158]

The appeal moves Stephen, and so while he rejects it, he also converts both the call and the power into his sense of the artist. Thus, at the moment of his vision, as he comes to believe that he was destined, or called, to be an artist, he responds as though to the call of God: "—Heavenly God! cried Stephen's soul, in an outburst of profane joy" (*P*, 171). And in chapter 5, he has gained a kind of power of exorcism as he drives the echoes of his demons—his father, his mother, "the screech of an unseen maniac"—"out of his heart" (*P*, 175–76), so that his soul can live.

Both artist and priest work through words and forms: the artist through words and literary conventions, the priest, through liturgy and ritual, to form the God on earth, the logos. The appeal of both kinds of power is substantially the same, but the priest's power is apparently inhuman. Stephen wonders at his rejection of the priesthood, "at the frail hold which so many years of order and obedience had of him" (*P*, 161), but the readers should not. Stephen's fiction—the ordering of his life—includes a woman as transfigurer. As we have seen in chapter 1, each time Stephen believes that he has found his transfiguration and hence his destiny, an important symbol of that experience has been female. In chapter 2, Stephen accepts the whore as the vision of his soul's transfiguration as he is born into "another world," and faints into the swoon of rapture: "In her arms he felt that he had suddenly become strong and fearless and sure of himself" (*P*, 101). In chapter 3, he finds his rebirth into faith achieved first through the fiction of Emma and later his vision of the Virgin interceding in heaven for him. Thus, by recurring patterns we are led to expect that his birth into his proper vocation will be marked by a vision of a woman; no woman appears as the priest suggests a religious vocation.

Eventually, it is Stephen's vision of the female of the beach that approves and confirms the creation of his new, artistic soul and marks his conversion to the service of art. That vision occurs only after he contemplates words:

> —A day of dappled seaborne clouds.
> The phrase and the day and the scene harmonised in a chord. Words. Was it their colours? He allowed them to glow and fade, hue after hue: sunrise gold, the russet and green of apple orchards, azure of waves, the greyfringed fleece of clouds. No, it was not their colours: it was the poise and balance of the period itself. Did he then love the rhythmic rise and fall of words better than their associations of legend and colour? Or was it that, being as weak of sight as he was shy of mind, he drew less pleasure from the reflection of the glowing sensible world through the prism of a language manycoloured and richly storied than from the contemplation of an inner world of individual emotions mirrored perfectly in a lucid supple periodic prose? [*P*, 166–67]

In this pasage Stephen attempts to separate words from "the glowing sensible world" in order to associate them with the "inner world," and to transform the day into art, not into the material of art, but into a musical notation or a part of harmony, arranged into satisfying relations by the artist. In several ways the passage reflects Stephen's association with his Aesthetic or symbolist predecessors. First, this passage links Stephen with a specific kind of artist. James Naremore, in "Style as Meaning in *A Portrait of the Artist*," comments on the passage:

> . . . it does call to mind Pater and the decadents. . . . On another level of secondary meaning the passage catches perfectly the attitudes of the

young men of the eighties and nineties, a new generation disillusioned by
the abortive Victorian attempts to reconcile culture and civilization, a
group of artists who ultimately rejected the "reflection of the glowing
sensible world" in favor of the "contemplation of an inner world of individual emotions." The notions about aesthetics that are implied by this
passage are pretty clearly out of Pater.[10]

Some more specific links can be seen in the passage. In the musical
metaphor (the chord) Stephen follows Swinburne, Pater, Wilde, and
Yeats. That idea of harmony is like Swinburne's use of the term to
discuss the relationship between inner and outer music. Harmony

> goes beyond either "external" or "inner" music. When thoughts, words,
> deed sing together, when external and "inner" music blend, the result is
> harmony.[11]

Similarly, the purest form of art for Pater is music; Wilde, following
Pater's lead, says, "Music is the perfect type of art" (5:163). Yeats, too,
finds the chord a descriptive term for language in "The Symbolism of
Poetry."

Third, Stephen, like the early Yeats, seems to want here what the
young Yeats called a "poetry of essences" ("The Autumn of the Body,"
E & I, 193–94). Even if words reflect, for Stephen, the sensible world,
they do so through a prism: they distort, break up into purer shades,
the material of life. Language transmutes, through its associations, life
into pure and carefully demarcated colors. Yeats associated this function of language and the desire of a poet to find a poetry of essences with
decadence ("The Autumn of the Body," *E & I*, 193). Decadence or
symbolism, or a poetry of essences removes the human elements of
change, uncertainty, and flux from the world and provides a secure and
ordered vision. The rejected language is "richly storied" and "manycoloured" because of its previous use; to reject that element of language
is to reject what language acquires through history and public use—
associations and varying meanings we bring to words because of our
experience of them in contexts other than the immediate one. Just as the
priest chooses the fixed world of eternity over the hazardous, temporal
world, so Stephen-artist seeks the same kind of nontemporal existence
in words.

This passage also fulfills one of the preconditions Yeats established
for achieving the meeting "at the trysting place of mortal and immortal." He says that no one "has ever plucked that rose, or found that
trysting-place" before achieving "the mastery of unlocking words" (*E &
I*, 255–56), or before the quester for the rose has "come to the understanding of himself" (*E & I*, 256). Stephen's meeting with the immortal
and mortal, the girl on the beach, comes *after* he discovers his vocation,
after he "understands" himself. He has seen his destiny:

Now, at the name of the fabulous artificer, he seemed to hear the noise of dim waves and to see a winged form flying above the waves and slowly climbing the air. What did it mean? Was it a quaint device opening a page of some medieval book of prophecies and symbols, a hawklike man flying sunward above the sea, a prophecy of the end he had been born to serve and had been following through the mists of childhood and boyhood, a symbol of the artist forging anew in his workshop out of the sluggish matter of the earth a new soaring impalpable imperishable being? [*P*, 169]

It is this vision, "the call of life to his soul," which creates his affirmation of his priesthood of art: "Yes! Yes! Yes! He would create proudly out of the freedom and power of his soul, as the great artificer whose name he bore" (*P*, 170). The imagery of resurrection is also traditionally the imagery of conversion. And Stephen's conversion occurs before he is allowed a vision of the rose, the girl on the beach; one discovers the self, as Yeats suggests, before the immortal vision is permitted. Yeats's perception, like Stephen's, is not specifically religious, but it derives from a pattern of religious myth.

Thus Stephen's vision of the girl seems to mark or confirm his vocation, but neither the girl nor Stephen's vision of her creates in him that sense of destiny. The girl is "the angel of mortal youth" (*P*, 172); she is, like Yeats's rose, a meeting of time and eternity (mortal and angel). This is, then, Stephen's trysting-place and has all the images of the trysting-place Yeats described.

Stephen's "angel of mortal beauty" stands in a long line of inspirational figures who almost inevitably are female. She is perhaps most closely related to Rossetti's figure of the soul in "Hand and Soul."[12] Stephen has been seeking the outward manifestation of himself that would appear at the moment of transfiguration, that would remove doubt and timidity, create mystical ecstasy, and confirm a method of life. In Rossetti's "Hand and Soul," a young artist named Chiaro seeks to discover how he should use his talent. Finding that fame doesn't satisfy him, he turns to painting with a moral purpose. As he inserts a "moral grandeur" into each picture, his paintings become sterile and lifeless, just as Stephen's self-conscious morality and religiosity result in his developing a sterile image of his prayers and piety pressing "like fingers the keyboard of a great cash register" in heaven (*P*, 148). During his similar period of producing only sterile images, Chiaro's soul appears to him.

A woman was present in his room, clad to the hands and feet with a green and gray raiment. . . . It seemed that the first thoughts he had ever known were given him as at first from her eyes, and he knew her hair to be the golden veil through which he beheld his dreams. Though her hands were joined, her face was not lifted, but set forward; and though the gaze was austere, yet her mouth was supreme in gentleness. . . .

"I am an image, Chiaro, of thine own soul within thee. See me, and know me as I am. . . . Seek thine own conscience (not thy mind's conscience, but thine heart's). . . .

"Chiaro, servant of God, take now thine Art unto thee, and paint me thus, as I am, to know me: weak, as I am, and in the weeds of this time; only with eyes which seek out labour, and with a faith, not learned, yet jealous of prayer. Do this; so shall thy soul stand before thee always, and perplex thee no more."[13]

Rossetti's Pre-Raphaelite muse is "supreme in gentleness," the woman through whose eyes Chiaro has been given his "first thoughts" and through whose golden hair "he beheld his dreams." This woman dispells Chiaro's perplexity and allows him to find the appropriate mode of art for him. Although the soul here is a very early Pre-Raphaelite woman and Stephen's bird girl is a late version, Stephen, like Chiaro, ascribes to his vision the power to permit art, to remove doubt ("timidity"), to assure him that he has been transfigured. Even the important physical attributes are the same: the hair and the eyes. Chiaro's woman is more obviously chaste, being "clad to the hands and feet with a green and gray raiment"; yet Stephen's woman "responds" to him "without shame or wantonness" (*P*, 171). Each man seeks his soul; each man believes he has found it. Chiaro's soul arrives explicitly to deliver a message about art: "Take now thine Art unto thee, and paint me thus, as I am, to know me!" Stephen has also wanted to find "the unsubstantial image which his soul so constantly beheld" (*P*, 65) and he, too, is released to art, claiming later "I will try to express myself in some mode of life or art as freely as I can and as wholly as I can" (*P*, 247). As the Rossetti passage implies, vision or sight and hence eyes are the crucial attributes of the poet/artist. Stephen's concern with his eyes and his vision (metaphorically and literally) is perfectly consonant with that aesthetic tradition.

In Swinburne's "Hesperia," Joyce could have found images that appear both in this scene on the beach and in the villanelle. In part because other poems in Swinburne's *Poems and Ballads* are used or alluded to in *A Portrait,* and in part because the seabird girl is verbally transfigured into the temptress of the villanelle, who is much like some of the women in Swinburne's poems, this poem appears to be a source for Stephen's vision, despite the fact that Swinburne does not appear to be writing specifically about poetry. The persona in "Hesperia" "beholds" a young woman in a dream "as a bird." He remembers

The delight of thy face and the sound of thy feet,
     and the wind of thy tresses,
   And all of a man that regrets, and all of a maid
     that allures.

She is described as a "manifold flower"; her "silence as music"; her "eyes . . . are quiet, . . . hands . . . tender." More importantly, perhaps, he feels that his heart, "baffled and blind," has moved toward her, and that the effect of his woman-vision is a reawakening; he may be

> Closed up from the air and the sun, but alive, as a
>   ghost rearisen,
> Pale as the love that revives as a ghost rearisen
>   in me.[14]

The relationship in Swinburne's poem between the speaker and the woman is more clearly destructive than the relationship between Stephen and his beach-girl; Stephen's villanelle, however, overtly describes the destructive elements of his muse.

What all of this means is not necessarily that Joyce had Yeats or Rossetti or Swinburne in mind when he wrote of the epiphany on the beach, but that he used stock images of a specific tradition; each of these Aesthete poets defines the relationship between some poet and a woman-inspiration-soul in much the same terms, employing the same images, so that while not every reader will hear the similarities with each of these poets, he can recognize Stephen's ancestors and brothers. The figure of the woman is a particularly strong indication of Stephen's artistic inheritance, and I will come back to that symbol and its nineteenth-century analogues later in chapter 3.

Stephen's conversion to artisthood, like his adopting of the priest as a metaphor for the artist, then, has its roots in the Pre-Raphaelite–Aesthetic tradition. The themes, images, symbols, and even in some cases the plots are repeated by Joyce to establish that Stephen is not just any young artist, but an artist who embraces the kind of art Joyce himself rejected in *Dubliners* and *Ulysses*, and even in *A Portrait* itself.

Once having created this symbol of the artist, Stephen elaborates on it; both his own inclinations and what he perceives as necessary for an artist-priest lead to his withdrawal from the mundane world. His isolation begins long before his vision on the beach. As a child he has detached himself from life (*P*, 67) and recognized himself as different from other boys. Pater's Marius and Wilde's Dorian Gray share this detachment, and Yeats, too, had seen the allure in it. "I had . . . experienced every pleasure because I gave myself to none, but held myself apart, individual, indissoluble, a mirror of polished steel" (*Mythologies*, p. 268). The Pre-Raphaelite Brotherhood was, in many ways, a retreat from the world for artistic purposes; for those men, the ugliness of their environment made detachment a necessity. For Arthur Symons, "the artist has no more part in society than a monk in domestic life."[15]

More clear than these parallels is the parallel between the ways in which Oscar Wilde and Stephen describe the isolation of the artist;

Wilde wrote: "the imagination spreads, or should spread, a solitude around it, and works best in silence and isolation" (5:113). The artist should

> be left alone, to create a new world if he wishes it, or, if not, to shadow forth the world which we already know, and of which, I fancy, we would each one of us be wearied if Art, with her fine spirit of choice and delicate instinct of selection, did not, as it were, purify it for us, and give to it a momentary perfection. [5:113]

For Wilde, then, the best artist is, like Stephen, one who wishes to "press in [his] arms the loveliness which has not yet come into the world" (*P*, 251), and barring that to purify life. Wilde also suggests how art protects Stephen and why Stephen chooses art as the ordering principle of his life. In "The Critic as Artist," Gilbert says,

> It is through Art, and through Art only, that we can realise our perfection; through Art, and through Art only, that we can shield ourselves from the sordid perils of actual existence. [5:185]

Stephen, too, wants some protection from the squalor of his own and his family's life.

The artist does not act, for to do so is to limit his vision. "Unlimited and absolute is the vision of him who sits at ease and watches, who walks in loneliness and dreams" (5:187); Stephen's isolation and loneliness and essential passivity tie him repeatedly to Aestheticism. He rejects action as not providing the ecstasy he experiences in *viewing* the girl and determining his vocation. Wilde remarks that "we are never less free than when we try to act. . . . [Because action] has hemmed us round with the *nets of the hunter*" (5:190, italics mine). The forms of action open to Stephen—the priesthood of the Church, the nationalism of Davin, the stewardship of his financially bankrupt family and responses to their needs—are rejected in his famous proclamation, which uses the same image of the net that Wilde uses:

> When the soul of a man is born in this country there are nets flung at it to hold it back from flight. You talk to me of nationality, language, religion. I shall try to fly by those nets. [*P*, 203]

> I will not serve that in which I no longer believe whether it call itself my home, my fatherland or my church. [*P*, 246–47]

Thus Wilde and Stephen favor a life analogous to the contemplative life of the priest, one estranged from the work of men. The nets Stephen speaks of are nets not because they are irrelevant, impotent forces, but because they mean so much to Stephen—in that way, those forms of action imprison him. Wilde's comments differ from Stephen's in at least one crucial way: Wilde uses paradox and intentional ambiguity. Wilde's aesthetic theories are presented not in his own voice but through dialogue. Wilde, in other words, knows the limits of the radical theories he presents and even contradicts himself from one dialogue to another or from the dialogues to *The Picture of Dorian Gray*.[16] When Stephen makes similar statements or takes similar stands, he gives no indication of understanding their paradoxical nature. Joyce called Wilde's theories "subjective Aristotle"; the echoes, lacking paradox and irony, are one way of characterizing Stephen.

This isolated, priestly artist who withdraws from the workaday world creates dangers for himself in accepting the role as priest and in isolating himself. Yeats wrote in "Poetry and Tradition" that

> Three types of men have made all beautiful things, [sic] Aristocracies have made beautiful manners, because their place in the world puts them above the fear of life, and the countrymen have made beautiful stories and beliefs, because they have nothing to lose and so do not fear, and the artists have made all the rest, because Providence has filled them with recklessness. [*E & I*, 251]

This recklessness causes Stephen to risk making a mistake—even to risk eternal damnation—in his role as artist. His sense of the beleaguered artist fighting against the world with the weapons of silence, cunning, and exile stems in large part from the clichés of Aestheticism: for instance, the artist, like Christ, was a martyr. In Stephen's own life the image of martyrdom begins with the Promethean-like punishment suggested by the eagles who "will come and pull out his eyes" (*P*, 8). Stephen develops this role mentally as he equates his own imagined death with the death of Parnell while he is in the Clongowes infirmary. And when Stephen determines to be a priest of art, neither he nor earlier advocates of the metaphor ignore the role of the priest as surrogate for Christ, performing the ritual Christ first performed on Maundy Thursday. Thus, through their metaphor or fiction they identify with Christ. Yeats assumes that artists are martyrs or risk martyrdom. In *Mythologies*, the artist becomes the crucified outcast, the Christ for the modern world (147ff). Martyrdom appears again in Yeats's essay, "Ireland and the Arts." There Yeats asserts: "And certainly if you take from art its martyrdom, you will take from it its glory. It might still reflect the passing modes of mankind, but it would cease to reflect the face of God" (*E & I*, 207–8). Thus, though Yeats does not quite assert so boldly the analogy to Christ as Stephen does, he perceives that quality of self-sacrifice that Stephen insists upon, and in talking about the crucifixion of the outcast, he implies the analogy. Similarly, Rossetti, an early Aesthete, believed artists risked martyrdom[17]; Wilde, Yeats, and others, later Aesthetes, both reiterated the belief and assumed it: Persecution of the artist almost obsesses, as it does Stephen, the partisans of the tradition.

In contrast, Joyce wrote Stanislaus Joyce in 1905—before he began *A Portrait*—that while "not like to die of bashfulness," he was not "prepared to be crucified to attest the perfection of my art. I dislike to hear of any stray heroics on the prowl for me."[18] What is happening, then, is that Joyce associates Stephen with a tradition through a metaphor explicit in the tradition; he shows us how Stephen extends too legalistically the metaphors beyond their applicability and how he commits a prime rhetorical error in his inability to perceive the fact of analogy and instead perceives analogy as fact. In his esthetic theory (see chapter 5), Stephen completes the logical argument and becomes God.

Stephen's artist-crucified-Christ-priest gains freedom and the right to express himself through his rejection of all of the beliefs and institutions of society. Like the early Yeats, Stephen believes that the primary task of the artist is self-expression. Yeats began with that theory: "I thought when I was young . . . that the poet, painter, and musician should do nothing but express themselves" (*E & I*, x). In Wilde's dialogue, "The Critic as Artist," Gilbert claims that we love those who confess themselves, like Rousseau, to the world through art (5:108), and that "the highest Criticism really is, the record of one's own soul" (5:154), and that criticism is an art (5:153). According to Gilbert, "the world will never weary of watching that troubled soul in its progress from darkness to darkness" (5:109). Wilde maintains that "emotion for the sake of emotion is the aim of art, and emotion for the sake of action is the aim of life, and of . . . society" (5:186). For Wilde, this distinction between life and art, and society and art is the root of the artist's martyrdom. As art enables man to think and feel it threatens society. Stephen's position, then, is the position of the young artist of Yeats's and Wilde's day: a position essentially of narcissism and self-indulgence.

Stephen ultimately identifies the artist with the Daedalian figure of the artificer, who is his new "father." Just as the priest joins a family, the order, or a nun "marries" Christ, so Stephen chooses a new family, a new ancestry. The imagined Daedalus, a maker of wings to escape labyrinths, reveals to Stephen his artistic vocation, and when Stephen makes his declaration of flight, he associates the imagery of nets and flight with Daedalus. It is clear that Joyce used the Daedalian myth for more than the figure of a hawklike man. Daedalus, imprisoned in his own labyrinth, escaped through his art: he made wings and flew above the imprisonment. The analogy has consequences or implications that Stephen does not explicate or apparently understand. For instance, Daedalus becomes imprisoned in his own work of art, and hence must use his own artistry to escape the nets he has produced. Similarly,

Stephen, as well as the country in which he lives, has erected nets. It is his art, his selection, and his shaping that create the nets of religion, family, and nationalism. Not every soul is trapped by and in Ireland. Although the politics of Ireland were confusing, frequently frustrating, and often tragic, Davin as well as real people such as Maud Gonne and W. B. Yeats managed to find some satisfactions in political involvement. Although poverty in Dublin was extensive, some students in *A Portrait* are apparently finding jobs. Although the Church was repressive, some characters such as Cranly found ways to live within or despite those constraints. And although personal relationships appear to be impossible for Stephen, Davin, Cranly, and E.C. attempt to form relationships with him. Stephen creates the nets he feels as much as he finds them. By 1905, before Joyce began this version of Stephen's story, he could see his own escape from Irish constraints in terms other than those of a young man. He wrote his brother:

> If you look back on my relations with friends and relatives you will
> see that it was a youthfully exaggerated feeling of this maldisposition of
> affairs which urged me to pounce upon the falsehood in their attitude
> towards me as an excuse for escape. [*Letters*, 2:89]

Stephen, just as the young Joyce did by his own testimony, participated in his own imprisonment. Concomitantly, he chose to see his name as Daedalus, although his family name is different.

Even the choice of Daedalus as a metaphor for the artist associates Stephen with Aestheticism. John Ruskin may have been one source for the metaphor, and although Ruskin does not belong so centrally to the Aesthetic-decadent tradition of Wilde and the 1890s, his partial sponsorship of the Pre-Raphaelites makes him part of the tradition. More germane to this study is Pater's discussion of Daedalus in *Greek Studies*. Daedalus is "the mythical, or all but mythical, representative of all those arts which are combined in the making of lovelier idols than had heretofore been seen."[19] Stephen is not unique in seeing Daedalus as the artist, nor is he stupid. The intelligence of Stephen is manifested concomitantly with his limitations. But it is Joyce who shows us how the image of Daedalus, the fabulous artificer, in itself undercuts Stephen's perception of his position. The ominous quality of the image pattern suggests once again the failure we see in Stephen's maturity: he, because he created or participated in the creation of the nets, carries them with him when he escapes to Paris. We should recall that from his first identification with Daedalus in chapter 4, Stephen has failed to see himself as Icarus, although he has seen himself as Daedalus's son. He has skipped over the dangers to himself. The boys' shouts, "O, cripes, I'm drownded!" which counterpoint Stephen's recognition, suggest that he, like Icarus, will end in the water having tried to fly too high. And the last reference of the novel, "old father, old artificer, stand me now and ever in good stead" (*P*, 253), again suggests that Stephen is a fallen or soon to be fallen son, not a successful artist. In *Ulysses*, these implications become explicit: the negative or ominous connotations of the myth, deemphasized in *A Portrait*, become the dominant connotations. Stephen falls: "seabedabbled."

Thus, from the beginning, Stephen shapes a role for himself that works out of the Aesthetic tradition of literature available to him as a young man: he adopts the roles Symons, Yeats, Wilde, Rossetti, and Pater used or constructed to explain art and the artist, roles based primarily upon an artist-priest analogy. To suggest that Joyce accepted all of these proclamations in 1916 is to ignore altogether *Dubliners* and his letters; Joyce, in writing that collection of stories, indicates his own movement away from a decadent, abstracted, and esoteric artistry—that is, a movement into what he considered maturity. In Stephen, Joyce presents an artist who uses and exaggerates these Aesthetic stances, accepting metaphor and analogy and suggestion as fact. He chooses one kind of artistry without the counterbalancing concerns Joyce reveals in *Dubliners*, where sympathy and compassion and connection with and among human beings, not isolation and aloofness, are the desired traits of man. It was not until *Ulysses* that Joyce brought two theories of art into direct confrontation, but in *A Portrait* he insisted upon Stephen's limitations in part by creating Stephen as the perfect type of the decadent-Aesthete poet.

Nonetheless, Stephen is this kind of poet and must define for himself what such a poet does, how he interacts with the raw material for his art, what the artistic process is. And in that process, just as in the figure he creates, Stephen belongs to, sums up, and exaggerates the tradition of the "last romantics"—Yeats's term for the artists of the 1880s and 1890s.

Notes

1. William Butler Yeats, *Essays and Introductions* (New York: The Macmillan Co., Collier Books, 1959), p. 163. Hereafter cited parenthetically *(E&I)*. George L. Geckle, "Stephen Dedalus and W. B. Yeats: The Making of the Villanelle," *Modern Fiction Studies* 15 (1969): 87–96, has demonstrated that Joyce used this essay by Yeats directly in *A Portrait;* in this case, however, I do not argue that Stephen's response comes directly from Yeats.

2. *The Poems of Tennyson*, ed. Christopher Ricks (London: Longmans, 1969).

3. See previous discussion, chapter 1.

4. *Letters*, ed. Richard Ellmann, 3 vols. (New York: Viking, 1966), 2:90. The other two poets Joyce mentioned are Wordsworth and Shakespeare. Stanislaus Joyce tells us in *My Brother's Keeper: James Joyce's Early Years* (New York: Viking, 1958) that "among the older poets he [James] had progressed from his boyish hero-worship of Byron through Shelley to Blake" (p. 99). *Letters* will hereafter be cited parenthetically *(Letters); My Brother's Keeper* will be cited as *MBK*.

5. See David J. DeLaura, "Pater and Newman: The Road to the 'Nineties," *Victorian Studies* 10 (1966): 39–69, for a discussion of Newman's relationship to the aesthetics of the 1890s.

6. Karl Beckson, "A Mythology of Aestheticism," *English Literature in Transition* 17 (1974): 233.

7. Matthew Arnold, "The Study of Poetry," in *Selected Essays,* ed. P. J. Keating (Suffolk: Penguin, 1970), pp. 340ff.

8. Oscar Wilde, "The Tomb of Keats," *The Complete Works,* 12 vols. (Garden City, N.Y.: Doubleday, Page & Co., 1923), 12:304. The essay originally appeared in *Irish Monthly* for 1877.

9. Arthur Symons, *The Symbolist Movement in Literature* (London: W. Heinemann Ltd., 1899), pp. 122, 10.

10. "Style as Meaning in *A Portrait of the Artist," James Joyce Quarterly* 4 (1967): 334–35.

11. Thomas Connolly, "Swinburne and the Music of Poetry," *Publications of the Modern Language Association* 72 (1957): 685.

12. *The Works of Dante Gabriel Rossetti,* ed. with Preface and Notes by William Michael Rossetti (London: Ellis, 1911; reprint ed., New York: Adler's Foreign Books, Inc., 1972), pp. 449–556.

13. Ibid., pp. 553, 555.

14. *The Complete Works of Algernon Charles Swinburne,* ed. Sir Edmund Gosse, C. B. and Thomas James Wise, 20 vols. (New York: Russell and Russell, 1925), vol. 1.

15. Symons, *The Symbolist Movement,* p. 84.

16. Compare, for instance, the statement that life imitates art with the statement that literature is "the perfect expression of Life" or the statement that art is neither moral nor immoral with the obviously moral closure of *Dorian Gray.*

17. See Frederick Shields, "Some Notes on Dante Gabriel Rossetti," *The Century Guild Hobby Horse* 1 (1886): 144.

18. *Letters,* 2:83. Nonetheless, Joyce knew and feared this element in the artist's self-perception. In another 1905 letter to Stanislaus he mocked the vision of the betrayed artist in a parodic prayer (*Letters,* 2:110). By 1905, then, he was able to see both how he might have shared or indeed still shared such a perception and the ludicrousness of the position.

19. See Charles T. Dougherty, "Joyce and Ruskin," *Notes and Queries* 198 (1953): 76–77. See also Sidney Feshbach, "A Dramatic First Step: A Source of Joyce's Interest in the Idea of Dedalus," *James Joyce Quarterly* 8 (1971): 197–204.

Walter Pater's comments on Daedalus are, I think, most illuminating. Pater continues:

The old Greek word which is at the root of the name Dædalus, the name of a craft rather than a proper name, probably means to work curiously—all curiously beautiful wood-work is Dædal work. . . . But it came about that those workers in wood, whom Dædalus represents, the early craftsmen of Crete especially, were chiefly concerned with the making of religious images. [*Greek Studies: A Series of Essays* (London: Macmillan and Co., 1910), pp. 237–38.]

3

Transmuting the Daily Bread

"A priest of eternal imagination, transmuting the daily bread of experience into the radiant body of everliving life." (Stephen Dedalus, *A Portrait*)

"Had he not come to Rome partly under poetic vocation, to receive all those things, the very impress of life itself, upon the visual, the imaginative, organ, as upon a mirror; to reflect them; to transmute them into golden words?" (Marius, *Marius the Epicurean*)

"We have had beautiful and imaginative work in which the visible things of life are transmuted into artistic conventions." (Wilde, "The Decay of Lying")

"This [knowledge] enabled me to make my little book a fanciful revery over the transmutation of life into art." (Yeats, *Mythologies*)

By the end of the nineteenth century, poets and critics associated with Aestheticism or symbolism consciously or unconsciously substituted art for life, valued the art product more than the events or emotions of life, attempted to live in and through art. Pater directed readers to fill their lives with art and song, claiming that they were more rewarding and predictable than the passions of life; Morris and Ruskin believed that industrialized society could be reformed by surrounding workers with art and by making workers artisans; Wilde, through his characters in the dialogues, rebuked Nature and Life while exalting Art and in *Dorian Gray* presented a fantasy of man becoming eternal art. Yeats sounded as though he believed art would usher in the earthly paradise for the Irish.[1] In practice, these dicta, beliefs, or hopes were doomed: human beings, society, nature, and tangible reality don't know or accept or follow the artist's or the critic's script. The appeal of these theories about art as it affects one's experience stems from the way they attribute control and power to the imagination, control and power that offer the means of reducing threat and increasing private satisfactions.

Stephen chooses to see art as the transmuting of life into something eternal. In the finest art, according to Dedalus, life is "purified in and reprojected from the human imagination" (*P*, 215). While *to transmute* denotes simply to alter or change, Stephen, Yeats, Wilde, and Pater use the term in a more specific sense: to change the substance, the essence. When Pater wrote of Marius's desire "to transmute [all those things, the very impress of life] into golden words," he meant to change the substance of life; when Yeats wrote of the process, he spoke specifically of alchemy—a "part of a universal transmutation of all things into some divine and imperishable substance" (*Mythologies*, 267). To use this precise word is to conjure up visions of alchemists, priests, and magicians. But the word *transmute* has an interesting history in nineteenth-century science too. Lamarck used it to denote a kind of evolution; the very reasons that caused Darwin and other scientists to reject the term and the theory help us to understand the distinction this word choice makes between Aesthetes and realists. Lamarck supposed "that as simple lowly organisms exist today without having been perfected or made complex, they must have arisen recently by spontaneous generation."[2] Spontaneous generation is more analogous to miracle than is the alternative, or Darwinian view. "Lamarck's theory of evolution was the last attempt to make science out of instinct," and thus belonged "to the contracting and self-defeating history of subjective science" while "Darwin's [belonged] to the expanding and conquering history of objective science."[3] Lamarck believed that organisms change through acts of will and desire, that evolution occurs through some felt need of the organism rather than by the random variation proposed by Darwin. These theories of will and need, personal choice and conscious intent, led scientists to reject Lamarck's theory and the term associated with it, *transmutation*. That Aesthetes and symbolists rejected the random nature of history and change proposed by contemporary science is, thus, indicated through (among other things) this one word choice: in it is encapsulated their rejection of an entire and dominant theory of historical change, adaptation, and human will. As the realists and naturalists emphasized the impinging social or cultural contexts of their characters and observable, external details, and in doing so imitated scientific method, so the Aesthetes and symbolists emphasized spiritual, essential, personal contexts and the unobservable truths. In doing so, they imitated alchemical and religious methods. The verb *to transmute* captures that method and that approach to literature.

Let me begin, then, by looking at the verb *to transmute*, as it informs our understanding of the aesthetic, moral, and psychological concerns of the Aesthetes and their heir, Stephen Dedalus.

In "*Rosa Alchemica*" Yeats remembered that he was attracted to alchemy in part because he believed that alchemists "had sought to fashion gold out of common metals merely as part of a universal transmutation of all things into some divine and imperishable substance; and this enabled me," Yeats wrote, "to make my little book a fanciful revery over the transmutation of life into art, and a cry of measureless desire for a world made wholly of essences" (*Mythologies*, 267). Stephen, Marius,[4] and Yeats use the same verb, *to transmute;* Stephen and Yeats consider the product "imperishable" and "impalpable" (*E&I*, 260); and Stephen, like Yeats, seeks to transmute the vulgar into the pure, life into art.

Oscar Wilde concurred:

> Art takes life as part of her rough material, recreates it, and refashions it in fresh forms, is absolutely indifferent to fact, invents, imagines, dreams, and keeps between herself and reality the impenetrable barrier of beautiful style, of decorative or ideal treatment. ["The Decay of Lying," 5:27]

> It is the function of Literature to create, from the rough material of actual existence, a new world. ["The Critic as Artist," 5:151]

Like Stephen, Wilde through his speakers focused on the recreative, transmuting nature of art, with life as the raw material; in his view, life—of itself—is insignificant. "We have had beautiful and imaginative work in which the visible things of life are *transmuted* into artistic conventions, and the things that Life has not are invented and fashioned for her delight" ("The Decay of Lying," 5:31, italics mine). Thus Wilde added his voice to those urging young artists to transmute life into art.

Yeats, Pater, and Wilde seem to continue, albeit sometimes unhappily, to see life and art as separate; Stephen collapses the distinction. He attempts to change his life into art, as they did, but he attempts to destroy any life—to live art rather than living life, and by doing so to remove the threats that his actual life creates. John V. Hagopian comments on the relationship between art and life:

> Works of art . . . are made of language which embodies the feeling-quality of human experience. In fact, one might say that works of art—and only works of art—make it possible to contemplate highly-charged human experiences with detachment and objectivity. In the hurly-burly of everyday life, experiences are rarely isolated from myriads of other experiences and irrelevant stimuli, and shaped into perceivable gestalts.[5]

So long as we continue to make a distinction between that unshaped life and art, we can accept that aesthetic. But if that theory makes art better than life and if we can live in art, then logically we should attempt to move into that better existence. Practitioners of Aestheticism and symbolism, in their emphasis upon the superiority of art to life, covertly desired to be rid of this life in favor of art. Dorian Gray's desire to have his picture age while he remained forever young and untouched by human and temporal existence represents the logic of Aestheticism. Yeats's admiration for *Axel* had the same motive: he liked best the line, "As for living—our servants will do that for us." Implicit in the devaluation of life in favor of art is the denial of the claims of human beings upon other human beings. In Hagopian's words, we can "contemplate highly-charged human experiences with detachment and objectivity": but that contemplation is inactive. We do not encounter people merely by contemplating them. Dorian's detachment from his own actions, figured in the changing face of the portrait, is the perfect image for artistic detachment that spells emotional and human isolation. Such an art becomes an escape from life, perhaps a refusal to live in this threatening world. Transmuting, the changing of essence or substance, seems to promise a transfiguration of the sordid world.

The very words Joyce associates in *A Portrait* with this process are symptoms of Aestheticism. The figure who performs the art, the priest, the descriptions of the process—eucharist, cry, mystery, reprojection, purification—and the end products—the hymn, the word made flesh, imperishable, impalpable—all these defined an aesthetic attitude at odds with the mass culture of the period. Most of them imply a rejection of rational explanation or logical or consequential order—in direct opposition to the descriptive, experimental, and scientific terms that realists and naturalists used. At the same time, to use these words is to identify, as Stephen does, with people in Elizabethan or medieval times, and thus Stephen removes himself from the linear, "progressive," sequential operations described by nineteenth-century scientists. Finally he escapes time altogether into a realm of nontime, art.

But even the attempt to escape time is an attempt conditioned by history. Yeats wrote in 1901: "Nobody can write well, as I think, unless his thought or some like thought, is moving in other minds than his, for nobody can do more than speak messages from the spirit of his time."[6] In his thoughts and in his very word choices, Stephen "speak[s] messages from [one of] the spirit[s] of his age." Yeats's own announcements help to establish the pervasiveness of this magical or miraculous theory of creation represented by the priest-artist's words, and Yeats even commented upon the opposition between science/realism and magic/symbolism:

> The scientific movement which has swept away so many religious and philosophical misunderstandings of ancient truth has entered the English theatres in the shape of realism and Ibsenism, and is now busy playing ducks and drakes with the old theatrical conventions. . . . Outside the theater [,] science[,] having done its work, is beginning to vanish into the obscurity of the schools, but inside there is still so much for it to do that many forget *how impermanent must be its influence, and how purely destructive its mission there,* and write and talk as if the imaginative method of the great dramatists, of Kaladasa [sic], of Sophocles, of Shakespeare, and of Goethe was to let its house on a lease for ever to the impassioned realisms of M. Zola and of Dr. Ibsen in his later style [which Yeats did not approve of], or to the would-be realisms of Mr. Pinero or

Mr. Jones. The barricades are up. . . . Those among the younger generation whose temperament fits them to receive first the new current, the
new force, have grown tired of the photographing of life, and have returned by the path of symbolism to imagination and poetry, the only
things which are ever permanent. [Frayne, 1:322–23][7]

Later Yeats insisted on the miraculous nature not just of art, but of
progress, that scientific term, itself:

All life is revelation beginning in miracle and enthusiasm and dying out as
it unfolds in what we have mistaken for progress. It is one of our illusions,
as I think, that education, the softening of manners, the perfecting of
law—countless images of a fading light—can create nobleness and beauty,
and that life moves slowly and evenly towards some perfection. Progress
is miracle, and it is sudden, because miracles are the work of an all-
powerful energy; and nature in herself has no power except to die and to
forget. [Frayne, 2:199]

Although Yeats used the word *progress*, he denied the evolutionary
principle that undergirded the nineteenth-century concept of progress;
he, too, denied linear time, and he denied to nature, the natural world,
any particular importance.

The desire to transmute and create something "imperishable" and
better than life is a desire to create something that is immune to the
ravages of the passing of the moment, or something that will expand the
moment, prevent its so rapid passage, as Pater suggests. Stephen's beach
girl expands the moment of ecstasy for him as he forgets time in its
linear manifestation. That instant of ecstasy acts like Pater's image of
passion, the flame that expands the interval, overcomes time, and provides the most intense experience of life. Yeats, following, one supposes, Pater's writings, calls the instant the "Great Moment": "And we
artists, who are the servants not of any cause but of mere naked life . . .
[are] Artificers of the Great Moment" ("Poetry and Tradition," *E & I*,
260). Pater's "visions," or expansions of the interval, Stephen's
epiphanies and Yeats's "Great Moments" are not merely parts of aesthetic theories, as Pater makes evident in his "Conclusion." We find
these ways of perceiving time attractive because by using them we gain
emotional or psychological control over time and hence recognize what
popular magazines in this century urge us to recognize, that the *quality*
of the time spent counts more than its quantity; in doing so, they lull us
into believing that quantity or the measured and inexorable passing of
time can be controlled, altered, or negated.

One of the difficulties in dealing with this language-thought matrix
is that these aesthetic-moral theories have informed much of our education and much of our own cultural context—as the allusion to popular

magazines that urge parents to work on the quality rather than the quantity of time with their children suggests. Thus, we can believe slow-motion films; we can *believe* novels such as Virginia Woolf's where one "minute" can last eighteen pages. Creating, or believing that we can create, time outside of a communal sense of time liberates us from mechanistic notions; it may also mislead us into a false sense of control over what the nineteenth century would call "natural process." In consequence we live in a world of humanly created, mutually exclusive, but coexisting "realities": "scientific" and "psychological" time. Ruth Temple sees Pater's "Conclusion" as specifically addressed to this problem: "Like so much of Pater's writing, it expresses the impact of science on modern man, and in its preoccupation with the fleeting nature of experience, the isolation of human beings, the relation of consciousness to the objects of consciousness, it outlines the program of the modern psychological novel."[8] At the same time, a point that Temple does not dwell upon, "modern" science, although it might isolate man, diminishes his uniqueness within the material world, makes his individual problems either relatively unimportant or not *his* in some essential way. Aesthetes responded defensively, attempting to move man outside that world of flux and change and of the irrelevance of the single man into a world of art object and nonchange and significant, miraculous transformations performed by the single man. That pattern is most obvious in Stephen Dedalus.

Stephen's artificer expands and creates the great moments such as his epiphany on the beach into prose poems. What Stephen does in the villanelle is to transmute, or transubstantiate, himself into a poem, just as Christ transforms himself into bread and wine. And the creation of the villanelle is an incarnation, complete with the annunciation by Gabriel (*P*, 217), during which the Godhead becomes the *logos*, or Word. Thus through art Stephen becomes important and able to survive the encroaching world of everyday Ireland.

All of these pronouncements and attitudes share a reactionary and defensive rejection of contemporary science and a rejection of the value or indeed the existence of external nature, at least as an entity separate from man and worthy of study. At the same time, these men deny the beauty of the "natural" world, a denial that separates these postromantics from their kinsmen earlier in the century. Wilde, as he frequently did, stated this attitude with less equivocation than most in "The Decay of Lying":

VIVIAN:. . . . What Art really reveals to us is Nature's lack of design, her curious crudities, her extraordinary monotony, her absolutely unfinished condition.

. . . .

VIVIAN:. . . . At present, people see fogs, not because there are fogs, but because poets and painters have taught them the mysterious loveliness of such effects. There may have been fogs for centuries in London. I dare say there were. But no one saw them, and so we do not know anything about them. They did not exist till Art had invented them. [5:7, 47–48]

Granting that Wilde may not share his character's thoughts completely, he is still expressing the extreme of the position adopted by Aesthetes. This rejection of nature in favor of patterned art is consonant with the rejection of time. In their word choices, they demonstrate that for them human fulfillment does not and cannot occur within time. While they reject external and shared nature and time, they accept and promote an elitist role for the artist; the artist is specially chosen, endowed with peculiar powers, and a unique individual in the midst of the great mass. The metaphors these same men chose for the poet, the priest, the magician, or the alchemist come from the hierarchial organization of secret societies or the Church. The central, informing metaphor of artist as priest insists upon the artist's superiority as a mediator, a controller of existence, and a leader. The ultimate control of the essential world by these artists-priests would be no less arrogant and elitist than the economic or political control of other elitists: they would create worlds that the rest of us would live in, they would create what is true or "there."

What is illuminating about Joyce's *A Portrait* is not that he used peculiarly apt words to describe art, but rather that he realistically dramatized—complete with motives and consequences—how and why a young artist adopts transmuting as the metaphor for writing and he dramatizes realistically several acts of transmutation. Wilde, in *The Picture of Dorian Gray*, for instance, gives the reader no reason for Dorian's hatred of his early life—no external or internal justification for turning himself into art. Dorian dreams of becoming eternally young like art merely because he fears growing old (a fear we all share, granted, but not a strong enough fear for isolating ourselves from people). Wilde, unfettered by realistic urges, can simply assume that the picture can age and the protagonist remain young. Joyce, unlike his youthful counterpart Stephen and unlike the Aesthete Wilde, used realism, even naturalism, to depict Stephen's development. He shows us how and why words become magical, at least for this boy; why this boy refuses to accept his inherited language; how and why women become symbolic figures that resemble first Pre-Raphaelite women and later the femmes fatales of decadence. He provides at least a limited understanding of the human motives behind Aestheticism by providing one example of an Aesthete in progress. What I wish to turn to, then, are the steps that Stephen takes in order to become a transmuter—the ways he deals with language and word, image, and symbol.

All words derive their power from the larger entity we call *language;* they efficiently name or designate or abstract only within an accepted and communal pattern that ascribes meaning to them. The first necessity for controlling words and meaning is, for Stephen, the separation of words from the constructs of language that make them mean not what the artist intends, but what the culture dictates. In Stephen's mind and experiences, language is created by others. As long as he is comfortable in that society, he is complacent about its prefabricated language:

> God was God's name just as his name was Stephen. *Dieu* was the French for God and that was God's name too. . . . But though there were different names for God in all the different languages in the world and God understood what all the people who prayed said in their different languages still God remained always the same God and God's real name was God. [*P*, 16]

As Stephen grows older, he begins to make finer distinctions than this one; no longer is language a national product—soon he sees different languages among the members of his extended family. At Christmas dinner, Dante argues with his father and Casey; the argument, about Parnell's disgrace and the Church's condemnation of him, centers on different languages. Of the twenty-eight uses of the word *language* or *languages* in the novel, eight occur in this passage. When Casey and Simon attack the priests for meddling in politics, Dante Riordan counters, "Nice language for any catholic to use!" (*P*, 31). She quotes the Bible in support of her position and concludes, "That is the language of the Holy Ghost" (*P*, 32). Then the real battle ensues; Dante's language is, according to Si Dedalus, "very bad language if you ask me" (*P*, 32). When the argument becomes focused on what Stephen will or will not remember from the Parnell scandal, the priests' condemnation, and the present argument, the focus is totally on language:

> —O, he'll remember all this when he grows up, said Dante hotly— the language he heard against God and religion and priests in his own home.
> —Let him remember too, cried Mr Casey to her from across the table, the language with which the priests and the priests' pawns broke Parnell's heart and hounded him into his grave. [*P*, 33–34]

Both languages here are shrill and biased. Stephen, unable to choose between the languages that disrupt his world and denote communal assumptions and associations, retreats into contemplating Eileen and parts of the litany of the Blessed Virgin.

After this scene, Stephen is never at home in any language pattern. Joyce uses the word *language* almost exclusively in negative contexts. In chapter 3, the priest warns of "the language of those fiendish tormentors" and hopes that the boys assembled for a retreat will never "hear that language" (*P*, 124). Stephen dreams of his own hell where goatish creatures encircle him; "soft language issued from their spittleless lips. . . . They moved in slow circles, circling closer and closer to enclose, to enclose, soft language issuing from their lips" (*P*, 138). In contrast, words can at least sometimes be associated with the good and the safe: "One who would redeem them . . . the Second Person of the Most Blessed Trinity, the Eternal Word" (*P*, 118). Stephen, then, by chapter 3, associates language with diabolical forces; it encloses, threatening to damn him. It is no longer the certain English of his childhood, but a vehicle for inflicting pain.

As Stephen appears to be moving toward the priestly orders, he feels disconcerted by certain priests he knows. Priests, who had had the Word in chapter 3, now appear to side with language: "Lately some of their judgments had sounded a little childish in his ears and had made him feel a regret and pity as though he were slowly passing out of an accustomed world and were hearing its language for the last time" (*P*, 156). Clearly Stephen associates language with the world in which it is appropriate and communal; as he begins to reject the world, he focuses on its language. In the same ways, he rejects Gaelic. Just before the end of chapter 4 and the beach scene, Stephen rejects the idea that "language manycoloured and richly storied" (*P*, 167), e.g., language whose associations are historical and legendary and popular accounts for his love of phrases. In chapter 5, Stephen walks "among heaps of dead language," while individual words on shops bind "his mind like the words of a spell" (*P*, 178–79).

When he rejects the dean of studies' language as one in which he has not "made or accepted" the words, when he rejects as one of the nets the language of Ireland, he is rejecting that shared means of communication. Like his weapons, "silence, cunning and exile," this rejection does not, on the face of it, make much sense for a would-be poet.

Stephen desires to create a new language—one that uses the words of the rejected tongue, but embeds in them new meanings, again part of a cultural movement. Rossetti, Morris, Pater, and Yeats had also sought a new language: Rossetti and Morris anachronistically, Pater through purifying vocabulary and style, Yeats in seeking his own style—a unique poetry. Like Stephen, Yeats rejected the views of Dr. Hyde and his cohorts who argued that the "new" language should be the "old" one, Gaelic.[9] Arthur Symons, in analyzing what he called the "decadent movement," opined that the desire to discover and communicate perfect truth perfectly lead to a rejection of old language patterns:

> : . . this endeavor after a perfect truth to one's impression, to one's intuition—perhaps an impossible endeavor—has brought with it, in its revolt from ready-made impressions and conclusions, a revolt from the ready-made of language, from the bondage of traditional form, of a form become rigid.[10]

The only kind of language that Stephen seems to find compatible by chapter 4 is either his own or that of sound, music, tastes. His own "violent or luxurious language" of escape "from the cold silence of intellectual revolt" (*P*, 181) is positive because it stings Davin into a story of a peasant woman. And in contemplating the Elizabethans (another indication of Stephen's essentially backward vision) he notes another kind of language: "He tasted in the language of memory ambered wines, dying fallings of sweet airs, the proud pavan" (*P*, 233). Note, however, that this language, momentarily given assent, is non-verbal, artistic, imaginative, historically anachronistic, and separate from Stephen's world. Furthermore even these phrases are shortly dismissed as being "like the figseeds Cranly rooted out of his gleaming teeth" (*P*, 233), hardly a positive association. Even the attractive language of the earlier time—like the language that attracted the Pre-Raphaelites—must be spit out of the artist's mouth. What Stephen wants is a system of words unlike the words of the dean of studies, words that Stephen himself has "made or accepted" (*P*, 189).

Early in the novel we catch a glimpse of how that process is possible. When Stephen takes long walks with his father he listens to "his elders" speak "constantly of the subjects nearer their hearts, of Irish politics, of Munster and of the legends of their own family" (*P*, 62). During these conversations, Stephen responds to words:

> Words which he did not understand he said over and over to himself till he had learned them by heart: and through them he had glimpses of the real world about him. [*P*, 62]

That is, Stephen neither asks his elders to define the words nor does he look them up in the repository of cultural meanings, the dictionary; instead, he seeks the meanings within himself, almost without reference to others' meanings, and then, having "made" meanings for the words, uses them as windows on the world. Such a method of acquiring and then understanding words is almost, though not quite, a total rejection of the cultural language. Stephen accepts the communal sounds, but he attaches to those sounds idiosyncratic meaning.

Like the Pre-Raphaelites and the decadents, Stephen finds that the language of the contemporary world does not suffice for beauty nor for the creation of sensuous poetry. They had seen the nineteenth century as a time without beauty, without conventions adequate for expressing

their vision, without a language that was beautiful. Their response was
to create a new poetic language, to turn to the Middle Ages for a
reference system that allowed them to communicate, and thus to separate their art from the age in which it was created. They created a new
language or a new mode by using the old elements, such as colors in
painting and words in literature, to construct new patterns that allow
communication. Stephen discovers in words, one element of language, a
tremendous power—for instance in the word *foetus* on a desk in Cork:

> On the desk before him he read the word *Fœtus* cut several times in the
> dark stained wood. The sudden legend startled his blood. . . . His recent
> monstrous reveries came thronging into his memory. They too had
> sprung up before him, suddenly and furiously, out of mere words. [*P*, 89–
> 90]

Words create the reality of Hell in chapter 3, transmuting Stephen's
own anxieties into external threats; and finally the Word—*claritas*—
becomes the third stage of apprehension and the escape from the imprisoning forces of his country, just as the Word, Christ (another *claritas*),
is the essence of and liberates the Church.[11] If he can separate words
from language, Stephen can create meaning for those words himself;
that is, he can supply a system, a new language, within which the words
have meanings. But words must stand in some relationship to each
other, to the speaker, and to the audience in order to have perceivable
meaning. For Stephen that relationship is created by rhythms he can
choose and control.

Rhythm

What I have been describing is a pattern of responses to external
threats and internal fears. Stephen's world is insecure; Ireland does not
provide, nor can his fictional parents, a bastion of safety for a young
man of Stephen's temperament. Like an autistic child, who rocks in
response to his world, Stephen uses rhythm to lull himself into security;
more accurately, perhaps, Stephen uses rhythm as we all do—when we
rock an infant, when we find dancing (at least the old fox-trot) a reassuring activity, when we beat on a punching bag to a staccato rhythm.
Mere alternation of strong and weak beats soothes; more sophisticated
are the rhythms of jump-rope, or the rhythms of Beethoven's Fifth. But
the root of the reassurance is the same: a desire to control random and
unordered experience. Art, perhaps, always has this function: Spenser's
stanzas, with their elaborate regularity, seem to control the profusion of
images, overwhelming stimuli, and moral conflicts merely by their

regularity. Children's stories, like the one that opens *A Portrait*, announce their beginning and their ending, reassuring the listeners that the story has a perceivable beginning and perceivable ending: the formulaic quality of openings and endings encourages us to believe that, indeed, they lived happily ever after. Formulae provide a kind of rhythmic marking. Just as words are, early in Stephen's life, ways of understanding the given world, so rhythm is first a means of controlling physical and psychological "facts" and only later becomes overtly aesthetic. We can see the parallels between Stephen and the symbolists and Aesthetes *only* after Joyce has demonstrated the psychological needs Stephen has that produce his concept of rhythm. As he demonstrates those needs and Stephen's responses to them, Joyce posits one way of understanding why Aesthetes adopted certain attitudes about rhythm.

As a small boy, Stephen employed rhythm to lessen an attack of disease as he "shut and opened the flaps of his ears" and compared the noise he created to a train going in and out of a tunnel (*P*, 13). He notes the same rhythmic pattern in the sequence of school and vacation, and associates school/vacation with "tunnel, out; noise, stop" (*P*, 17). All of these effects give him some control through physical manipulation and intellectual understanding over the parts of his life that threaten him. As he begins to discover an aesthetic and emotional satisfaction in controlling the rhythm and pattern of events and impressions from the sensible world, he makes the external world less threatening and more pleasing. By perceiving a relationship between the negatives (noise, school) and the positives (stop, vacation) he provides certainty to his life. While he cannot prevent the negatives, they begin, through his pattern of relationships, to guarantee the eventual arrival of the positives; school, though miserable, holds in it the promise of vacation and home. Disparate and threatening elements of the environment, elements that, like words, exist externally to Stephen, can be divested of their threat and can acquire positive value as harbingers of positive elements. And Stephen has created, by establishing these relationships, predictability and beauty. There is satisfaction in that.

On the trip to Cork, Stephen discovers another pattern or rhythm that shields him from the terrors of his life.

> The neighbourhood of unseen sleepers filled him with strange dread as though they could harm him; and he prayed that the day might come quickly. His prayer, addressed neither to God nor saint, began with a shiver, as the chilly morning breeze crept through the chink of the carriage door to his feet, and ended in a trail of foolish words which he made to fit the insistent rhythm of the train; and silently, at intervals of four seconds, the telegraph-poles held the galloping notes of the music between punctual bars. This furious music allayed his dread and, leaning against the windowledge, he let his eyelids close again. [*P*, 87]

The threats (unseen sleepers) are controlled by the regularity of rhythm, which casts an incantation over him. Later he discovers the same kind of alternation—a variety of rhythm—in Shelley's poetry:

> Art thou pale for weariness
> Of climbing heaven and gazing on the earth,
> Wandering companionless . . . ?

> He repeated to himself the lines of Shelley's fragment. Its alternation of sad human ineffectualness with vast inhuman cycles of activity chilled him, and he forgot his human and ineffectual grieving. [*P*, 96]

As Stephen associates rhythm with meaning, he begins to associate it with literature and just as importantly with a sense of avoiding "human and ineffectual grieving"; thus rhythm allows Stephen to escape human limitations and to move into eternal "cycles." Nonetheless, it is the "alternation" or rhythm of the elements, their relationship, that allows the escape. Although he cannot create the elements in a relationship of rhythm, just as he cannot create words, he can create the relationship, the context, the rhythm, or the language system. It is the order that attracts him, just as the order of Shelley's lines and meaning still the riot of his own mind and as he tried to use money to create order in his family's life (*P*, 98). Consistent with this desire to create order, he attempts after his religious "rebirth" to order his life:

> Sunday was dedicated to the mystery of the Holy Trinity, Monday to the Holy Ghost, Tuesday to the Guardian Angels, Wednesday to Saint Joseph, Thursday to the Most Blessed Sacrament of the Altar, Friday to the Suffering Jesus, Saturday to the Blessed Virgin Mary. [*P*, 147]

His obsession with order becomes most clear in this effort to order religion into perceivable and predictable patterns: "he drove his soul daily through an increasing circle of works of supererogation" (*P*, 147). This imposed, artificial scheme provides order, pattern, and rhythm to his life.

Even the choice that Stephen makes between the priesthood of the Church and the priesthood of art is a choice between rhythms of life, hence between relationships among elements. He uses the metaphors of rhythm: the "chill and order" of the Jesuits contrasts with the "agile melody" of music (*P*, 161, 160). The elements of the Jesuit order, its silence, its ritual, its sense of indelible vocation, its power, its transubstantiating role, its isolation, etc., all these elements remain the givens in Stephen's world.

He increasingly associates rhythm with literature in chapter 4; his phrase "A day of dappled seaborne clouds" finally pleases him because of "the poise and balance of the period itself," "the rhythmic rise and fall of words" (*P*, 166). The rhythm, the order, the control: the highest marks of literature and what interests Stephen. Finally in chapter 5 Stephen comes to a purely literary sense of rhythm. First, the villanelle depends upon rhythm for its creation: "The verses passed from his mind to his lips and, murmuring them over, he felt the rhythmic movement of a villanelle pass through them" (*P*, 217–18). Rhythm generates form, just as it formed experience all the way back at Clongowes. Form is analogous to rite or liturgy; the Mass contains and shapes the elements as the villanelle contains and shapes the elements; and the form proves the magic.

Only at this point in Stephen's fictional life does Joyce allow us to draw analogies between Stephen's use of rhythm and the uses the Aesthetes and symbolists put it to. The timing seems to me crucial: Stephen is no longer a child but he is not yet a mature man. The comment is implicit: such notions about rhythm are adolescent, immature. The clichés about adolescence ring true here: a period of threat, insecurity, anxiety, rebellion against the "adult" world; Stephen reacts to his adult world—Ireland—as the Aesthetes and symbolists responded to theirs—Victorian prosperity, science, change. And the Aesthetes/symbolists and Stephen use rhythm to deny and escape those worlds.

Yeats in "The Symbolism of Poetry" outlines the importance of rhythm for composition:

> The purpose of rhythm, it has always seemed to me, is to prolong the moment of contemplation, the moment when we are both asleep and awake, which is the one moment of creation, by hushing us with an alluring monotony, while it holds us waking by variety, to keep us in that state of perhaps real trance, in which the mind liberated from the pressure of the will is unfolded in symbols. [*E & I*, 159]

And he claims that the proper rhythms for symbolic poetry are not "energetic rhythms" but, instead,

> those wavering, meditative, organic rhythms, which are the embodiment of the imagination, that neither desires nor hates, because it has done with time, and only wishes to gaze upon some reality, some beauty. [*E & I*, 163]

We shall return to this essay by Yeats, but to the point here are Yeats's comments upon rhythm as it influences or makes possible the creation of symbols and poems. First, Stephen acts out literally the injunction that is only metaphorical in Yeats's essay: he attempts to expand that moment between his sleep and his waking in order to write the villanelle; "the rhythmic movement of the villanelle" prolongs his contemplation of E. C. and his writing.[12] He shrinks from the world and tries to keep his state of half-sleeping. "Soon he would sleep" (*P*, 222). And, like the visions suggested by Yeats, Stephen's villanelle is separate from any time, and separates him from desire and from hate, and leads him to contemplate only beauty, as E. C. loses all the human and temporal qualities assigned to her and becomes only the "temptress of the villanelle."

Stephen's childhood interest in rhythm, then, despite the lack of reference to or parallel with writings of the Aesthetic tradition he represents, leads directly to his adolescent concept of rhythm, which is very much like that of Yeats. Like the words of transmutation, this rhythm functions in part to control time and the elements of life in order to assuage fears and escape from the uncertainties of life, to "have done with time." What Joyce demonstrates through Stephen over and over is an avoidance of life; Stephen's motivations for choosing this kind of rhythm, for assigning it such importance, have directly to do with his sense of the impinging, frightening, and uncontrolled external world. Art thus alleviates fears because it changes the relationships among elements of our world and, more importantly, allows the artist to determine just what those relationships are. As we shall see later, not all the threats Stephen perceives in his world are totally false, nor are those real threats completely dissipated by his artistic manipulation.

Symbolism

> All sounds, all colours, all forms, either because of their preordained energies or because of long association, evoke indefinable and yet precise emotions . . . and when sound, and colour, and form are in a musical relation, a beautiful relation to one another, they become, as it were, one sound, one colour, one form, and evoke an emotion that is made out of their distinct evocations and yet is one emotion. ["The Symbolism of Poetry," *E & I*, 156–57]

Rhythm assists in controlling meaning by establishing relationship; symbols mysteriously are meaning—or so one might believe after reading Symons, Yeats, and Stephen Dedalus. The process that attributes meanings, emotional and intellectual, to symbols is perhaps finally mysterious because it is private and never fully articulated. Symbols are an attempt to change or modify the "meaning" attached to reasonably concrete entities, and, particularly for the modern writer, to change the meaning of the words that indicate those concrete entities from a communal and generally rather vague or limited meaning value to a personal and precise meaning however suggestive and expansive: Yeats's "indefinable and yet precise emotions" (*E & I*, 157). By necessity, then, any time we analyze symbols we limit them, we destroy some of their resonance, we translate into definable terms the indefinable. In short, we simplify. But creating symbols can also be used to simplify an individual's experience; the more they simplify, the greater the danger that they stereotype rather than capture complex associations. And the more they stereotype experiences and emotions, the more easily they are manipulated. Stephen's symbolic birds suggest harbingers of destiny, aesthetic fathers, the artist, the art object itself, betrayal, loneliness, and perhaps drowning. The bird-Daedalus thus may create for the reader complex, indefinable, and yet precise emotions and ideas. Another of Stephen's symbols seems to me less a symbol and more a stereotype. Women are not human beings, but Pre-Raphaelite figures who ensnare and yet liberate the artist; women all look very much alike, they all have the same designs on the artist. The symbol of the artist-priest is neither so complex nor so delicate as the bird-Daedalus symbol, nor is it a stereotype as the woman symbol is. The most suggestive and evocative of these symbols is the least like the symbols of Aestheticism and symbolism. A symbolist-Aesthete poet must create symbols, and Stephen creates them rather consciously. Here Joyce appears to have dropped one of his allusive hints at influence; in chapter 5 Stephen contemplates a line from Nash. He remembers: *"Darkness falls from the air"* (*P*, 232), contemplates the line with "a trembling joy, lambent as a faint light," and then realizes that he has improperly remembered the line, *"Brightness falls from the air"* (*P*, 234). Of all symbolic lines, this one is not precisely the most obvious; Yeats quotes the line more than once, and more importantly, he quotes the line in "The Symbolism of Poetry," the essay that describes the mood, setting, time, and concept of rhythm that inform the villanelle. Yeats uses the line as an example of symbolism, of beautiful poetry that evokes intellectual and emotional responses. George Geckle, in "W. B. Yeats and the Making of the Villanelle," convincingly argues both that Joyce knew this essay and that he used it as a pattern for Stephen's composition.[13] The Nash allusion draws one more connection to Yeats's essay, but Stephen's mistaking of the line suggests that Stephen's perception is not even accurate about his tradition; when he forms symbols from that tradition, we cannot even be sure that he perceives the literary realities accurately, much less the "objective" facts of his environment.

One of the novel's symbols can be used as a test case. Stephen views women at the end of the novel much as the Aesthetes and decadents viewed them. Joyce devoted much energy to that symbol in *A Portrait,* perhaps in part because he shared with his culture ambivalent feelings about women, and perhaps in part to investigate, to objectify why and how he came to have these destructive views of them: perhaps by using a fictional character he could understand and deal with his own limits.

Two related forces produce Stephen's vision of a temptress, his personal needs and the literature of his culture. This figure's positive attributes link her with inspiration figures, contemporary muses, and

Beatrices; her negative aspects with the devouring femme fatale and Salomé. The relationships between his personal needs and the literary portraits of women which allow him to find in the external world similar women are complicated. In one sense, Stephen's psyche makes him receptive to almost clichéd views of women; in another sense, Stephen shares with his culture and its writers some emotional needs that caused them to perceive women in similar ways. As Joyce dramatized why and how Stephen comes to see women as he does, he imitated the nineteenth-century development of a symbolic woman from an essentially benign or positive figure to a devouring and negative one such as the women we see in the works of Swinburne and Wilde. Stephen's creation of his symbol, thus, recapitulates on an individual level a process that culminates in poems such as Swinburne's "Faustine" or "Laus Veneris," where we find ravenous destroyers, insatiable monsters whose only apparent desire is to destroy the male suitor-lover-poet. That this cultural phenomenon has psychic roots should be clear: women are feared by Wilde, Swinburne, Yeats, whatever attractions or powers they may possess for these men; at the same time, the fact that cultural views affect the individual view developed by children is also clear, as the cult of the Western hero and children's imitation of that figure make clear in our own time and country.

Stephen's first encounters with women are domestic and essentially positive—his mother smells nicer than his father. But we hardly finish the first page of *A Portrait* before Dante begins to demand obedience from the young boy. By the second page, a bifurcated vision is established. Stephen views Eileen as positive; he plans to marry her. But Dante and Stephen's family see her as negative, tempting him both sexually and religiously because she is a Protestant. And their threats create Stephen's first sense of sin or deviance or guilt. He must apologize or, like Prometheus, be attacked by eagles; here the eagles will "come and pull out his eyes" (*P*, 8). Without insisting upon a Freudian pattern of interpretation, we do see that the eagles, in this context associated with the women who invoke them as appropriate chastizers (Dante and, presumably, Stephen's mother), threaten to maim him for at least pseudosexual behavior. Eileen herself plays much the same role as Rossetti's blessed damozel in chapters 1 and 2 of *A Portrait;* that is, she entices Stephen while she seems to be a virgin. So, too, does Rossetti's blessed damozel, who sits in heaven among the saints and yet who lures the speaker with her sensual, not spiritual charms. Through Eileen's blond hair and white hands, Stephen comes to understand the litany of the Blessed Virgin, *Tower of Ivory, House of Gold;* the litany itself, based on the Song of Songs, mingles holy and sexual imagery.

Eileen had long thin cool white hands too because she was a girl. They were like ivory; only soft. That was the meaning of *Tower of*

and spiritually destroying the seraphim: she persists in being the *"Lure of the fallen seraphim."* Similarly, Swinburne's Faustine is never satisfied with the earthly lover or the earthly experience of love. She lures only to destroy, and would destroy a true lover:

> You'd give him—poison shall we say?
> Or what, Faustine?[16]

In "Laus Veneris," the woman's "gateways smoke with fume of flowers and fires,/With loves burnt out and unassuaged desires"[17]; while Stephen's temptress's *"eyes have set man's heart ablaze,"* which produces the *"smoke of praise";* both women are insatiable. Swinburne's persona claims,

> I dare not always touch her, lest the kiss
> Leave my lips charred.[18]

Yet both men seek that which destroys them, and both have given up Christ for the love of a devouring woman. In Swinburne's poem, the knight claims his sin is greater than other men's, "For I was of Christ's choosing, I God's knight,/No blinkard heathen stumbling for scant light."[19] Stephen, too, has rejected the Church and Christ for the muse-temptress of chapter 4, and both have chosen a woman who comes out of the sea: "As when she came out of the naked sea" in Swinburne's poem. Both forget "fear and all weary things," end "prayers and perished thanksgivings," and both sense that they may risk eternal damnation for their choice: "As after death I know that such-like flame [the flame of desire] / Shall cleave to me for ever."[20] For Swinburne and Stephen this symbolic woman has mixed meanings: however destructive she is, she is essential to their life and art. As Swinburne said in a defense of his poems, "But not at once, or not for ever, can the past be killed and buried; hither also the huntress follows her flying prey, wounded and weakened, still fresh from the fangs of passion; the cruel hands, the amorous eyes, still glitter and allure . . . the feet are drawn back towards the ancient ways. Only by lifelong flight, side by side with the goddess that redeems, shall her slave of old escape from the goddess that consumes."[21]

These "cruel hands" and "amorous eyes" which Swinburne draws attention to occur in many poems associated with the decadent 1890s and in Stephen's own descriptions of the woman. Stephen has focused on the eyes of his beach girl (the eyes there function to lure Stephen into his glorious fall)[22] and on the fingernails of Eileen, associated with ivory and with the Virgin, hence with both the redeeming and consuming goddess. Ernest Dowson's poem "I Was Always a Lover of Ladies' Hands" represents one of the many ways in which the poets of the nineties used the image:

I was always a lover of ladies' hands!
   Or ever mine heart came here to tryst,
For the sake of your carved white hands' commands,
   The tapering fingers, the dainty wrist;
. . . .
They are pale with the pallor of ivories
. . . .
I know not the way from your finger-tips,
   Nor how I shall gain the higher lands,
The citadel of your sacred lips:
   I am captive still of my pleasant bands,
   The hands of a girl, and most your hands.[23]

Here the citadel is the kind of sacred Tower of Ivory that Stephen envisions, and the ivory hands parallel the fingernails of Eileen. Wilde uses the same image in describing his Sphinx: "Curving claws of ivory."[24] Thus, the hand of ivory that captivates the persona and the poet can be cruel, as in Swinburne or Wilde, or relatively benign, as in Dowson, but it is always a force that controls the artist and as such is potentially dangerous. The point is not that Stephen has read Dowson, Wilde, or even a specific Swinburne poem (although the parallels are striking with Swinburne's poem), but that Joyce is associating Stephen with the "tragic generation," as Yeats called the Aesthetic poets of the 1890s.[25] How Stephen constructs the female figure is reasonably clear; her analogues in Wilde, Swinburne, Dowson, and Yeats associate Stephen with those writers; at the same time, Stephen's process, rooted in his initial threatening encounters with women, illuminates the psychosocial context that influenced Joyce and the other writers. That all of these men have such terrifying visions of women points less, I think, to an enormous coincidence that all the men had the same idiosyncratic psychological problems than to cultural conditions that exacerbated and directed emotional tensions present in most people in most eras. To analyze satisfactorily what conditions—economic, religious, social, political—fostered these visions of women as powerful and destructive, as decorative and stylized, as either pure and fragile or demonic would take me beyond the scope of this book. Some causes—obvious or otherwise—do, however, suggest themselves.

On one side, the condition of women improved in the nineteenth century. The power of the Victorian mother—and her symbol, Queen Victoria—gave women, at least imaginatively, more power than they had had in the eighteenth century. Property rights and legal rights were just beginning to be granted to them, and women were entering professions long closed to "respectable" women. The clichés of the time have some kind of significance. "The hand that rocks the cradle rules the Empire," for instance, asserts that the real power behind British imperialism was female. And certainly women dictated social and moral codes. But, in spite of these sources of power and independence, the work of middle-class women shrank. Perhaps as other workers became more specialized in their tasks, women did too: the multiple jobs of the woman—teacher, nurse, mate, domestic servant, mother—were spread increasingly in the middle class to professional nurses, teachers, and servants. I suspect, as this happened, as middle-class women performed less physical labor, they felt less valued and perhaps responded in part by becoming more manipulative emotionally, seeking to recapture past value in the only sphere open to them, the family. Women could trade only with their beauty, their "cultural graces," their emotional support- iveness: their traditional accomplishments, largely domestic, were no longer important. A woman who could spin and weave, who could cook and farm, who could nurse and teach, was no longer desirable to a middle-class man: he hired people with those skills. Women may thus have learned to develop other, more emotional skills—and those skills, properly acquired, can manipulate and threaten men. Those skills, now labeled passive-aggressive, almost call for the defensive reaction we see in the images of women created by nineteenth-century writers: castrat- ing women; supportive, benevolent muses or lovers; decorations for elegant drawing rooms; moral dictators; innocent children who foster man's ego by their very dependence. As Virginia Woolf wrote, such a woman was above all pure.[26] Trading on that virtue, almost trading out of necessity, such women may well make their men (husbands, friends, children) feel both humiliation and awe. Required sexual purity must aggravate the normally ambivalent relationships between men and women—must create fears and anxieties on both sides. H. G. Wells and others who advocated liberating sexuality responded to the negative effects of the requirement.

The more narrowly defined the role for "respectable" women be- came, the less meaningful work they had to do, the more they were encouraged to develop emotional skills, perhaps the more stereotyped their images in literature became. As the skills of many women were measured not by what they could do, but rather by what they could make other people feel and do, the more destructive became the literary images of women. To alleviate the threats—real and imagined—writers made women beautiful and passive things; consigned to what their cul- ture saw as trivial, women sought escape through more and more polit- ical equality with men; that attempt increased the threats.

Whether or not these speculations account for the development of literary femme fatales, it is obvious that many men transcribed their own fears into that figure, that the view of women explicit in those figures marred more than one man's life; it is possible that such a view cohered with homosexuality among writers and artists. But my concern here is with Joyce and what he has done. He shows us at least one reason, one pattern of causes for such a distorted vision—providing, that is, an individual pattern of motivation that explains and recapitulates the process his culture went through. He demonstrates that men had realistic and accurate reasons for fearing women: Stephen *is* threatened by Dante and his mother, the Church does deny any sexual contact with—any right to touch—women. And he, probably from personal experience, understands how destructive such sexual responses are; he shared them; the villanelle was Joyce's own, but by the time he wrote *A Portrait* he knew enough about his own psyche to dramatize the responses and their implications and to reject the villanelle from his collected poems. Even Stephen understands that he substituted an artistic vision for a woman. He records in his diary that he has turned off his emotional response to E. C. and turned on "the spiritual-heroic refrigerating apparatus, invented and patented in all countries by Dante Alighieri" (*P*, 252).

Thus Stephen creates a symbol of a threatening force—women—that contains and assuages his sense of threat and fears. His similarity to the nineteenth-century Aesthetes is reinforced by his choice of poetic form; as he completes his vision in the villanelle, he chooses a poetic form that very few other English poets use, except those of the nineties. And through his creation of symbol the nineteenth-century Aesthetic movement is "explained" or "analyzed" dramatically. Stephen writes out of a pattern of fear, a pattern that often concurred with homosexuality, and a pattern that bequeathed to the twentieth century one of the more damaging visions of women as devouring seductresses, necessary and necessarily evil.

At the same time, the tradition judges Stephen, for these other writers could claim that they were creating art works that did not reflect their own visions (a claim I clearly only half believe), while Stephen is confusing his life with art and his poetic creature with flesh and blood creatures such as E. C. Stephen is not just transmuting life into art, he is also destroying life as a separate and separable entity.

What he has been looking for throughout *A Portrait* is a *raison d'être*, both in terms of a vocation and a manner or method of organizing the world, of distancing those voices which threaten to humble his pride and destroy his youth. Art gives him that order. Art shapes and selects the empirically perceived world into the most satisfying relations of the sensible. Words interest Stephen more for their ability to describe or reflect the inner world than to reflect the world of appearances. Images, and then symbols, patterned and related to each other through the artist's sense of rhythm, control the outside world and give it the meaning the artist has internally, rejecting elements that conflict with the artist's sense and amalgamating crucial and mundane elements of his life.

Although the artist may in a work of art limit the meaning of symbols and things external to a character, to attempt to do so in one's life has serious pitfalls. Like Wilde, Stephen makes Pater's sense of style a way of living as well as a way of writing. From the earliest recognition that each boy walks differently, Stephen perceives and judges his experiences on the basis of external elements of style, or the outward and visible signs of inward and spiritual realities. But those inward realities are always Stephen's not the realities of the girl on the beach, the hawk flying above it, or the boys swimming. Those boys become "characterless" when naked (*P*, 168) because their identifying outward signs are gone. Cranly becomes the "image of the head and face, . . . a priestlike face" (*P*, 178) because Stephen is in the habit of confessing to him. Each of these boys becomes only the outward and visible sign of Stephen's mind or emotions, and any differentiating aspects are rejected by Stephen's inner world. E. C. loses all individuality and becomes, like the women of Clane, a symbol of the Irish race, a "batlike soul" (*P*, 221). In the final chapter, Stephen attempts to reduce her to an abstract symbol. In a similar way, he shapes and distorts all his experience into aesthetic patterns that are satisfying. His is a symbolic, or sacramental, and solipsistic vision. His first efforts are amateurish, but as the novel proceeds and his symbols are defined, he uses them to aid in transmutation and change, control and escape; and in doing so, he usurps the realities of his life.

Usurpation

The three instances of "literary" creation in the novel demonstrate Stephen's increasingly conscious use of symbols and art to change reality. In the infirmary at Clongowes, Stephen imaginatively converts both his own feared death and Parnell's death into rudimentary art. Should he die, the rector would be resplendent "in a cope of black and gold," "the bell would toll slowly" (*P*, 24), and his audience, the other boys, would respond emotionally. The poetry of *Dingdong! The Castle Bell!*, his funeral music, creates a "tremor" in him as he thinks, "How sad and how beautiful" (*P*, 24). Parnell's death becomes for Stephen a dreamvision of the sea and sorrow, with Dante "walking proudly and silently past the people who knelt by the waters' edge" (*P*, 27). In each case—his own imagined demise and Parnell's real death—the personal emotion is objectified and witnessed as artistic and distanced rather than felt as an emotional and immediate experience; in each case, the original participant in the emotion portrayed, Stephen, becomes the observer. Parnell's death becomes a subject of Stephen's prose poem.[27] In contrast, Simon Dedalus weeps for the fallen leader. To make the death of the chief, or one's own death, into a literary experience is to change it and to control it; eventually to create literature that denies by absorbing and displacing reality.

The first consciously literary effort, dedicated to E.C., performs the same corrective surgery on life:

> . . . by dint of brooding on the incident, he thought himself into confidence. During this process all these elements which he deemed common and insignificant fell out of the scene. There remained no trace of the tram itself nor of the trammen nor of the horses: nor did he and she appear vividly. The verses told only of the night and the balmy breeze and the maiden lustre of the moon. Some undefined sorrow was hidden in the hearts of the protagonists as they stood in silence beneath the leafless trees and when the moment of farewell had come the kiss, which had been withheld by one, was given by both. [*P*, 70–71]

Suffering, like other poets of the 1890s, "some undefined sorrow," Stephen uses the same kind of atmosphere and sense of a decayed world that beclouds and denies specificity to poetry as they did. Stephen disappears, or becomes only a "protagonist," not himself but another. Stephen changes himself, makes himself better in his own eyes as the figure becomes fainter, and changes the sense of an experience; he makes his life into art that is better than life, just as he later reshapes his encounter with Cranly. Specificity and reality, for Stephen, are symptoms of the external and threatening world; becloud the issue or event and life improves. Pater's criticism and Wilde's dialogues show us less of the psychological motives for preferring art to life than we can see in this scene.

By the time Stephen composes the villanelle, his abilities to alter life are much more sophisticated and his choice of subject and form reflects more overtly his literary ancestors. His symbolic temptress, as I have demonstrated earlier, simultaneously marks Stephen as a product of his culture and is a response to his idiosyncratic vision. The villanelle form, with its intricate rules, forces a clearly identifiable, artificial scheme on the writer within which he is free to create; and the villanelle form, particularly in English, is more confining than, say, the sonnet. The form, in other words, provides ordering principles as complex as the ritual of the Church and fulfills Stephen's recurrent need for order. Convention guarantees a kind of beauty, order, or austerity befitting an artist-priest. His choice of a French form of poetry is part of his rejection of Ireland and his acceptance of the *fin de siècle* world that looked to Paris and the French for art and life patterns. Thus in the villanelle Joyce demonstrates again the conflation of personal needs and cultural influences.

Stephen writes his poem out of "bitter and despairing thoughts" that "the radiant image of the eucharist" unite, creating "a hymn of thanksgiving" (*P*, 221). By writing the poem he believes that he controls the girl: "Conscious of his desire she was waking from odorous sleep, the temptress of his villanelle" (*P*, 223). Charles Rossman and Bernard

Benstock have recently discussed this poem at length. Rossman's analysis, countering that of Robert Scholes,[28] concludes that the poem indicates Stephen's inability to produce art: "The villanelle is not a serious sign of Stephen's artistry, but a repudiation of the conditions and prerequisites that would enable Stephen to grow into artisthood" as Stephen ignores the real E.C. and real life and substitutes for them his "fear of his own physicality, and his hope of overcoming it." Like Rossman, I believe that the villanelle "duplicates the psychological function of the earlier poem to E.C."; that is, to change life and make it less threatening. As Rossman asserts, "Psychologically, the poem substitutes for life."[29] While Scholes argues that the poem marks Stephen's movement—from an Aesthete to an artist—Rossman sees this inability to deal with life, that which Stephen must in his own words "purify" and "reproject" in order to be an artist, as a symptom of his failure. That symptom is, precisely, the symptom of the Aesthetes: a detachment from life, a substitution of art for life, a refusal to move emotionally into time and flux. Rossman, like Scholes and other commentators, must use the rest of *A Portrait* to explicate the poem: it is not a clear, radiant image separate from the rest of the world.

There is, however, important information about Stephen and his vocation here, which makes looking at the poem again useful:

Are you not weary of ardent ways,
Lure of the fallen seraphim?
Tell no more of enchanted days.

Your eyes have set man's heart ablaze
And you have had your will of him.
Are you not weary of ardent ways?

Above the flame the smoke of praise
Goes up from ocean rim to rim.
Tell no more of enchanted days.

Our broken cries and mournful lays
Rise in one eucharistic hymn.
Are you not weary of ardent ways?

While sacrificing hands upraise
The chalice flowing to the brim,
Tell no more of enchanted days.

And still you hold our longing gaze
With languorous look and lavish limb!
Are you not weary of ardent ways?
Tell no more of enchanted days.

[*P*, 223–24]

First, of course, Stephen is the composer of "*Our broken cries and mournful lays,*" which are turned into the "*one eucharistic hymn*"; the poet is the writer of hymns to a god. But the god is not the god of the Church; the temptress takes over the role of the responsive God. The hymn then becomes the chalice *"flowing to the brim,"* which is sacrificed to the god-temptress, the *"lure of the fallen seraphim."*[30] If the hymn, the sacrifice, the eucharist is offered to the temptress by the poet, the sacrifice is the poet himself—he is ablaze: *"Your eyes have set man's heart ablaze."* This fire produces the *"smoke of praise"* in stanza three, which is transformed into a hymn in the next stanza, and into the sacrifice of stanza six. So the poet becomes the poet-sacrificer-sacrificed to the god-woman. Like Christ, in a way he sacrifices himself to himself, since the temptress is the product of his mind. The figure of a woman is also art. The girl on the beach is the temptress of art, the angel sent to prove his vocation.

Art thus becomes the *"lure of the fallen seraphim"* and like Prometheus, the artist, at odds with his gods for taking what is godlike, fire-art, to man, blends both messianic and rebellious attitudes. Stephen is not only Christ, but also Satan (the *fallen* seraphim). As Bowen notes:

> . . . in his denial of accepted national, religious, and moral standards [he] becomes Satanic in his own mind, just as his exile and suffering for his newly created conscience cause him in his own mind to become analogous with Christ. As Satan he rebels but as Christ he is ripe for betrayal, saving the race, and transubstantiation into art, his saving wine and wafer. The hymn which celebrates all this is Stephen's villanelle, a song about himself and his miraculous transformation by and of himself into the very song which celebrates the transformation, and ultimate blend of life and art.[31]

But the blend is Joyce's, not Stephen's. Stephen has consecrated, transubstantiated himself into art with himself as priest at the ritual. The lonely world of art is like the lonely altar at which Stephen imaged himself celebrating Mass. But to have sacrificed oneself in this manner is to make oneself as immortal as art: it is to change life and humanity into other, nonhuman entities. Art is, for Stephen, artifice and self-conscious transmutation of the self into art, and performed to escape the "bitter and despairing thoughts" that plague mortal and human existence.

Joyce uses one of the few direct references to Yeats's prose in *A Portrait* to make Stephen's relationship to the decadent 1890s in this villanelle clearer, just as he uses the villanelle form to indicate the same relationship. George L. Geckle has pointed out some of the similarities:

> Stephen's whole development as a young man *"weary of ardent ways"* reflects the influence of such *fin de siècle* poets as Dowson, Swinburne, Symons, and Wilde, but especially the Yeats of the 1890's.[32]

Geckle argues persuasively that the time of the composition of the villanelle echoes Yeats's insistence, in "The Symbolism of Poetry," upon creation in "the moments between sleeping and waking." Yeats and Pater both point to the prolonging of "the moment of contemplation."[33]

A second, important connection to Yeats's essay resides in the ways in which we must read and understand Stephen's symbols. If they make sense, they do so because of the context—the whole novel—in which they appear. That is, the reader of the novel understands the villanelle because its images have been constructed and developed through the narrative of the novel. Hence we perceive precise, emotional associations for the smoke of the censer, or the lure of the seraphim, or the lavish limbs of the girl *because* those images are defined by the boy's swinging of the censer and his dreams about it, or the temptress Eileen, or the girl on the beach with fuller thighs. To the extent that we understand the villanelle, we do so because of the idiosyncratic associations of the novel; it is not a poem, it is a passage in a novel. In one sense, then, the private language created by Joyce in the novel, Stephen's own language, allows the villanelle to communicate, and to change E.C. and all the other women of Stephen's life into temptresses, and Stephen into a Promethean-priest-artist.

Another important way of seeing how prevalent are the images used to describe Stephen's writing of the villanelle is to compare his method of composition with that described by Cardinal Newman in "Literature" and Stephen's image of fire with Newman's similar image. Discussing how the artist "uses" eloquence and ornament, and while denying that those elements of style are added after the original conception, Newman insists upon the inevitability of ornament, and on its inseparability from content: "It is the fire within the author's breast which overflows in the torrent of his burning, irresistable eloquence."[34] Stephen translates Newman's metaphor into literal statement just as he has translated Yeats's metaphor of the moment between sleep and waking; that is, Stephen represents his heart as being literally *ablaze*. In the same essay, Newman indicates that form arises with emotion: "Not the words, alone, but even the rhythm, the metre, the verse, will be contemporaneous offspring of the emotion or imagination which possesses" the artist.[35] Stephen "felt the rhythmic movement of a villanelle pass through them [his first verse]. The roselike glow [his emotion] sent forth its rays of rhyme; ways, days, blaze, praise, raise" (*P*, 217–18). Stephen does, that is, precisely what Newman claims all great poets do. Stephen is, once again, hardly original—if we know the cultural contexts of the late nineteenth century.

But what seems to concern Joyce equally is Stephen's unconscious transmutations, his failure to perceive accurately individuals and events. He misinterprets reality. Early in chapter 2 he finds in *The Count of*

Monte Cristo a partial substitute for the desired and as yet unfulfilled mystical moment, an escape from his depressing environment. Literature is satisfying and protective because it changes his life psychologically, because it allows him to be not Stephen Dedalus but a romantic hero, and because it allows him to be morally superior to a world that from his point of view judges him and his father negatively. Literature changes Stephen's experience by reconstructing it.

Similarly, his own mystical moments all reconstruct or construct experience: his encounter with the whore is treated in semireligious and ritualized ways; his religious rebirth is artistically created through the power of words; the girl on the beach is transformed into a demigoddess. In chapter 5, Stephen modifies his experience of sensuous detail into art or literary experience:

> . . . as he walked down the avenue and felt the grey morning light falling about him through the dripping trees and smelt the strange wild smell of the wet leaves and bark, his soul was loosed of her miseries.
>
> The rainladen trees of the avenue evoked in him, as always, memories of the girls and women in the plays of Gerhart Hauptmann; and the memory of their pale sorrows and the fragrance falling from the wet branches mingled in the mood of quiet joy. [*P*, 176]

Thomas Grayson has insisted upon the disparity between Stephen's theory of three phases of apprehension and his own acts of apprehension:

> In Stephen's transubstantiation of experience the movement is from a concrete and corporal or sensual image—the rain laden trees—to an abstract or artistic image—Hauptmann's women and girls—and finally to what for him must be regarded as a "pure" experience—the experience of a "pale sorrow" which mingles in "a mood of quiet joy." This for Stephen is an "Esthetic image." The attainment of this aesthetic image is through a process which has three states. . . .
>
> But in the passage we have been considering Stephen is not engaged in apprehension in the sense of its being constituted of three activities [as Stephen outlines them in the aesthetic theory]. He does not perceive, recognize, and become satisfied. On the contrary, he casts most of his perceptions of reality out of his heart with an execration. He does not perceive; he engages in literary fantasy.[36]

Grayson points to two important facets of Stephen's character, his rejection of reality and his substitution of art for reality. Stephen undercuts his own esthetic theory by his failure to use it. Just as important, Grayson's explication indicates how Stephen usurps reality in creating his emotional symbols and how he creates stereotyped, predictable responses: The rainladen trees *always* evoke a literary reference. Similarly, when he needs justification for his own emotional and intellectual isolation as artist, he discovers cunning as a jesuitical quality, and thus priests become in his thought cunning, and so do artists. Yet, earlier, he had disbelieved the description of the Jesuits as crafty (*P*, 155, 186). Once more Stephen's symbols predetermine the reality he perceives and they change life.

Stephen's most sophisticated and important work of art is his life, or his reconstruction of his life that we know as *A Portrait*. He tries to control impressions, information and meaning. It is not merely a Faustian attempt to aggrandize himself, but a reflection of his mind that insists that meaning be attached to every chance occurrence if that occurrence is to be immortalized as part of his life and work. The process of creating symbols allows Stephen to attach significance to women, or birds, to create a particular kind of betrayed-martryed-glorified artist. By the end of the novel Stephen is consciously altering the facts of what happened. For instance, we have Davin's report to make it clear that Stephen misinterprets E. C.[37] The most striking reshaping of actual experience is, however, the conversation with Cranly and its record in the diary that forms the last section of the novel.

If we compare the discussion with Cranly over Stephen's refusal to make his Easter duty with the diary entry in which Stephen records the discussion, we can see the extent to which he is selecting, interpreting, even distorting the dross of his existence into art.

> 20 *March:* Long talk with Cranly on the subject of my revolt. He had his grand manner on. I supple and suave. Attacked me on the score of love for one's mother. Tried to imagine his mother: cannot. Told me once, in a moment of thoughtlessness, his father was sixtyone when he was born. Can see him. . . . Hence Cranly's despair of soul: the child of exhausted loins. [*P*, 247–48]

Nothing in the conversation indicates that Cranly has "despair of soul." He may be less fascinating than Stephen because he is better adjusted to his environment or because we don't see his mind working, but he is certainly not in despair. Second, Stephen is hardly "supple and suave." Nor does Cranly have a "grand manner on." Far from that, Cranly tries to end the conversation before Stephen is ready to. "Stephen, struck by his tone of closure, reopened the discussion at once" (*P*, 243). When Stephen has revealed his real fear of blasphemy, he insists upon continuing the conversation. He saves face by equating his fear of blasphemy with his fear of "dogs, horses, firearms, the sea" (*P*, 243). It is apparent that the equation is not true. When he admits that he has confessed, revealed his soul, to Cranly—when, that is, he says, "You made me confess the fears that I have" (*P*, 247)—he tries to recoup by insisting upon what he does not fear. Then Stephen, in his diary entry, having neglected more of the conversation than he comments on, resorts to an *ad hominem* attack on Cranly. He never defeats Cranly in argument, which may be more annoying since he, not Cranly, began the argument and continued the discussion. So Stephen reshapes the occurrence in his diary and both accounts appear in the novel so that the diary entry will change our perception of the encounter and of Stephen. The irony is that Stephen cannot make his perceptions fit the facts. At the same time, something else happens. As Stephen's record of his life approaches the present, the time during which he narrates his story, his control diminishes and we notice more clearly errors in the narration: past events are more easily and surreptitiously controlled; time allows Stephen as it allows all of us to change and alter the events of our life. By the time we read of the diary entries, Stephen no longer has the luxury of mulling over and ordering his life; thus those entries are much closer to "raw" material. The temporal point of view of most of the novel is just prior to the dates the diary records; thus most of the novel is remembrance, filtered and selected and qualified by the present self-perception of Stephen; the disjuncture between diary and previous narration stems in part from that circumstance.

The process of turning oneself into art in order to escape the unpleasant truths of life and finally life itself is the process that Oscar Wilde depicted Dorian as following when he becomes his own portrait. Stephen's psychological motives, much clearer than Dorian's or Wilde's, or Pater's, help us understand both the ways in which *A Portrait* works and the ways in which certain kinds of theories about art are the product of psychological needs, assuage threats from the environment, and permit self-aggrandizement.

Stephen, without much awareness of the dangers, accepts the shared tendencies of an entire tradition, and in doing so usurps human and living perception through aesthetics. He trades life and love and emotions for art; in that trade he has given up precisely the raw materials of any art, even that art which he seeks to define and create. The contradiction here dooms Stephen as it doomed many poets of the 1890s to incomplete and sterile art.

Notes

1. Among the writings that prompt this remark are Pater's "Conclusion," Ruskin's studies of the Gothic and his later semisocialist writings, Morris's attempts to promote in his writing and speaking and more practical efforts beauty in the workplace, Wilde's "Critic as Artist," and Yeats's "Ireland and the Arts." The idea is not limited to these writers.

2. Sir Gavin de Beer, "Biology before the *Beagle*," in *Darwin*, ed. Philip Appleman (New York: W. W. Norton & Co., 1970), p. 5.

3. Charles Coulston Gillispie, "Lamarck and Darwin in the History of Science," in *Darwin*, ed. Philip Appleman (New York: W. W. Norton & Co., 1970), pp. 47–48, 49.

4. *Marius the Epicurean* (London: Dent, 1934), p. 103. Hereafter cited parenthetically *(M)*.

5. "Literary Criticism as a Science," *Topic: A Journal of the Liberal Arts* 12 (Fall 1966): 54.

What Stephen tries to do is make his life a "perceivable gestalt," rather than having to deal with the "hurly-burly of everyday life." Hagopian insists that one cannot even "use . . . the emotions derived from literature" as Stephen does, for instance, with *The Count of Monte Cristo* and Hauptmann's women.

6. *Uncollected Prose by W. B. Yeats*, ed. John P. Frayne and Colton Johnson, 2 vols. (New York: Columbia University Press, 1970, 1976), 2:257. Hereafter cited parenthetically (Frayne).

7. I have corrected punctuation in this passage: Frayne's text reads, "Outside the theatre science having done its work."

8. Ruth Temple, "The Ivory Tower," in *Edwardians and Late Victorians*, ed. Richard Ellmann, English Institute Essays 1959 (New York: Columbia University Press, 1960), p. 40.

9. Walter Pater, "Style," *Appreciations* (London: Macmillan and Co., 1910), pp. 5–38. W. B. Yeats, *Autobiography* (New York: The Macmillan Co., Collier Books, 1965), especially pp. 135, 247; hereafter cited parenthetically *(Autobiography)*.

Both Morris and Rossetti comment upon language and reference systems. William Morris on language and the necessity for creating a new art: (1) Letter to Fred Henderson, quoted in E. P. Thompson, *William Morris: Romantic to Revolutionary* (London: W. Heinemann Ltd., 1967), Appendix. "You see things have very much changed since the early days of language: once everybody who could express himself at all did so beautifully, was a poet for that occasion, because all language was beautiful. But now language is utterly degraded in our daily lives, and poets have to make a new tongue each for himself" (879).

(2) *William Morris, Artist, Writer, Socialist*, ed. May Morris (London: Blackwell, 1936). "I think one reason why there is so much to be said for that Art which deals with the life of the past, or rather with the artist's imagination of it, is because so can the artist have at his back that traditional combined idea of Art which once was common to the whole people" (306).

(3) "When an artist has really a very keen sense of beauty, I venture to think that he can not literally represent an event that takes place in modern life. He must add something or another to qualify or soften the ugliness and sordidness of the surrounding life in our generation" (ibid., 304).

(4) Morris sees the need not for redoing medieval art but laying "hold of the substance" of art as it was practiced; perhaps "uniting to the beauty which medæval art attained the realism which modern art aims at; to sculpture, uniting the beauty of the Greek and the expression of the Renaissance with some third quality not yet discovered" (*Collected Works*, ed. May Morris, 24 vols. [London: Longmans, 1910–1915], 23:91–92).

10. "The Decadent Movement in Literature," *Harpers New Monthly Magazine* 87 (November 1893): 859. See also Hugh Kenner's *The Pound Era* (Berkeley, Calif.: University of California Press, 1971) for a discussion of this shared "need" for a new language. Kenner uses Joyce as an example, but not as I am here.

11. Hughes T. Bredin, "Applied Aquinas: James Joyce's Aesthetics," *Éire-Ireland* 3 (1968): 65.

12. Geckle, "Stephen Dedalus and W. B. Yeats: The Making of the Villanelle," *Modern Fiction Studies* 15 (1969): 87–96, discusses how Yeats's concept of rhythm informs this passage. See discussion below.

13. Ibid.

14. "The Blessed Damozel," *The Works of Dante Gabriel Rossetti*, ed. with Preface and Notes by William Michael Rossetti (London: Ellis, 1911; reprint ed., New York: Adler's Foreign Books, Inc., 1972).

15. *Collected Works*, 1:111.

16. "Faustine," in *The Complete Works of Algernon Charles Swinburne*, ed. Sir Edmund Gosse, C. B. and Thomas James Wise, 20 vols. (New York: Russell and Russell, 1968), 1:243.

17. "Laus Veneris," *The Complete Works*, 1:348.

18. Ibid., p. 349.

19. Ibid., p. 347.

20. Ibid.

21. "Notes on Poems and Reviews," *The Complete Works*, 16:362.

22. See discussion, chapter 1. See also Archie Loss's essay, "The Pre-Raphaelite Woman, the

Symbolist *Femme-Enfant,* and the Girl with the Flowing Hair in the Earlier Work of James Joyce," *Journal of Modern Literature* 3 (1973): 3–23. Mr. Loss connects Stephen's woman with the women of Pre-Raphaelite painting.

23. *The Poems of Ernest Dowson,* ed. Mark Longaker (Philadelphia: University of Pennsylvania Press, 1962), p. 56 ("Ad Manus Puellae").

24. Oscar Wilde, "The Sphinx," *Works,* 1:289–308.

25. Yeats used this phrase as the title of one section in his *Autobiography.*

26. "The Angel in the House," in *The Death of the Moth* (New York: Harcourt, Brace, Jovanovich, 1942).

27. In connection with Stephen's transformation of the experience of death into an aesthetic experience, Dante Gabriel Rossetti's poem "My Sister's Sleep" is interesting. In that poem the focus of emotion shifts from the sister's death to the emotional and finally aesthetic experience of the speaker. For an explication, see James G. Nelson's "Aesthetic Experience and Rossetti's 'My Sister's Sleep,'" *Victorian Poetry* 7 (1969): 154–58.

28. Robert Scholes, "Stephen Dedalus: Poet or Esthete?" *Publications of the Modern Language Association* 79 (1964): 484–89.

29. Charles Rossman, "Stephen Dedalus' Villanelle," *James Joyce Quarterly* 12 (Spring 1975): 292, 289, 284, 282. See also Bernard Benstock's "The Temptation of St. Stephen: A View of the Villanelle," *James Joyce Quarterly* 14 (Fall 1976): 31–38. Benstock refines or, as he says, nudges Rossman "over the edge"; but he does not really disagree with him.

30. Stephen's villanelle uses many of the motifs that he has noted earlier in the novel. For instance, the chalice flowing to the brim first appears in chapter 1. After some schoolmates had been caught, apparently for smuggling, Stephen hears the "pock" of the cricket bats (*P,* 45). At the end of the chapter the sound is repeated: "In the soft grey silence he could hear the bump of the balls: and from here and from there through the quiet air the sound of the cricket bats: pick, pack, pock, puck: *like drops of water in a fountain falling softly in the brimming bowl*" (*P,* 59, italics mine). So from the first chapter of the novel, the image of the chalice flowing to the brim is part of Stephen's image patterns, ready to reappear whenever he sees or contemplates similar experiences.

Or, the prayer starting to heaven "not as a number but as a frail column of incense or as a slender flame" (*P,* 148) reappears in the poem as *"Above the flame the smoke of praise"* which flies upward to heaven as the eucharistic hymn.

The temptress herself, with *"languorous look and lavish limb"* is a reworking of Stephen's vision on the beach: there the girl whose eyes held his had "thighs" that "were fuller" (*P,* 171).

31. Zack Bowen, *Musical Allusions in the Works of James Joyce: Early Poetry through "Ulysses"* (Albany, N.Y.: State University of New York Press, 1974), p. 31.

32. Geckle, "The Making of the Villanelle," p. 90.

33. Ibid., pp. 91, 93.

34. *The Idea of a University,* ed. I. T. Ker (Oxford: Clarendon Press, 1976), p. 234.

35. Ibid.

36. "James Joyce and Stephen Dedalus: The Theory of Esthetics," *James Joyce Quarterly* 4 (Summer 1967): 314, 318–19.

37. Davin, attempting to convince Stephen to return to the Gaelic class, insists that E. C. is not interested in Father Moran: "—O, come now. . . . Is it on account of that certain young lady and Father Moran? But that's all in your own mind, Stevie. They were only talking and laughing" (*P,* 202).

4

The Failures of Aestheticism

Joyce implies his assessment of the human failures of Aestheticism in the prayer of Stephen's mother; she prays that he "may learn in my own life and away from home and friends what the heart is and what it feels" (*P*, 252–53). While the artistic failures are, for example, implicit in a poem that makes sense only as a passage in a novel, the human failures are dramatized in details of the plot. For instance, when Stephen leaves Dublin for Paris, he calls upon Daedalus: "Old father, old artificer, stand me now and ever in good stead." In the imagery of the novel, that appeal identifies Stephen as Icarus, the son who flies sunward until the wax on his wings melts and he tumbles into the sea. Early in *Ulysses*, we find Stephen recognizing that identification: "You flew. . . . Paris and back. Lapwing. Icarus. *Pater, ait.* Seabedabbled" (*U*, 210). Stephen knows, in the later novel, that he has been Icarus, not Daedalus; he knows his escape has failed.

Stephen Dedalus fails to show compassion and charity, fails to recognize the claims and even the existence of other human beings, fails to recognize his own emotional needs. Adherents of Aestheticism with their solipsistic vision, their belief that the artist is a special soul destined to live separate from the rest of humanity, faced the same failures, and lived disastrous lives. A. C. Swinburne's later years were marked by emotional disorders and virtual incarceration. Oscar Wilde, after a long and very public career, ended disgraced and exiled. Less public, but just as tragic, were the lives of younger men who chose to associate themselves and their art with Aestheticism. W. B. Yeats, looking back to the 1890s in his *Autobiography*, catalogued and explored the failures and misfortunes of his contemporaries, especially of Lionel Johnson and Ernest Dowson:

> Though I cannot explain what brought others of my generation to such misfortune, I think that . . . I can explain some part of Dowson's and Johnson's dissipation—
>
> > What portion in the world can the
> > artist have,

Who has awaked from the common dream,
But dissipation and despair?

[*Autobiography*, 208]

Yeats associated these men's art with their lives—apparently without remembering that he too was a poet and yet did not end miserably. These men "live[d] lives of such disorder"; but they also lived lives of isolation—from each other even. Yeats marveled that he did not know that Johnson or Dowson drank heavily, that he did not know that Johnson's "conversations" with famous men were fictional— "dreaming" that "was made a necessity by his artificial life" perhaps. Having discovered Johnson's alcoholism, Yeats even urged him "to put himself . . . into an Institute"; he recalls that "the last time" he saw "Dowson he was pouring out a glass of whiskey for himself in an empty corner of my room and murmuring over and over in what seemed automatic apology 'The first to-day' " (*Autobiography*, 202, 203, 206, 208). While Yeats did not know what caused these tragedies, he did associate them with art and with Walter Pater:

> If Rossetti was a subconscious influence, and perhaps the most pow-
> erful of all, we looked consciously to Pater for our philosophy. Three or
> four years ago I re-read *Marius the Epicurean* . . . it still seemed to me, as I
> think it seemed to us all, the only great prose in modern English, and yet I
> began to wonder if it, or the attitude of mind of which it was the noblest
> expression, had not caused the disaster of my friends. It taught us to walk
> upon a rope, tightly stretched through serene air, and we were left to keep
> our feet upon a swaying rope in the storm. . . . I think none knew as yet
> that Dowson, who seemed to drink so little and had so much dignity and
> reserve, was breaking his heart for the daughter of the keeper of an Italian
> eating house, in dissipation and drink; and that he might that very night
> sleep upon a sixpenny bed in a doss house. [*Autobiography*, 201–2]

These men, "distant" in their "relations to one another," could not find even among fellow poets a community. What Yeats outlined, then, was the effect, or the possible effect, of Aestheticism upon human beings— but those human beings presumably chose Aestheticism for personal reasons, just as they chose to respect Pater as their "sage." They believed "that life is ritual," but ritual is distanced, formulaic, indifferent to idiosyncratic needs and the needs of a specific time. When life is perceived to be ritual, it is too close to "Life is art" for comfort. And the storms of real life make tightrope walking impossible.

The potential villain in this case had himself worried about his influence. Pater deleted the "Conclusion" to *The Renaissance*, a crucial statement of English Aestheticism, in the second edition, because he feared that "it might possibly mislead some of those young men into whose hands it might fall," and claimed, "I have dealt more fully in

Marius the Epicurean with the thoughts suggested by it."[1] In the "Conclusion," Pater was unconcerned about the morality of a life spent in moments of high passion and had emphasized the isolation of the individual; in contrast, in *Marius,* his focus changes—he concerns himself with moral issues and the demands of the community as much as with the claims of the individual in his prison of a mind. The fear of misleading young men, then, is probably a realistic fear that young men, without any overt concern with the morality of life or the community in which they live, would be led by Pater's prose to adopt a life separate from other people and separate from considerations of morality or ethics. In a later essay, Pater had more accurately stated his position: at the end of "Style" he claimed that great literature must deal with great and good ideas and emotions.[2] But the "Conclusion" makes no reference to such ethical judgments—and could, indeed, mislead young men who chose to follow Pater as their sage.

In fiction, at least, it did. One of Dorian Gray's rationales for his behavior—behavior marked by its indifference to all moral and social values—is virtually a quote from the "Conclusion":

> . . . there was to be . . . a new Hedonism which was to recreate life. . . . Its aim, indeed, was to be experience itself, and not the fruits of experience, sweet or bitter as they might be.[3]

Pater had written: "Not the fruit of experience, but experience itself, is the end."[4] Dorian Gray draws one unspoken but possible corollary to Pater's doctrine: "A new Hedonism." Dorian, reading Huysmans and quoting Pater, is the epitome of an Aesthete and fulfills Pater's fears; Wilde provides for the modern reader one example of how Aestheticism fails by dramatizing it in his novel.

During Joyce's boyhood, there were two influential Aesthetes: Walter Pater and Oscar Wilde. In the popular imagination, Wilde was the more visible. From the performance of Gilbert and Sullivan's *Patience* on, Wilde was the example par excellence of bohemian artists. His successful and highly publicized tours to America, his personal and professional flamboyance, and his influence on innumerable young artists were probably enough to make his name equivalent to "the artist." But his trial in 1895 and his subsequent conviction on charges of homosexuality were notorious. For the average man in the street, Arnold's philistine, he was the obvious whipping boy, the perfect example of what was wrong with artists: "See, we told you. Art is not for men; artists are perverted, immoral; they threaten the social structure." However, Pater, while particularly famous among the educated classes, was the sage, the prophet for the poets of the 1890s, as Yeats's testimony makes clear. A writer, writing about the artist in the early part of the century, would assume that his audience knew these two artists at least by reputation. Joyce, merely through his title, could associate

Stephen with Dorian Gray and Marius—and probably with George Moore, whose *Confessions of a Young Man* was another novel about a young artist. But even if Joyce did not hold such an expectation, to write another novel about the growth of the artist was to invite comparisons with these other novels, much as a novel about young men who went off to war invited, a generation later, comparisons with other novels about young men who went off to war.

When we turn to Pater's *Marius the Epicurean* and Wilde's *Picture of Dorian Gray*, we find that Joyce described, like his predecessors, the liabilities of the Aesthetic life as failures of contact—personal and artistic—between the artist/seer and the audience/community. I chose these two novels as most likely analogues to Joyce's because Pater and Wilde appear to have shared Joyce's analysis.[5]

Fatherless and Exiled

The image of the alienated artist, cut off from his society and rejected by it, coheres with the metaphor of the poet-priest. More to the point, exile and alienation are chosen responses, responses that are defensive. In discussing Tennyson's "Ulysses," R. F. Storch describes the general psychological truth expressed through exile:

> . . . if one feels rejected and abandoned this [exile] seems to ease the burden. . . , and one can even assume moral superiority by rejecting the other instead of feeling rejected: I am now cutting myself off voluntarily because the ancestral hearth does not provide conditions for self-fulfillment. . . .

> Ulysses is the spokesman not merely of an individual fate, but also of a type of exile who in the nineteenth century becomes nearly identical with the figure of the poet, who spurns "a savage race/That hoard, and sleep, and feed, and know not me." . . . The poetic imagination rejects the crassness of the time and in turn feels rejected by it. Stephen must see himself as exile, because he feels guilty. . . . The neglect of . . . pieties and loyalties is the condition of his uneasy freedom.[6]

Exile from one's nation (as Stephen Dedalus chooses) parallels exile from one's family and culture. The perfect metaphor for such an exile is the fatherless man, a man detached from his biological past and communal present, the odd man out. In *Dorian Gray, Marius the Epicurean*, and *A Portrait*, the protagonists are, in differing ways, fatherless: Marius remembers his father only vaguely, Dorian has never known his father, Stephen Dedalus—more realistically—murders his father psychologically by supplanting him with Daedalus (a figure that is both a father and the self).

False or nonexistent fathers create some of the protagonists' difficulties. A false father, Lord Henry, perverts and destroys Dorian Gray by leading him away from life into refined patterns, into an intense desire for youth and beauty, and into a dangerous rejection of moral standards. When Dorian and Lord Henry first meet when Basil Hallward is painting Dorian's portrait, Hallward warns Dorian about Lord Henry: " 'Don't . . . pay any attention to what Lord Henry says. He has a very bad influence over all his friends' " (*DG*, 37). But Lord Henry does influence Dorian: he encourages him to " 'get rid of . . . temptation' " by yielding to it. " 'Resist it, and your soul grows sick with longing for the things it has forbidden to itself, with desire for what its monstrous laws have made monstrous and unlawful' " (*DG*, 39). "Words spoken by chance, no doubt, and with wilful paradox in them—had touched some secret chord that had never been touched before" in Dorian (*DG*, 40). And it is Lord Henry who makes mortality and age so repulsive to Dorian: " 'You have the most marvellous youth, and youth is the one thing worth having' " (*DG*, 45). Dorian initially rejects the idea: " 'I don't feel that' " (*DG*, 45), but as Henry elaborately describes his age—its wrinkles and ugliness—and the transitory nature of Beauty, he tempts him to a fall. " 'Live! Live the wonderful life that is in you! . . . A new Hedonism—that is what our century wants. You might be its visible symbol. . . . The world belongs to you for a season' " (*DG*, 47). When Basil finishes the portrait, Dorian looks at it and realizes, "Yes, there would be a day when his face would be wrinkled and wizen, his eyes dim and colourless, the grace of his figure broken and deformed. . . . The life that was to make his soul would mar his body. He would become dreadful, hideous, and uncouth" (*DG*, 51–52). In response, he wishes to exchange places with the portrait:

> "I shall grow old, and horrible, and dreadful. But this picture will remain always young. . . . If it were only the other way! If it were I who was to be always young, and the picture that was to grow old! For that—for that—I would give everything! Yes, there is nothing in the whole world I would not give! I would give my soul for that!" [*DG*, 52–53].

The Faustian pact has been offered; later Dorian realizes that it was accepted. Lord Henry functions more and more as Mephistopheles, encouraging Dorian to deny the consequences of his actions. When Dorian emotionally destroys his first love, the picture reflects his actions: "The face appeared to him to be a little changed. The expression looked different. One would have said that there was a touch of cruelty in the mouth" (*DG*, 166). At the end of the novel, Dorian recognizes that his pact had ruined him: "Ah! in what a monstrous moment of pride and passion he had prayed that the portrait should bear the burden of his days, and he keep the unsullied splendour of eternal youth! All his failure had been due to that" (*DG*, 398). Like Dorian, Stephen is

prepared to sacrifice his soul for art: in order to "express myself in some
mode of life or art as freely as I can and as wholly as I can. . . . I am not
afraid to make a mistake . . . perhaps as long as eternity too" (*P*, 247).
Lord Henry had tempted Dorian into a desire to escape time—and
humanity. Life becomes for Dorian "the greatest of the arts" (*DG*, 236).
Just as Stephen Dedalus has escaped the consequences of his inability to
kiss E. C. on the tram steps by converting the experience into a poem,
just as Stephen escapes the truth of Cranly's arguments at the end of *A
Portrait* by making Cranly an image of his precursor, so Dorian escapes
experience and life by becoming a walking, breathing portrait of youth
and beauty. And it is the false father who encourages this escape. Lord
Henry urges Dorian " 'to become the spectator of one's own life' "—
and hence " 'to escape the suffering of life' " (*DG*, 203).

Marius's problem is different; he knew his real father only briefly
and hence his self-identity is, in part, achieved only when he is reconciled to his dead father at the grave. And that reconciliation is, crucially,
prior to his ambiguous conversion to Christianity at the end of the
novel. By the time he goes off to school, early in the novel, Marius is an
actual orphan because his mother has died. He has only vague memories
of "the father, dead ten years before, of whom, remembering but a tall,
grave figure above him in early childhood, Marius habitually thought as
a genius a little cold and severe" (*M*, 7). For the father, religion had been
"in the main a matter of family pride" and that faith is "sustained by a
native instinct of devotion in the young Marius" (*M*, 4). Marius's faith is
different from his father's; Pater ambiguously asserts that "the very
absence from those venerable usages of all definite history and dogmatic
interpretation had already awakened much speculative activity" (*M*, 6)
in the young boy. Why Marius does not have this history or interpretation is never clear, although Pater seems to associate the father's absence
with Marius's skeptical faith:

> The devotion of the father then had handed on loyally . . . a certain
> tradition of life, which came to mean much for the young Marius. The
> feeling with which he thought of his dead father was almost exclusively
> that of awe; though crossed at times by a not unpleasant sense of liberty,
> as he could but confess to himself, pondering, in the actual absence of so
> weighty and continual a restraint, upon the arbitrary power which Roman
> religion and Roman law gave to the parent over the son. [*M*, 11]

The father's death (or absence as Pater seems to focus on it) allows
Marius a freedom of belief and action that would not have been allowed
by the Roman religion. His mother, who dies during his teens, is remembered more positively. "She died away from home, but sent for
him at the last, with a painful effort of her part, but to his great grati-
tude, pondering, as he always believed, that he might chance otherwise
to look back all his life long upon a single fault with something like

remorse, and find the burden a great one. For it happened that, through some sudden, incomprehensible petulance, there had been an angry childish gesture, and a slighting word, at the very moment of her departure, actually for the last time" (*M*, 24–25). By the fourth chapter, Marius is alone in the world, a spectator among his school friends, viewing rather than participating in school activities. His isolation at school is consonant with his lack of contact with parents.

Very near the end of the novel Pater makes much clearer the alienation of son from father. Marius visits his father's grave:

> That hard feeling, again, which had always lingered in his mind with the thought of the father he had scarcely known, melted wholly away, as he read the precise number of his years, and reflected suddenly: He was of my own present age; nor [sic] had [sic] old man, but with interests, as he looked round him on the world for the last time, even as mine to-day! And with that came a blinding rush of kindness, as if two alienated friends had come to understand each other at last. [*M*, 257]

It is this experience, this mental reconciliation with the father, which allows Marius to feel sympathy with other people. Shortly after, he contemplates his own life of detachment and contemplation: "His own temper, his early theoretic scheme of things, would have pushed him on to movement and adventure. Actually, as circumstances had determined, all its movement had been inward; movement of observation only, or even of pure meditation; in part, perhaps, because throughout it had been something of a *meditatio mortis,* ever facing towards the act of final detachment" (*M*, 258). His vision, that is, has always moved toward the dead—the father and his own death. Reconciliation with the father precedes human connection. His Christian friend Cornelius arrives: "It was just then that Marius felt, as he had never done before, the value to himself, the overpowering charm, of his friendship. 'More than brother!'—he felt—'like a son also!' . . . Identifying himself with Cornelius in so dear a friendship, through him, Marius seemed to touch, to ally himself to, actually to become a possessor of the coming world; even as happy parents reach out, and take possession of it, in and through the survival of their children. For in these days their intimacy had grown very close" (*M*, 258–59).

This closeness, this touching, is available to a man who has not felt emotional closeness since the death of his mother. The freedom he feels because he has no father allows him to reject his traditional religion— one part of his past—because "the pursuit" of his ideal "demanded entire liberty of heart and brain," and "that old, staid, conservative religion of his childhood certainly had its being in a world of somewhat narrow restrictions" (*M*, 29). To achieve this liberty, Marius, like Stephen, must divest himself of emotional attachments: "It had always been his policy, through all his pursuit of 'experience', to take flight in time from any too disturbing passion, from any sort of affection likely to quicken his pulse beyond the point at which the quiet work of life was practicable. . . . He felt that the mental atmosphere within himself was perceptibly colder" (*M*, 247). Marius has chosen to avoid human contact, here contact with or commitment to a woman. Freedom and isolation go hand in hand. The early freedom from the father has, as its necessary corollary, isolation from hereditary culture and faith but also isolation from contemporary faith and current friends.

Stephen and Marius find early an almost religious necessity to be silent and separate; Marius "secluded himself . . . from others . . . in a severe intellectual meditation, that salt of poetry, without which all the more serious charm is lacking to the imaginative world" (*M*, 72). Stephen contemplates Aristotle, Aquinas, Augustine, attempts to form an aesthetic theory, rejects his classmates, refuses to sign a peace petition, and refuses to join the Gaelic revival: one of his classmates calls him an "antisocial being" (*P*, 177), and the label rings true. Stephen needs and wants the same isolated freedom from the voices of his father and his mother, from "the screech of an unseen maniac," from "voices offending and threatening to humble the pride of his youth" (*P*, 175–76); his flight from Dublin is imaged as an escape from imprisoning nets. But, as it does with Marius, that freedom means emotional coldness: E.C.'s overtures must be denied as Stephen turns on "the spiritual-heroic refrigerating apparatus" (*P*, 252). Stephen recapitulates the isolation of Dorian from friends and society, which permits freedom but costs Dorian his humanity.

Both Pater and Joyce overtly use the metaphor of exile, tying the exile to a lack of fathers. Marius leaves his family home, and all the certainties associated with it, to go to Rome, the decadent center of the pagan world, just as Stephen goes to Paris, the decadent center of the modern world, leaving behind the certainties of Ireland. And, indeed, both men undertake the journey at least in part for artistic reasons. Marius

> had . . . come to Rome partly under poetic vocation, to receive all those things, the very impress of life itself, upon the visual, the imaginative, organ, as upon a mirror; to reflect them; to transmute them into golden words. [*M*, 103]

Stephen and Marius are both transmuters. Stephen goes "to encounter . . . the reality of experience" and to transmute that daily bread into art. Dorian's exile is totally psychic, not physical; yet, he is as effectively separate from his society as Stephen and Marius.

That separation, imaged in fatherlessness and exile, lies at the root of emotional and artistic failure. Wilde, Pater, and Joyce appear to agree that false fathers—inappropriately chosen fathers—and the absence of the real father cut young men off from human contact and emotional connection while allowing them freedom. In Wilde, that freedom amounts to license; in Wilde, the protagonist is more severely and completely isolated than Stephen or Marius is. If one symbol or way of imaging the limitations of Aestheticism as a philosophical basis of life can be seen in the artistic treatment of women, another perhaps as crucial one can be seen in the absence of fathers, the biological transmitters of culture and community. But Joyce is more realistic than Pater or Wilde; he demonstrates that in most young men's lives the supplanting of the father is a chosen, mental act. For Dorian and Marius accidents of fortune leave them without appropriate fathers or father figures. Stephen, by choice, rejects the father supplied by fortune, and in rather a normal, adolescent way, mentally replaces the father with a demigod—Daedalus. Near the end of *A Portrait*, Joyce associated fathers once more with Ireland. A friend of Stephen's, who has just returned from western Ireland, tells a tale of an old Gael, an image of the rejected fatherland. Stephen comments in his diary on the man and his tale:

> I fear him. I fear his redrimmed horny eyes. It is with him I must struggle all through this night till day come, till he or I lie dead, gripping him by the sinewy throat till . . . Till what? Till he yield to me? No. I mean him no harm. [*P*, 252, Joyce's elipses]

This figure of fatherland is the cultural father—a more potent force now than the biological father, a force still to be struggled against. Joyce has exaggerated the idea of fatherlessness, but he has also made it clearer and more realistic.

The Dangers of Aestheticism

Perhaps because Wilde draws extensively on Huysmans's *À Rebours*, Dorian Gray is more overtly an Aesthete than Marius or Stephen Dedalus. All three characters share the major assumptions of Aestheticism: art is purer and more perfect than life, words have magical or alchemical power, and the artist's mission in life is predetermined. For Stephen, art is life "purified and reprojected from the human imagination"; for Lord Henry, the virtue of art is that in it "the mere shapes and patterns of things" become refined; they gain "a kind of symbolical value, as though they were themselves patterns of some other and more perfect form whose shadow they made real" (*DG*, 71). Dorian gains that symbolical value by becoming the unsullied, eternally beautiful portrait. Marius shares this emphasis upon purity and perfection: "The products of the imagination must themselves be held to present the most perfect forms of life—spirit and matter alike under their purest and most perfect conditions" (*M*, 85). Yet, for Marius and Stephen, this perfection is only a reflection of the inner perfection. Stephen's meditation upon "a day of dappled seaborne clouds" ends in his commending the phrase as "an inner world of individual emotions mirrored perfectly in a lucid supple periodic prose" (*P*, 166–67). Marius believes that "the word, the phrase, [is] valuable in exact proportion to the transparency with which it conveyed to others the apprehension, the emotion, the mood, so vividly real within himself" (*M*, 89).

That art should mirror the inner life is not, in itself, a terribly original or daring idea. To the extent that the inner life is chosen over the outer life—almost in rejecting the outer life—the theory is more original, at least in the nineteenth century. But what makes these artistic theories conjoin with Aestheticism is the belief, one current by the 1880s in certain circles, that words are magical or alchemical—a belief that Yeats and Mallarmé and Symons shared. Marius does not, at least not overtly. Dorian and Stephen think of words as separate from a human being that produces them. Dorian's temptation comes from words—but he focuses not on Lord Henry, who produces them, but rather on the words themselves:

> Words! Mere words! How terrible they were! How clear, and vivid, and cruel. One could not escape from them. And yet what a subtle magic there was in them! They seemed to be able to give a plastic form to formless things, and to have a music of their own as sweet as that of viol or of lute. Mere words! Was there anything so real as words? [*DG*, 40–41]

Stephen's epiphany in Cork, that he shares "monstrous reveries" with other (and in this case, past) young men, arises from "words":

> A vision of their [other students'] life, which his father's words had been powerless to evoke, sprang up before him out of the word cut in the desk. . . . His recent monstrous reveries came thronging into his memory. They too had sprung up before him, suddenly and furiously, out of mere words. [*P*, 89–90]

This passage is curious because in it Joyce distinguishes between the words that are powerless and words that have tremendous power. The distinction here has to do with human agents: on the one hand, words produced by an ordinary father are powerless; on the other, words produced by an unnamed, imaginary figure and words that "spring up" in the inner life of the artist as a young man are powerful. Although special persons, or the unprompted workings of a mind, may produce powerful words, their particular and unique power attaches not to the utterer but to the words themselves: in this sense they are "mere words." Dorian and Stephen both find that power threatening; Dorian claims there is no "escape from them"; Stephen later feels that the words on stores "bound his mind like the words of a spell" (*P*, 178). In each case, the words are separate from people—or appear to be. These no-

tions about words at least assume that words are not controlled by
people, but by some supernatural force, sometimes an artistic force.
And, thus, for the artist to control words he cannot be "mere man"—he
must have some supernatural power too. Like the sages who could read
and control the ancient runes, the modernist artist is special in that he
can control and read the word—a task that most of us cannot accomplish.

For Marius and Stephen this control is the domain of the poet/
priest. And their art has only a vague relationship to external realities.
Marius's "first, early boyish ideal of priesthood, the sense of dedication,
survived through all the distractions of the world, and when all thought
of such vocation had finally passed from him, [it moved] as a ministry,
in spirit at least, towards a sort of hieratic beauty and order in the
conduct of life" (*M*, 16). Poetry becomes for Marius a sacred mission;
his early religion came "to count with him as but one form of poetic
beauty" (*M*, 26). He conceives of winning fame as "a poet perhaps" (*M*,
28). He "feels himself to be something of a priest, and [sees in] that
devotion of his days to the contemplation of what is beautiful, a sort of
perpetual religious service" (*M*, 150–51). He thinks of fulfilling "the
desire of the artist in him . . . by the exact and literal transcript of what
was then passing around him, in simple prose, arresting the desirable
moment as it passed, and prolonging its life a little" (*M*, 94). But when
Marius actually produces his prose, it does not transcribe the world
around him accurately at all. Marius discovers himself enfolded in "a
very delicate poetry"

> . . . as passing into the poet's house he paused for a moment to glance back
> towards the heights above; whereupon, the numerous cascades of the
> precipitous garden of the villa, framed in the doorway of the hall, fell into
> a harmless picture, in its place among the pictures within, and scarcely
> more real than they—a landscape piece, in which the power of water
> (plunging into what unseen depths!), done to the life, was pleasant, and
> without its natural terrors. [*M*, 186]

The prose poem, the artistic shaping here, makes the scene "harmless"
and devoid of "natural terrors"; similarly, Stephen's ability to change
his encounter with E. C.—to make himself one of the kissers rather
than the rejector of the kiss—follows the same patterns. The realities—
tram, trammen, and horses—disappear; the boy who could not kiss the
girl is supplanted by a boy who does kiss the girl. Both poets remove
the threatening aspects of experience; they control and make static—in
poems or pictures—the terror of experience; by doing so, they distort
and remove the truth of their experience. Like Dowson's melancholy
lyrics, Marius's picture and Stephen's poem are vague. Dorian's status
as art object specifically allows him to escape into a static, nonthreaten-
ing world.

But words and the ability to manipulate them are not the only requisites for artistry. One of the most distressing aspects of decadence and Aestheticism to the philistine was that the followers or adherents appeared to recognize no limits on the kinds of behavior and experience permissible. Like *enfants terribles,* the decadents shocked the bourgeoisie and claimed that all experience was good and necessary: "Not the fruit of experience, but experience itself is the end." Dorian, Stephen, and Marius seem to demonstrate that belief: each wants experience, and yet for all of their overt and verbal dedication to it, none of them joins in the life around him. The philistine view was wrong, because of a paradox in Aestheticism. Each watches as a spectator from the earliest sections of the novels; each seeks to control or modify time as it passes—or to escape time; each wishes to separate his life from the life of the common man. That confusion, or paradox, is implicit in the "Conclusion" to *The Renaissance.* Although Pater had called upon his readers to experience life, and hence expand their brief interval on this earth, he ended by suggesting that life was not the best place to find experience:

> . . . our one chance lies in expanding that interval, in getting as many pulsations as possible into the given time. Great passions may give us this quickened sense of life, ecstacy and sorrow of life, the various forms of enthusiastic activity, disinterested or otherwise, which come naturally to many of us. Only be sure it is passion—that it does yield you this fruit of a quickened, multiplied consciousness. Of such wisdom, the poetic passion, the desire of beauty, the love of art for its own sake, has most. For art comes to you proposing frankly to give nothing but the highest quality to your moments as they pass, and simply for those moments' sake.[7]

Contemplating art, a spectator sport, is the highest form of experience and passion. This passage is perhaps the most crucial document of Aestheticism. In it, Pater promulgates the paradox of inactivity and detachment fulfilling the desire for experience and passion, and fulfilling that desire best: "The wisest, at least 'among the children of this world,'" spend their interval "in art and song." It is no wonder that Pater worried about the effect of the essay on young men.

What is or was wrong with the kinds of lives the Aesthetes lived, the kinds of art they produced? The principal writers knew—Wilde and Pater knew, even if they could not act on the knowledge. Not unlimited, amoral experience, but isolation, failures of compassion, inability to connect with other human beings—these qualities of Aestheticism, in part chosen and in part predestined—produced unhappy lives and second-rate art.

Of the three writers—Joyce, Wilde, and Pater—Joyce is the least overt about how serious the failures are. Wilde, the most obviously damaged human being, is the most overt. In *Marius*, Pater had chosen a narrative point of view that allowed him to comment on the limitations of Marius's philosophy:

> . . . if certain moments of their lives were high-pitched, passionately coloured, intent with sensation, and a kind of knowledge which, in its vivid clearness, was like sensation—if, now and then, they apprehended the world in its fullness, and had a vision, almost "beatific", of ideal personalities in life and art, yet these moments were a very costly matter: they paid a great price for them, in the sacrifice of a thousand possible sympathies, of things only to be enjoyed through sympathy, from which they detached themselves, in intellectual pride, in loyalty to a mere theory that would take nothing for granted, and assent to no approximate or hypothetical truths. [*M*, 153]

This passage, and others like it, state, I think, the real difference between the philosophy of the "Conclusion" to *The Renaissance* and the philosophy developed in *Marius*. Pater believed that Marius's Cyrenaicism is a "subjective and partial" ideal—one that holds special attraction for the young (*M*, 149). Marius could choose it because of his father's absence. But Pater, although sympathizing with it and with the young men who held such ideals, believed that "by its exclusiveness, and by negation rather than positively, . . . such theories fail to satisfy us permanently; and what they really need for their correction, is the complementary influence of some greater system, in which they may find their due place" (*M*, 151), even if young men must go through the narrower ideal first. The "greater system" in Pater's novel may well be Christianity, although the attractions that the faith holds for Marius are almost purely aesthetic: the beauty of the service and of the worshippers attracts him.

In Wilde's novel, the failure is imaged physically: Dorian kills the painter of his portrait in order to avoid detection (killing this creator is like killing a father) and finally stabs the portrait itself, trying to kill the evil charm. In doing so, he commits suicide. His life of isolation and utter and complete freedom leads to absolute self-destruction. Having made his Faustian pact, he discovers that art, given a life of its own, is fatal, destroying his own life. He tells Basil, " 'There is something fatal about a portrait. It has a life of its own' " (*DG*, 214). Art and being an artist is dangerous in this novel. Basil is murdered to prevent the revelation of the portrait; Dorian claims that the portrait " 'has destroyed' " him (*DG*, 286). Wilde explicitly connects perfect art and inhumanity. Just before Dorian's suicide, Lord Henry and Dorian discuss the portrait:

> " . . . I never really liked it. . . . It used to remind me of those curious lines in some play—'Hamlet,' I think—how do they run?—

> " *'Like the painting of a sorrow,*
> *A face without a heart.'*

Yes: that is what is was like!" [*DG*, 388]

Wilde makes the statement even stronger in Lord Henry's response: " 'If a man treats life artistically, his brain is his heart' " (*DG*, 388), and in Lord Henry's reference to the Bible: " 'What does it profit a man if he gain the whole world and lose . . . his own soul' " (*DG*, 389). Although Lord Henry is right when he asserts that " 'life has been your art' " (*DG*, 393), Dorian rejects that life, vows " 'to be good' " and claims that art has " 'poisoned' " him (*DG*, 394). Dorian sees the "living death of his own soul" (*DG*, 400), he sees that "of the lives that had crossed his own it had been the fairest and the most full of promise that he had brought to shame" (*DG*, 398). The claims of the heart, and the claims of morality, and the claims of others had been rejected; and he has paid the price—the death of the soul—even an unintended manifestation—of his emotional and spiritual death. I think it worthwhile to acknowledge here that many readers find Dorian's suicide, the moral element of Wilde's novel, too neat, too abrupt, too much a way out of a novel that could go no further; that is, many readers sense that Wilde's own sympathies approve less of the moral "punishment" than of the experimentation and life that precedes it. Even granting that reservation, Wilde's novel makes it clear that Wilde did understand and was concerned about the implicit failures of Aestheticism.

In both Wilde's and Pater's novels, the conversion to wider sympathy—or the recognition that the Aesthetic life is deadly because it is indifferent to the claims of others—is unconvincing. Pater's own commentary convinces the reader, but Marius's only visible act of sympathy comes after reconciliation with his father and somewhat melodramatically ends with his death, a death caused by his loyalty to Cornelius and, through Cornelius, to Christianity.

In *A Portrait,* no conversion or even recognition is apparent. In part that difference stems from Stephen's fictional age at the end of the novel. Joyce did not so overtly dramatize the failures of Aestheticism—and dangers of rejecting the family—in *A Portrait,* for he cut his tale off short. Only in *Ulysses* can we see Stephen as fallen, as Icarus, into the sea between Dublin and Paris. What we do see in *A Portrait* is the implicit failure. First, in Stephen's argument with Cranly, Cranly argues that Stephen should communicate at Easter simply to please his mother. When Stephen objects, Cranly proposes one truth: "— Whatever else is unsure in this stinking dunghill of a world a mother's love is not. Your mother brings you into the world, carries you first in her body. What do we know about what she feels? But whatever she feels, it, at least, must be real. It must be. What are our ideas or ambitions? Play. Ideas! Why, that bloody bleating goat Temple has ideas" (*P*, 241–42). Joyce appears to have agreed with Cranly, for he once told his brother that there were two certain things in this world: a mother's love for her child and the hypocrisy of men.[8] As importantly, Cranly argues emotionally—from compassion and charity: make your Easter duty and give your mother a break. Second, at the end of the novel, Stephen records his mother's prayer: "that I may learn in my own life and away from home and friends what the heart is and what it feels" (*P*, 252–53). Her prayer reinforces Cranly's principles of emotional connection and sympathy. There is no melodramatic end here, except the one Stephen creates for himself; no murders, no magical transformation of people into art or art into people, no fantasyland of unlimited success, no plague come to end a novel. Joyce's novel is persistently realistic; he chose to impose the rules he perceived in his own life on the characters and events of his novels; Wilde and Pater did not. And in Joyce's novel, family and financial responsibilities and emotional attachments are not conveniently out of the way; Stephen has insufficient money to extricate himself completely from the environment that produced him, and his family, at least for a while, continues to live and disapprove of his choices. That is, Stephen's quandary is more realistic. How does one pursue perfect beauty in a fallen world? Joyce attempted to dramatize what he thought would happen to a young man in reasonably normal circumstances who embraced this kind of life, this kind of art. He differed less from Pater and Wilde and Yeats in his final judgment than he did in his realism—a violently anti-Aesthetic mode. He used the realistic storm and the realistic tightrope to plunge his character not into a circus pit, but into the real sea between Dublin and Paris.

Notes

1. Walter Pater, "Conclusion," *Studies in the History of the Renaissance* (London: Macmillan and Co., 1910), p. 233.

2. Walter Pater, "Style," *Appreciations* (London: Macmillan and Co., 1910), p. 38.

3. Oscar Wilde, *The Picture of Dorian Gray, The Complete Works*, 12 vols. (Garden City, N.Y.: Doubleday, Page & Co., 1923), 4:238–39. Hereafter cited parenthetically (*DG*).

4. Pater, "Conclusion," *The Renaissance*, p. 236.

5. James Hafley, in "Walter Pater's *Marius* and the Technique of Modern Fiction," *Modern Fiction Studies* 3 (1957): 99–109, discusses connections between Pater's and Joyce's works. Despite this study, which might have served as an introduction to extended discussion, little subsequent criticism has discussed the two novels. An exception is Robert Scotto's essay, "'Visions' and 'Epiphanies': Fictional Technique in Pater's *Marius* and Joyce's *Portrait*," *James Joyce Quarterly* 11 (Fall 1973): 41–50.

All novels about young artists do not seem to be analogous to Joyce's novel. For instance, Moore's novel, despite the title and subject, and despite the fact that Joyce knew much of Moore's work, does not share image patterns or specific concerns with *A Portrait*. Huysmans' *À Rebours* shares many themes with *A Portrait*, but Huysmans' novel is not similar in tone and does not really trace the development or education of a young man. According to Richard Ellmann, *James Joyce* (New York: Oxford University Press, 1959), pp. 78–79, Joyce read *La-bas* before 1902. "After an initial liking for Huysmans he began to complain that Huysmans in his later books was becoming 'more formless and more obviously comedian.'" As important is the fact that Huysmans' aestheticism is totally different in tone and morality from that in any of Joyce's works. Joyce's sense of Aestheticism is, I suspect, much more like the English garden variety than like Huysmans'; and that, I suspect, means that Joyce is, like Wilde, more conscious of moral issues than many of his Continental contemporaries.

6. R. F. Storch, "The Fugitive from the Ancestral Hearth: Tennyson's 'Ulysses,'" *Texas Studies in Language and Literature* 13 (1971): 294, 295, 296. Storch does not see any distance between Joyce and Stephen, and he does not see the novel containing any comment upon Stephen as Stephen falls into the pattern of self-deluding exile.

7. Pater, "Conclusion," *The Renaissance*, p. 239.

8. Stanislaus Joyce, *My Brother's Keeper* (New York: Viking Press, 1958), p. 91: "He declared bitterly that he believed in only two things, a woman's love of her child and a man's love of lies—of lies of all possible kinds—and he was determined that his spiritual experience should not be a make-believe."

5

Joyce and Stephen

Joyce's relationship to Stephen is admittedly complex and one of the central problems raised by *A Portrait of the Artist*. An analysis of that relationship is as complicated as the relationship itself. Most simply, Stephen both resembles Joyce and was depicted by Joyce as differing from him. Stephen attends the schools Joyce attended, they share friends, a poem ("The Villanelle of the Temptress"), some theories about art; both chose to leave Dublin for the broader vistas of Paris. Joyce was writing a kind of autobiography, but he wrote a portrait of *the* artist, not a portrait of *an* artist, not a record of any single, idiosyncratic development. He himself pointed out that the last words of the title, *as a Young Man*, were too often ignored.

Although the connections between the young Joyce and Stephen are undeniable, the distinctions between young Stephen, a type, and an older Joyce are crucial. Joyce generalized from his own experience, creating a type that, as Georg Lukács argues,[1] allows the reader to understand a particular social and cultural period without denying the individuality of the character. Stephen is a type of the Aesthete—adolescent, sensitive, and isolated from community. Creating the type allowed Joyce, perhaps, to analyze and overcome some of the limitations he perceived in Aestheticism.

In those limitations and in the broader range of aesthetic matters they introduce, we can see some of the complexity of Joyce's relationship to Stephen. J. Mitchell Morse claims that Joyce's "art, whose subject is the defeat of art by vanity, is joyfully free because he has fought his way through and beyond all the vanities by which lesser artists are inhibited. The most difficult of these for him to overcome was quite evidently the vanity of art for art's sake."[2] Morse's perception seems true, and yet Stanislaus Joyce remembered that Joyce's first stories "were neither adventurous nor romantic. They were already in the style of *Dubliners*" (*MBK*, 56–57). Certainly by the time Joyce wrote *A Portrait*, he had abandoned the kind of art favored by the Aesthetes, leaving "The Villanelle of the Temptress," a poem that never appeared in printed collections of Joyce's verse, to Stephen Dedalus.

Although some of Joyce's lyrics in *Chamber Music* are similar in style and matter to some of Yeats's poems in *Crossways*—for instance, "To an Isle in the Water"—by 1907 Joyce was tired of his own poetry: "I don't like the book but wish it were published and be damned to it. However, it is a young man's book. I felt like that" (*Letters*, 2: 219). Yeats himself had praised the poetry, but felt it was too early to know the extent of Joyce's talents, a commentary that suggests that Yeats, too, had seen it as "a young man's book."[3] *Dubliners* was altogether a different kind of art. Joyce clearly indicated in a letter to Grant Richards what "school" of aesthetics his stories belong to: "You will not be prosecuted for publishing it [*Dubliners*]. The worst that will happen, I suppose, is that some critic will allude to me as the 'Irish Zola'!" (*Letters*, 2: 137). These stories are, in manner and matter, more like the naturalistic fiction of Zola than like the early poems Joyce wrote, or Yeats's early poetry, or Pater's impressionistic essays. Joyce repeatedly urged publication of *Dubliners* because they were "a chapter of the moral history of my country" (*Letters*, 2: 134), a "first step towards the spiritual liberation of my country" (*Letters*, 1:63). Joyce's claim to his brother in 1906, before he wrote *A Portrait*, that "a page of *A Little Cloud* [a story written late in the composing of *Dubliners*] gives me more pleasure than all my verses" (*Letters*, 2: 182), his decision to exclude Stephen's poem from *Chamber Music*, his analysis of his poetry as "a young man's book," all these attest to his critical and extensive movement away from dreamy, symbolist poetry.

Joyce's rejection of Aestheticism can also be seen in his response to W. B. Yeats, a response no doubt affected by the fact of Yeats's prominence, by potential envy or jealousy, and by a natural rejection of artistic fathers. Of the writers in Ireland when Joyce was a young man, he preferred Yeats—reading, according to Stanislaus, everything Yeats wrote. Yet Joyce attacked Yeats, both for Yeats's use of Irish folk materials and for his Aestheticism. Joyce "laid the blame on Yeats's aestheticism for what he called 'the man's floating will' and wavering indeterminate personality" (*MBK*, 99). While the conflicting records of Joyce's meeting with Yeats do suggest that Joyce insulted the poet, Joyce himself insisted by word and deed that he admired and respected Yeats. Granting that ambivalence, it is possible to see why Joyce might have rejected Yeats on artistic grounds—despite the fact that much of Joyce's early poetry could be termed Aesthetic. The Yeats Joyce could know in 1900 was not the Yeats who wrote *Responsibilities* or any later volume. The Yeats of 1900 sat in London and dreamed of Innisfree; he wrote "The Stolen Child," a poem that contrasts the world of the faery—eternal, amoral, joyous—not with Ireland as Yeats knew it—its poverty and unhappiness—but with an idyllic countryside where one hears "the lowing/Of the calves on the warm hillside/Or the kettle on the hob/Sing peace" and where mice "bob/Round and round the oatmeal-chest."[4] That world was not Joyce's; Yeats's early art did not reflect the world as an urban citizen—such as Joyce—might see it. Nor did Yeats intend his art to reflect that world; Yeats sought, early in his career, to create beauty, not realism, and he found it in the romantic countryside. Richard Ellmann has pointed out that, while Yeats glorified the aristocracy and the rural peasantry, he had no use for Joyce's Dublin—urban, bourgeois, and modern.[5]

Stanislaus Joyce claims that romantic or Aesthetic art could not hope to satisfy Joyce because it did not correspond to the "admittedly debased" life "that passed before his steel-blue eyes" (*MBK*, 90, 92). Joyce's own letters confirm that need for precise realism; again I quote from letters concerning *Dubliners:* "I have written it for the most part in a style of scrupulous meanness and with the conviction that he is a very bold man who dares to alter in the presentment, still more to deform, whatever he has seen and heard" (*Letters*, 2: 134). Later Joyce complained of Seumas O'Kelly's *By the Streams of Killmeen*, quoting his own conclusions: " 'Maybe, begod, people like that are to be found by the Stream of Killmeen only none of them has come under my observation, as the deceased gent in Norway [Ibsen] remarked' " (*Letters*, 2: 196). Stephen Dedalus and the Aesthetes are devoid of such a dedication to realism.

Yet Joyce, too, saw himself in Stephen Dedalus and so saw some traits of Aestheticism in himself. That fact is not surprising for Aestheticism was a cultural response to conditions that impinged on Joyce as much as they did on others. He told Frank Budgen that he had not let himself off lightly in the character as he appears in *Ulysses*.[6] The evidence Stanislaus gathered might well be dismissed as created or selected to sustain and prove a particular perception of his brother—a perception that separates Joyce from Stephen—were it not for the letters and the novels. For instance, when Stanislaus Joyce records that his brother liked Ibsen (hardly a favorite, except in some of his "poetic" drama, of the Aesthetes) because of his aloofness, his concern for the everyday, his record of conflicts of ideals and his " 'fine pity for men' and a 'deep sympathy with the cross purposes and contradictions of life' " (*MBK*, 95–96), we can verify not the specific words but the attitude Stanislaus recorded by reading the letters. There Joyce consistently praised Ibsen; an early letter (1906) not only indicates that Joyce liked Ibsen but in it Joyce claimed affinity: "I fancy I[bsen]'s attitude towards litherathure [sic] and socialism somewhat resembled mine" (*Letters*, 2: 183). And much later, in 1939, Joyce remarked, "J. M. B. in his preface alludes to Ibsen as 'the greatest dramatist of our age'. I would go much further" (*Letters*, 3: 453). The letter quoted earlier represents Ibsen, like Joyce, as approving of realism—"the deceased gent" would share Joyce's disapproval of O'Kelly's characters. And Joyce's novels—*Dubliners*, *A Portrait*, and *Ulysses* certainly—are so firmly grounded in realistic and naturalistic detail that even Lukács, in an attack upon modernism for evading reality, admits that Joyce's subject occasionally forced him to escape the nets of modernism.[7]

That Stephen adopts the artist-priest metaphor is typical of Aestheticism, as chapter 2 above demonstrates. Because he is an Irish Catholic, the metaphor, for him, is even more alive with Catholic nuances than it would be for Yeats or Pater—and so the values associated with religion are more overt in *A Portrait*. To reject a call to the Catholic priesthood is, in that novel, not to be taken as an error. Joyce, too, rejected the Roman Catholic Church—although not for Stephen's precise reasons, a point to which I will return.

The director appeals to Stephen's desire for power, to his pride, to his desire to exalt himself above other people, even above the Blessed Virgin Mary as the priest alone has the power to "make the great God of Heaven come down upon the altar and take the form of bread and wine" (*P*, 158). But although Joyce shared Stephen's rejection of this kind of priesthood, when Stephen transfers the hubris and power hunger from one priesthood to another, Joyce is not one with his creature. In fact, at a similar age, Joyce only sometimes believed himself an artist.[8] And Stephen does transfer all the negative aspects of Catholic priesthood to the priesthood of eternal imagination. As he concludes his discussion of dramatic art (a discussion that does not appear in Joyce's own aesthetic notebooks), Stephen claims:

> The esthetic image in the dramatic form is *life purified* in and reprojected from the human imagination. The mystery of esthetic like that of material creation is accomplished. The artist, *like the God of the creation*, remains within or behind or beyond or above his handiwork, invisible, *refined out of existence*, indifferent, paring his fingernails. [*P*, 215, italics mine]

The material world, created by God, must be "purified" in the "human imagination" in order to be art. To make pure is, generally, to improve, to create the essence of, to remove adulterating elements; the artist, then, improves the creation of God, a creation that people have sullied. And, having done that, having become a deity himself, he vanishes, "refined out of existence." Like Yeats and Wilde, who rejected the natural world because it was not refined or patterned, Stephen sees the need to make life better. That makes the artist not merely a priest with the awful power to call God down on the altar, to absolve sin, etc., not merely a deity who creates, but better than the God of creation. In Stephen's mouth, Joyce placed a paraphrase of Flaubert, but Joyce refined away the limits Flaubert recorded in his analogy. For Flaubert did not speak of purifying life, nor did his artist become "refined out of existence." Art was *"une seconde nature"* and the artist proceeds by analogy, always present in his work, rather than as Stephen suggests "within or behind or beyond or above," a sequence of possibilities that moves the artist out of his work and into a superior, or heavenly, location. Furthermore, the famous passage of Flaubert's letters is prompted by his attack on specifically didactic passages of *Uncle Tom's Cabin:* Flaubert wanted slavery depicted but not the sermons he found there. And, finally, for Flaubert the effect on the audience—which is to be *"une espèce d'ébahissement"* (amazement)—is altogether absent from Stephen's comments at this point. Stephen's words exaggerate Flaubert's ideas—and further aggrandize the poet.[9]

Paradoxically, this self-aggrandizement results in self-destruction—the artist is "refined out of existence." Yet, that state is equivalent to God on the seventh day, when he rests. At the same time, the point crucial to me, the artist ceases to be human at all. He aspires to be god, to be nonhuman. The attempt to become like the gods led Adam and Eve not to the paradise of heaven, not to the paradise of Paris, but out of the paradise of Eden. Stephen, insofar as he chooses this kind of artisthood, chooses death because it offers an escape from time and flux, from the mire and blood of human experience, an escape to purity. That choice is motivated by fear and envy as much as it is motivated by self-confidence. Stephen, like Yeats, is prepared to be crucified for his art; Joyce is not (see *Letters,* 2: 83). Joyce has, it seems to me, taken the metaphor of a tradition, that the artist is a priest, and extended it logically. Above the priests are bishops and a pope, above them is God. Stephen will tolerate neither bishops nor a pope. He will be God.

This is a point difficult to make because the basic assumptions of my own craft as critic derive from much the same aesthetic assumptions. One effect of New Criticism has been to make us perceive the artist as a conscious craftsman, like a god aware of all he does. That is, from the image of the artist as priest, emphasized and popularized by the Aesthetes and perfected by Joyce and Stephen, New Critics and their admitted or tacit followers have implicitly assumed that writers are omniscient about themselves, their words, their motives, and their works *when they function as writers;* as human beings, in their roles as "mere" human beings, of course, these writers are expected to know nothing; any consulting of conscious intent is, then, irrelevant. However much we may admire the intricacies of *Ulysses* or *Finnegans Wake* (or *Absalom! Absalom!* or "The Waste Land"), and however much we may recognize the active craftsmanship of any work of literature, we are, I think, involved in an act of self-deception when we assume that all the pen strokes on a piece of paper and all the images produced by a writer are wholly conscious acts, never acts whose motives are unknown to the writer or which produce effects uncalculated by the writer or unseen by the critic. We are involved in an act of condescension and arrogance when we dismiss an expository or verbal statement of intent as irrelevant to our reading. In either case we are denying the humanity of the writer. Furthermore, we as readers—whether we are New Critics or not—seem to enjoy the same deification implicit in such a view of the artist; the better we read, the better we behold the mind of God, and eventually, perhaps, our mind will become united with the godhead as we proclaim the truth.

As disparate as a Jungian might seem from a New Critic, Jung shared such views of the artist. In *The Spirit in Man, Literature, and Art,* Jung asserted that the artist "is in the highest degree objective, impersonal and even inhuman—or superhuman—for as an artist he is nothing but his work, and not a human being"; he is "an impersonal creative process."[10] The "artist, like the God of creation," disappears in Jung's view as a human being, and is replaced with this superhuman force—objective, impersonal. Hence, to understand that creative process, as the critic hopes to do, the reader, too, must reject his own humanity. Criticism makes strange bedfellows. Some psychological critics arrive at their godhead from a different direction. As Jung pointed out, they study the man, not the artist; the writer becomes a bundle of frustrated instincts with but one positive outlet, art. This poor, fumbling human being can only be understood by a more enlightened being who can analyze his motives and discover "what he was really saying" beyond or below the surface. The critic, fully aware of all his own motives, perfectly conscious, omniscient not only about himself but about any author, proclaims the truth from his deeper, hidden storehouse of knowledge. The critic thus assumes a position as a kind of God. Oscar Wilde had proclaimed that the critic is an artist; if the artist is God, so is the critic. Between and among and around these Scyllas and Charybdises, modern critics wend their weary ways attempting to escape mortality and proclaim truths. We share some of the same emotional needs implicit in Aestheticism. Thus, it is easy to see the similarities between Stephen and Joyce, and to appreciate Stephen's aesthetic credo. It is far more difficult for us to focus on what separates Joyce from Stephen because it separates Joyce from many of our own critical principles. What we have difficulty acting out in our reading and criticism is the old-fashioned notion that a poet is a man speaking to men—that the relationship is one of equality and humanity—that both human elements of communication exist as human. It is that commonness and humanness that Stephen Dedalus rejects in his analysis of the artist and art; the imaginary kinsmen who call to him at the end of *A Portrait* have "white arms of the roads" and "black arms of tall ships"; their disembodied voices call to him: "Come" (*P*, 252). They are not, at least not recognizably, human.

Stephen's hubris and quest for godhead is consonant with Aestheticism and the practice of symbolist art. Joyce did not share it, at least not comfortably and at least not as an older man. But he did share with his creature some notions about art. Much of Stephen's esthetics in chapter

5 comes from notebooks Joyce kept in Pola and Trieste and Paris. And much of the esthetics is typical of the period. Two paradoxes of Aesthetic theory are writ large in Stephen's exposition: art has no effect on or connection with life, yet art spiritualizes man; the artist of Ireland rejects politically nationalistic art and yet is a higher nationalist, attempting to aid his countrymen. Concerning the first paradox, Wilde probably put the matter most clearly. In "The Preface" to *Dorian Gray*, Wilde claimed, "All art is quite useless." In the same preface, Wilde asserted that the "elect," those who are "cultivated," "find beautiful meanings in beautiful things"; the religious associations of the word *elect* are consonant with other comments Wilde makes. In "The Critic as Artist," Gilbert claims that "tragedy . . . cleanses the bosom of much 'perilous stuff,' " that it "purifies and spiritualises the man" (5: 131) and that literature is "the highest art" for words have "thought and passion and spirituality" (5: 133). That argument would seem to make the purpose of literature didactic or moral. Not so. The "purification and spiritualising . . . is . . . essentially æsthetic and is not moral"; nonetheless, through literature "common natures seek to realise their perfection" (5: 130, 151). Moral intentions have no place in proper art; they belong to those "baser forms of sensual or didactic art that seek to excite to action of evil or of good" (5: 194). This apparent contradiction between purifying and spiritualizing on one hand, and amoral or non-didactic art on the other, lies beneath much Aestheticism and many reading habits. The purpose of literature is to spiritualize, but it is not to improve the *moral* health of man. It is, in societal terms, useless.

We can use Wilde's position to clarify Stephen's. Stephen wishes to ennoble his countrymen:

> How could he hit their conscience or how cast his shadow over the imaginations of their daughters, before their squires begat upon them, that they might breed a race less ignoble than their own? [*P*, 238]

Yet that desire and his final intent, to "forge . . . the uncreated conscience of my race" (*P*, 253), are consonant for Stephen with static art, art that does not produce either "desire or loathing" (*P*, 205). Like Wilde, Stephen believes that the purpose of art is to spiritualize, but that art should not be didactic. If to say that Wilde's position clarifies Stephen's is, perhaps, to make too large a claim, at least Wilde's position suggests that Stephen echoes an existing cultural paradox or contradiction about the purpose of art rather than creating something new.

One paradox within the cultural period, then, is clearly presented by Wilde and echoed in *A Portrait:* and it underlies most modern critical practices. Stephen's relationship to nationalism is equally paradoxical. While fleeing an Ireland that he depicts as "the old sow that eats her farrow," Stephen plans to create "the uncreated conscience" of his "race"; while sailing to Paris, he claims that "the shortest way to Tara [the traditional and mythic center of Irish free government] was *via* Holyhead," the gateway to Europe and England; while rejecting the claims of conscience, he intends to "hit" the conscience of his countrymen or "cast his shadow over the imaginations of their daughters . . . that they might breed a race less ignoble than their own" (*P*, 203, 252, 250, 238). How an Aesthete could be a nationalist is a question that plagued Yeats at least in the years between 1890 and 1916; his provisional resolution assumed Wilde's distinction between moral and spiritual art. Yeats sought an art that would revitalize Ireland, an art that would help the Irish race "become a chosen race, one of the pillars that uphold the world" ("Ireland and the Arts," *E & I*, 210). His poets "were to forge in Ireland a new sword on our old traditional anvil for that great battle that must in the end re-establish the old, confident, joyous world" ("Poetry and Tradition," *E & I*, 249). Art was supposed to spiritualize the nation, to assist only indirectly in the political and economic battles that, for Yeats, were merely symptoms of the spiritual "great battle." Stephen's sword—his ashplant, the runic record of man's achievements, his art—will be forged in the smithy of his soul; in *Ulysses*, that ashplant shatters a chandelier that represents the new, deadening world of Ireland, Stephen's family, and his own guilt. Yeats's need to change Ireland, to fight that great battle, stemmed, like Stephen's need, in part from an inability to live in contemporary Ireland. Both artists chose weapons that are archaic—ancient, Germanic swords that would bring in the "old, confident, joyous world." Neither looked to the future so much as he looked to the past for a healthier society. Yeats and Stephen fundamentally agree: art is, in any physical sense of the word, useless. The swords are all metaphorical swords. Here Stephen adopts an attitude consonant with the attitudes of the most influential man of Irish letters.

A pennyworth of Wilde may help again to resolve, or at least to indicate the cultural resolution, of an apparent conflict. Wilde maintains that "emotion for the sake of emotion is the aim of art, and emotion for the sake of action is the aim of life, and of . . . society" (5: 186). As art enables man to think and to feel, it threatens society. In that sense it is revolutionary—although the particular words and metaphors that the Aesthetes used indicate that it is reactionary, that it, although subversive to present society, seeks to move back in time, to an earlier golden age. Wilde and Yeats, then, can stand as exponents of a kind of art, of a kind of purpose for art, that reveals the cultural conflict between amoral, static art and the forging of an uncreated conscience.

How fully Joyce shared these artistic ideas is, perhaps, impossible to determine. I suppose him to have shared some of them for he, too, spoke of aiding in the spiritual liberation of his country. Where he differed from Stephen's nationalism I put off until later in this chapter. There are, however, at least two crucial ways in which Joyce's early aesthetics in the notebooks and in *Stephen Hero* depart from Stephen's. The first, Joyce's theory of epiphany, has been discussed fruitfully by Irene Hendry Chayes.[11] She argued that epiphany, although not included as a theory in Stephen's discussion, underlies the structure of *A Portrait:* Stephen's epiphany at the end of chapter 4 is only the most obvious example. But there is another side to epiphanies; they "arise" from mundane reality, from a connection between the perceiver and something petty in the world he views. In an instant, sparked by apparently unimportant, everyday minutia, one *sees* a truth, an essence. Contrast this theory of truth finding with Yeats's and Stephen's. As Stephen conceives his villanelle, he is in a trance, the moment of vision comes as he is half asleep and half awake. As Geckle has demonstrated, that moment is Yeatsian.[12] It resembles the moment of trance that Yeats described in "The Symbolism of Poetry," the moment between "waking and sleeping" when, called by rhythm, symbols come to mind. For Yeats and Stephen, then, epiphanies come from trance, from moments when the "perceiver" is separate from everyday minutia. In contrast, Joyce found truths in conjunction with "realistic" perception; epiphany in Joyce's sense is antisymbolist; for that reason, Stephen's esthetics do not include the term or the idea.

A theory of "epiphany" is not the only topic Joyce denied his creature. In his notebooks, Joyce favored comedy over tragedy. In *A Portrait,* Stephen concentrates on tragedy as the crucial art form, ignoring comedy almost entirely. This distinction, too, aligns Stephen with Yeats rather than with Joyce. Yeats, at least in his early aesthetics, claimed that tragedy was finer than comedy for it works with the essential in man, destroying character (the crucial element in comedy) in order that the mythic passions might be displayed. Hence Yeats wanted masks—to avoid individual features of any actor—and rhythmic chanting—to avoid individual inflections. Comedy was lesser because it had to focus on delineated character and was tied to realistic detail. Thus he argued that

> tragedy must always be a drowning and breaking of the dykes that separate man from man, and that it is upon these dykes comedy keeps house. . . .
>
> . . . .
>
> We may not find either mood in its purity, but in mainly tragic art one distinguishes devices to exclude or lessen character, to diminish the power of that daily mood, to cheat or blind its too clear perception. If the real world is not altogether rejected, it is but touched here and there, and into the places we have left empty we summon rhythm, balance, pattern,

images that remind us of vast passions, the vagueness of past times. ["The Tragic Theatre," *E & I*, 241, 243]

At least for Yeats, then, the glorification of tragedy is consonant with his rejection of realism and his practice in *Crossways* and *The Rose* of eluding the world of the mortal moment. In contrast, even as early as 1903, Joyce claimed comedy as the highest, most perfect art.

> Desire, as I have said, is the feeling which urges us to go to something but joy is the feeling which the possession of some good excites in us . . . desire urges us from rest that we may possess something but joy holds us in rest as long as we possess something . . . a comedy (a work of comic art) which does not urge us to seek anything beyond itself excites in us the feeling of joy . . . tragedy is the imperfect manner and comedy the perfect manner in art. [*CW*, 144]

Denying Stephen this principle, or indeed much mention of comedy at all, twelve years after Joyce wrote this and just as Joyce was almost ready to write the obvious comedy of *Ulysses*, Joyce marked a genuine distance between himself and his creature in matters of aesthetics. Stephen, incapable of much joy, is incapable of comedy. By analogy, Joyce suggests that Aesthetes miss the perfect manner of art. Indeed, Yeats later became less impatient of character and comedy as well, one detail that suggests that the later Yeats was also less an Aesthete.

Although Joyce had argued, just as Yeats might have, for spiritual liberation as an "end" of art, he apparently believed liberation came through a nicely polished mirror (mimetic art) rather than through an art of essence. Yeats created, as Stephen Dedalus saw in *A Portrait*, "the loveliness which has long faded from the world" (*P*, 251); Stephen wishes to embrace and create "the loveliness which has not yet come into the world" (*P*, 251); Joyce wanted, in *Dubliners* at any rate, to give "the Irish people . . . one good look at themselves in my nicely polished looking-glass" (*Letters*, 1: 64). His realistic art is consonant with his political professions; a socialist critic could approve of the stories in that collection because they are rooted in faithful renditions of human life in Ireland.

On the subject of what kind of art one should produce, then, Joyce is not Stephen; but from at least one critic's point of view, realism is no less arrogant than Aestheticism. Homer Obed Brown in *James Joyce's Early Fiction* has rightly argued that even the realistic mode does not allow the artist to escape from self-aggrandizing roles.[13] In *Dubliners*, according to Brown's thesis, until "The Dead" the narrator (whom Brown seems to identify with Joyce) remains above and judging the creatures of his stories. To the extent that the primary judge is, in our tradition, God, Joyce despite the realism of *Dubliners* seems to equate the artist with an element of God. Yet, if one follows Brown's argument, it is difficult to see that Joyce ever rejected the role of judge or diagnostician in his later novels; he certainly becomes more sympathetic with his subjects, but he continues to see and record and analyze the characters and actions of his characters, using the only "eyes" he has. That element of hubris seems inevitable; no artist can avoid indicating both that he has a private view he believes in and that in fact he knows more than his characters do. To write for others implies an ability to communicate and to see something that others cannot. Thus, while I understand Brown's impatience with the failures of sympathy inherent in *Dubliners* and find his analysis accurate in many ways, he seems to ignore the contributions that the realistic mode makes to *A Portrait* and to *Ulysses*. The particular amalgamation of Aestheticism and realism that Joyce achieves in "The Dead," *A Portrait*, and *Ulysses* allows the author to share with his characters the traumas of life and makes him less splendidly isolated than the mode of *Dubliners*—or than the mode Stephen proclaims in *A Portrait*. At the same time, *A Portrait* remains a realistic novel, and if that implies that Joyce judges, then I am only saying that he, like all writers, does have some kind of attitude about each of his characters. The totally indifferent is, as Brown suggests, the totally superior.[14]

Despite some of the language in *A Portrait*, which, as almost all commentators agree, parodies or imitates Pater and other figures from the nineteenth century, Joyce concentrates on the probable, on establishing motives and circumstances that make Stephen and his fellows appear to be like the kinds of people we know. Unlike, for instance, two of the novels of the decadence, *Dorian Gray* and *À Rebours*, *A Portrait* depicts a society hampered and sustained by modes of conduct and belief that at least once existed. As Joyce depicted his young Aesthete artist, he used a style as realistic, as didactic, and as naturalistic as that of Zola, Tolstoy, or Hardy. The text of *A Portrait* provides not a moment of blinding insight into a character, nor a static, unemotional experience for the reader. Rather, we feel with Stephen the power of the sermons in chapter 3, and share with him the pain of Dolan's pandying, as well as the ecstasy with which he views his beach girl. Stephen's motivations are as realistically presented as his own mind can permit; we learn of economic, social, political, and religious realities of urban Ireland—and the squalor and deprivation and repression that those realities create for Stephen help motivate his choice of a vocation. As Joyce undercuts Stephen, he undercuts him by demonstrating the naturalistic or social and psychological causes for his vision: the very aptness and persuasiveness of the analysis embedded in the text have left many readers unsure about Joyce's own relationship to Stephen and to Stephen's ideas. Stephen is totally believable—reviewers and critics have always accepted him as such—while both Dorian and Des Esseintes exist in a never-never land and their authors demand that we not inquire too closely about their motives, their finances, their history, their families. Dorian's motives are simply not dealt with; why would a young, beautiful man want to escape society or move into the under-world of Victorian England? In contrast, Stephen "lives" in a human and historical and political world of time—of moments that pass inexor-ably; Dorian and Des Esseintes do not. Why Stephen wants and needs to escape the provincialism of Ireland is reasonably clear and perfectly understandable: the entire novel works to show us why, and very few readers are puzzled by his chosen exile. Joyce's own practice as an artist finally separates him from his artist as a young man.

Artistic choices and theories are, as I suggested at the beginning of this study, coherent with other aspects of behavior and personality, aspects that are enacted in a world of moments. Joyce's relationship to his creature, Stephen, is just as complicated when we turn to religious, political, and psychological consonants of Aestheticism.

Stephen's vocation makes him ineffective as a political being. For the Aesthetes, art is finally useless in the sense that, as Auden put it, it "makes nothing happen." The static nature of the artistic experience is not finally liberating—especially for an Irishman near the turn of the century. Pater's injunction to fill the moment before it passes, to pack passion into our interval before time and mortality end that interval, concluded with a recommendation to do it as "the wisest at least 'among the children of this world'" do with "art and song," for art "comes to you proposing frankly to give you nothing but the highest quality to your moments as they pass, and simply for those moments' sake."[15] If all art is quite useless and the purpose of art is to expand the too-fleeting intervals, that is, to hold the viewer-reader statically in the moment so that he can triumph over and deny the transitoriness of the world around him, this kind of art and its practitioners are necessarily ineffec-tive, impotent by choice, in the world of moments, the temporal world. Stephen's disengagement from the world is a necessary corollary of the Aesthetic view of art; but I suppose that that view is created and chosen at least in part in order to avoid worldly contact.

For an Irish writer in 1900, that ineffectiveness was particularly uncomfortable because he lived in a country that had been oppressed for centuries, among a people that had, repeatedly and unsuccessfully, at-tempted to revolt against the oppressor, and in a time when the land and people were moving rapidly. England had been pumping money into Ireland, in part to redress the inequitable taxation and spending policies of the Parliament: peasants were buying, with the help of English loans, the land they worked; England spent money providing technical assist-ance, education, and health care. Less material changes cohered with material improvements: the Gaelic League asserted the Irishman's right to his language, George Russell (better known as AE) promoted litera-ture and agriculture (the latter through cooperatives), Irish courts were now run by Irishmen. But the lot of the Irish was still less than comfortable; Arthur Griffith argued that no political or spiritual liberation could come until and unless economic independence was achieved. The Wildean and Paterian artist—if he was in any way a nationalist—must have felt torn.

Yeats's ambivalent relationship with Irish politics surfaces most overtly in his experiments for a national theater. In 1904 he produced *On Baile's Strand,* a play that speaks to contemporary Irish issues only tangentially (although great critical acrobatics can make the drama "relevant"); yet *Cathleen Ni Houlihan,* a contemporary play, is so avowedly "nationalistic" that Yeats wondered later if his play had sent men out to die in the 1916 uprising. The second play portrays Ireland in the person of the beautiful Cathleen, who calls men to leave their fiancés and families to serve a higher good, to fight for her. The destruction of humans implicit in this plot provides a tension that may have escaped its early audience. Yeats himself could never believe in violent revolution nor give himself wholeheartedly to political and economic nationalism. In the Cathleen play, the woman is an old hag revitalized, miraculously transformed into ideal beauty when young men rise up and follow her; this beauty—and the transmutation that causes it—are the only "rewards" promised the young men; that is, not a *political* motivation but an aesthetic one is envisaged. Nationalism is portrayed here as another way of escaping mortal moments and living where age does not wither—in a realm of eternal beauty—the unblemished Cathleen. In "Upon a House Shaken by the Land Agitation," Yeats agonized over the loss of wisdom and mirth and beauty implicit for him in the destruction of old families and old homes (most of which were, in Ireland, English or Anglo-Irish, Protestant, and the product of long centuries of colonial rule). That is, for Yeats, nationalism and economic change conflicted directly with the nobility of art, manners, and passion he most valued—a nobility that, like artists, he saw as one of the three sources of "all beautiful things." In "Easter 1916," he wondered about the latest group of Irish martyrs: "Was it needless death after all? / For England may keep faith / For all that is said and done."

Yeats saw the major benefit of the 1916 rebellion as tragic: "A terrible beauty is born." If we digress briefly, the oddity of Yeats's refrain and its depoliticizing of the revolution will be clearer. In tragedy, Yeats had argued, the individual and the real world are properly rejected—or at least diminished as much as possible—so that we can "into the places we have left empty . . . summon rhythm, balance, pattern, images that remind us of vast passions" and past times ("The Tragic Theatre," *E & I,* 243). That is, tragedy removes us from the here and now and places us into eternal and mythic realms of passion. That is precisely what his poem on the rebellion enacts. The men and women who marched in Dublin at a particular time and for particular reasons and who were killed in the real world were, to Yeats's mind, a mixed lot. Some were good—poets, idealists; some were once good and now at least in part corrupted by political involvement—for instance, a woman whose voice had grown shrill; at least one was, in his role as mortal, bad.

> This other man I had dreamed
> A drunken, vainglorious lout.
> He had done most bitter wrong
> To some who are near my heart.
>
> [ll. 31–34]

But, in Yeats's poem, these individual characteristics disappear as these people move outside of time: even the "drunken, vainglorious lout," John MacBride,

> . . . has resigned his part
> In the casual comedy;
> He, too, has been changed in his turn,
> Transformed utterly:
> A terribly beauty is born.
>
> [ll. 36–40]

Each individual has become a character in a passionate and beautiful tragedy. In his commemorative poem, Yeats spoke of Ireland's duty in response to this rebellion, the duty

> To murmur name upon name,
> As a mother names her child
> When sleep at last has come
> On limbs that had run wild.
>
> [ll. 61–64]

The result of the revolution may be political in the history books, but in Yeats's poem, the Irish are to be moved to revery, to contemplation of beauty—as a mother is moved when a child sleeps. Yeats does not in this poem suggest political or active response to the martyrdom. The revolution allows the martyrs to escape the world of Dublin, the "motley" of modern life—not to achieve anything in the world of moments. Yeats even asks if their deaths were needless. By doing so, he suggests the relative uselessness of active engagement in the world, an engagement that the Aesthetes eschewed but that these people attempted. The ultimate and insistent result of their action is, in this poem, not political; it is aesthetic: "A terrible beauty is born." Life had, for Yeats, as Oscar Wilde once claimed it did, imitated Art; Life had created tragedy.

However disconcerting such a reading of Yeats's poem may be, the form of the poem—especially its refrain—focuses us upon beauty just as the Cathleen play focuses us upon beauty. Both make political action less action in this world than action in the realm of art and eternity. These two examples of Yeats's ambivalent response to Irish political and national ferment display in miniature a conflict between the contemplative modes that Aestheticism celebrated and nationalism. In some ways, the larger history of the Abbey Theatre is a history of a conflict between politics—a variety of active nationalism—and art. Yeats saw art as nonpolitical just as Wilde and Stephen saw it.

The problem, particularly tough for an Irish nationalist writer to resolve, is one faced by all writers who as mere human beings have political and moral and economic views (however much denied, repressed or unconscious). More to the point here, we can, by focusing on the ways various artists cope with the problem, see that an artist's aesthetic values imply or cohere with certain political, social, and economic choices and attitudes. Stephen's advocacy of art that "induces or ought to induce" stasis in the viewer, that turns the artist into a god "invisible, refined out of existence, indifferent, paring his fingernails," is a prescription for paralysis in the everyday world. While the ordinary citizens of Dublin are paralyzed politically (in "Ivy Day in the Committee Room"), maritally (in "The Boarding House," "A Little Cloud," etc.), economically (in "Counterparts," "Two Gallants," and, indeed, in most of the stories), and spiritually (especially in "Grace"), the artist is, too. Stephen's paralysis is more obvious in *Ulysses,* where it is clear both that he has not created any art worth mentioning and that he is paralyzed emotionally and economically, than in *A Portrait.* Stephen's Aestheticism, like that of Pater, Wilde, Dowson, Johnson, because it urged an aloofness from common life and common man, corresponds to his refusal to sign the peace petition or to join the Gaelic League or to sympathize with Davin's semirevolutionary patriotism. Even more fundamentally his choice and perceptions about art force him to reject political and social action and concern with it. The poet must be above such issues—as McCann accuses him, "—Minor poets, I suppose are above such trivial questions as the question of universal peace" (*P,* 197). Significantly, Stephen's attempt to placate him finally focuses upon the uselessness of his signature, an act of writing and of identity.

Thus it is that Joyce dramatically portrayed the conjunction between Aestheticism and not only a rejection of political action but also a sense of total impotence in the world, a sense of ultimate uselessness. I do not mean to suggest that Joyce himself was terribly active as a political being. His attitudes and his values, however, are distinctly different from his creature's. To demonstrate that briefly, a letter to Stanislaus will do. He wrote to Stanislaus attacking the Church and commenting on politics. First the attack on the Church:

> For my part I believe that to establish the Church in full power again in Europe would mean a renewal of the Inquisition—though, of course, the

Jesuits tell us that the Dominicans never broke men on the wheel or tortured them on the rack.

The Church was, from Joyce's point of view, capable of tyranny and destruction, and was an element of the power structures that oppressed the ordinary man. Joyce portrayed the Church in *Dubliners* as paralyzing; the Church there destroys or helps to destroy the life of its members. In contrast, Stephen's reasons for rejecting the Church are essentially personal—he no longer believes and refuses to serve. Dramatically, the Church's effect on Stephen Dedalus in *A Portrait* is to terrify him into denying a crucial part of his humanity—his body and his mirth. While he comes eventually to feel that piety is lacking because, in part, it separates him from common humanity, he leaves not because the Church tyrannizes men, but because it hurts him. The hell sermons, recorded at such length in the novel, attest to the inhumanity of religion, at least in Joyce's eyes, which is confirmed by Joyce's rejection of the Church: he never reconciled with it.

When Stephen rejects the Catholic Church, he imitates his creator. What differentiates Stephen's rejection from Joyce's—and hence helps to define Joyce's relationship to his character—are the motives that prompt the rejection. In the same letter, Joyce linked the Church with other tyrannies, especially political ones:

> But can you not see plainly from facts like these that a deferrment [sic] of the emancipation of the proletariat, a reaction to clericalism or aristocracy or bourgeoisism would mean a revulsion to tyrannies of all kinds. Gogarty would jump into the Liffey to save a man's life but he seems to have little hesitation in condemning generations to servitude. [*Letters*, 2: 148: August 1906]

Stephen seems not in any way, either in *A Portrait* or in *Ulysses,* to share this interest in socialism, this kind of political concern, this kind of vocabulary, or this kind of analysis. He announces himself as above such issues.

To be an Aesthete is, then, to be simultaneously both arrogant and impotent, even Stephen's signature is "useless." At the end of *A Portrait,* Stephen focuses upon the arrogant and self-liberating aspects of Aestheticism; at the beginning of *Ulysses,* he focuses upon his own impotence in the battle with Mulligan, the usurper who wishes to Hellenize Ireland. Mulligan's desire itself is ironic; Mulligan mimics Arnold's compromise with the dirty work of the world, a compromise that allowed Arnold to speak to the issues of his day while remaining aloof from the philistines and barbarians, a compromise that cohered with Arnold's decision to cease writing poetry. Stephen's label for Mulligan, *usurper,* suggests that he wanted to Hellenize Ireland himself—or at least that he saw it as one method of creating the uncreated conscience.

(Perhaps more comically Mulligan is also a usurper because, while Stephen wished to hit the conscience of the women of Ireland so that they might breed a more noble race, Mulligan proposes a stud service for Ireland.) Stephen is powerless, as the milkwoman listens to Mulligan and ignores him. Even in *A Portrait*, Stephen is frustrated by a woman, like the milkwoman metaphorically associated with the soul of Ireland, who turns to a more "practical" man of the world (a priest) and ignores the poet. Stephen has wanted power to control himself and reshape his private, internal life. His desire to create the uncreated conscience is frustrated by the events in Paris and the conditions under which he returns to Dublin. But the more radical source of frustration is his own self-perception. As he had dreamed of being a priest in a church without worshippers (*P*, 159), so as a poet that isolation prevents any contact with his congregation, his readers, his society, the politics of life.

In direct contrast with Stephen, Leopold Bloom functions within his society, that is, politically. And all of *Ulysses* is, as Richard Ellmann suggests,[16] a political act on Joyce's part, though I would define *political* in less doctrinaire ways than Ellmann does. The first indication that *Ulysses* is a political act is the color of the cover itself. It is, according to Joyce's letters, a blue commemorating Greece. But it is also the color of the blue books that were governmental reports on sociological conditions and the results of investigations that might lead to legislation. Vivian in Wilde's "The Decay of Lying" condemns realists as writers of "Blue-Books." Thus, Joyce's insistence upon the color blue for his novel was perhaps one way of suggesting it was a sort of political investigation, an indictment of conditions—economic, medical, or social—affecting Ireland and freedom. The investigation is both widespread and condemning. For instance, the amount of work accomplished in Dublin during June 16, 1904, is minimal; many of the characters are out of work, the "unlabouring men" who lounge outside Daniel Bergin's in "Wandering Rocks" (*U*, 221), Bloom's compassion for whores who must earn their living some way, Bloom's reference to the "submerged tenth, viz., coalminers, divers, scavengers, etc." (*U*, 646–47), and the idle loungers of Barney Kiernan's and the newspaper office all testify to the economic disease of Dublin, where, at the turn of the century, "more than half of the population . . . had been classified under the heading of 'Indefinite and unproductive class.' "[17] Joyce's social analysis can been seen, too, in the plight of the Dedalus children, who seem to suffer physically as well as psychologically from their father's economic situation. Similarly, in "Wandering Rocks," Dilly confronts her father for money to feed the family and Simon responds by attacking her: "—Stand up straight for the love of the Lord Jesus. . . . Are you trying to imitate your uncle John. . . ? You'll get curvature of the spine. Do you know what you look like?" (*U*, 237).

Molly Bloom's worries about her husband's job are based, cer-

tainly, on her fears about his political opinions (as Ellmann points out),
but they are also based on the economic facts surrounding her. Individual men appear to be out of work because they are lazy: Simon
Dedalus seems unlikely to accept or perform work properly if he were
offered it. But as the American experience with unemployment suggests, repeated failures to find jobs disillusion and finally paralyze
women and men. The desperation of Corley, who is ready to carry a
sandwich board to earn money (*U*, 619), may placate readers who remember him as a character in "Two Gallants" who bilked a slavey out
of her money, but his plight, coupled with that of almost every adult
male in the book, points to unemployment and poverty as widespread
in Dublin as in any American ghetto in the 1970s. My analysis is not
rebutted by noting that between 1895 and 1915 the English government
spent relatively large amounts of money in Ireland to correct various
ills. Having "discovered" that Ireland was in terrible straits and that the
Irish had been seriously overtaxed, the British government attempted to
promote land acquisition (spending £108 millions in guaranteed loans to
small farmers so that they could buy the land their families had farmed
for generations), agricultural reforms, medical services, industrial development, education.[18] This exertion appears to have had a common
outcome—the revolution came after significant progress had been made
in Ireland; the riots of the 1960s in American cities followed much the
same pattern—the War on Poverty helped prompt rising expectations
that led, as much as the conditions themselves, to riots.

Joyce's concerns in *Ulysses*, then, included the economic and political circumstances of his countrymen. These concerns, alien to Stephen
Dedalus and more generally to the Aesthetes, and the character of
Leopold Bloom illuminate Joyce's relationship to Stephen, to the Aesthetes, and to the realists. Joyce's political concern should not surprise
readers familiar with the first "A Portrait": in that essay Joyce called for
regeneration in terms very different from Stephen's.

> His Nego [I deny], therefore, written amid a chorus of peddling Jews'
> gibberish and Gentile clamour, was drawn up valiantly while true believ-
> ers prophesied fried atheism and was hurled against the obscene hells of
> our Holy Mother: but, that outburst over, it was urbanity in warfare.
> Perhaps his state would pension off old tyranny—a mercy no longer
> hopelessly remote—in virtue of that mature civilization to which (let all
> allow) it had in some way contributed. Already the messages of citizens
> were flashed along the wires of the world, already the generous idea had
> emerged from a thirty years' war in Germany and was directing the coun-
> cils of the Latins. To those multitudes, not as yet in the wombs of human-
> ity but surely engenderable there, he would give the word: Man and
> woman, out of you comes that nation that is to come, the lightning of
> your masses in travail; the competitive order is employed against itself,
> the aristocracies are supplanted; and amid the general paralysis of an
> insane society, the confederate will issues in action.[19]

Many elements here sound like Stephen, but the differences are important; in *A Portrait*, Stephen's assertion that he *will not serve*, which is parallel to the *Nego* here, echoes Lucifer tellingly. The call for action is almost unknown to Stephen; and even the calmness with which Joyce could acknowledge the gifts of his civilization does not accord with Stephen's rebellion. But the most striking difference is the socialistic attitude, the "state" that "would pension off old tyranny," the "generous idea" that will liberate the "masses in travail," the call for a "confederate will," the indictment of the "competitive order": all these point to aspects of social change alien to Stephen's desire to use silence, exile, and cunning to create "the uncreated conscience of my race" (*P*, 253). Joyce probably agreed with Stephen and Blake that one must kill the priest and king in the imagination, but he was not sufficiently a "pure" poet to exclude those extranneous issues of contemporary debates that Yeats urged poets to ignore.[20]

Leopold Bloom's politics I wish to return to later, indicating only briefly at this point his difference from Stephen and his relationship to the ideas of Joyce. Like Joyce and Stephen, Bloom has grown up with the deprivations and oppression of nineteenth-century Ireland; like his creator, he has flirted with socialism in his youth. His economic theories are based upon a redistribution of capital, the requirement that all men must work, and loving the country where one is "well off." Speaking with Stephen in "Eumaeus," Bloom spins out his theories:

> But in the economic, not touching religion, domain, the priest spells poverty. . . . I want to see everyone, concluded he, all creeds and classes *pro rata* having a comfortable tidysized income, in no niggard fashion either, something in the neighbourhood of £300 per annum. That's the vital issue at stake and it's feasible and would be provocative of friendlier intercourse between man and man. At least that's my idea for what it's worth. I call that patriotism. *Ubi patria*, as we learned a small smattering of in our classical day in *Alma Mater, vita bene*. Where you can live well, the sense is, if you work. [*U*, 644]

Bloom's doctrine of work does not resemble Ruskin's or Carlyle's: he is not urging a metaphysical, spiritual benefit for working. As a puritan and a Jew, Bloom sees work as a duty as well as a right. What he objects to in the present condition of Dublin is that there is insufficient work and that the work accomplished does not earn a living. If he means literally that all creeds and classes should receive the same income, then Bloom is indeed radical.

Stephen objects to the word *work* and the implication that he, too, should have to work. In a passage seemingly overlooked by Ellmann in his discussion of Joyce's politics, Stephen reveals his true colors: "— Count me out, he managed to remark, meaning to work" (*U*, 644). If Stephen is a socialist—or even a democrat—then his rejection of work is inexplicable. Despite his fine rhetoric that suggests the problem lies with the king and church, Stephen's inability to live in society is internal. Bloom is not implying that Stephen must get his hands dirty: "—I mean, of course, the other hastened to affirm, work in the widest possible sense. Also literary labour, not merely for the kudos of the thing. Writing for the newspapers which is the readiest channel nowadays. That's work too. Important work" (*U*, 645). Stephen's supreme egotism, his refusal to have anything to do with patriotism or his country or his community, however defined, make it impossible for Bloom to understand him. He does not understand that Bloom is not arguing in this discussion of patriotism a typical Irish line at all. And, finally, Bloom seems unable to understand that Stephen rejects work itself. He claims, "All must work, have to, together" (*U*, 644). The conversation ends with Stephen's dismissal of the subject. Richard Ellmann comments on the same passage:

> later Stephen remarks somewhat testily to Bloom, "You think I am important because I belong to the Faubourg Saint Patrice [*sic*] called Ireland for short. But I think Ireland is important because it belongs to me." The State is the instrument of its members, not their enslaver.[21]

Ellmann, like Stephen, appears to have missed Bloom's point. Throughout *Ulysses,* Bloom avoids, as Ellmann points out, the standard Irish views about the British, and in this exchange defines patriotism and nationality not in terms that suggest the state should enslave but in fact that it should serve: as Weldon Thornton translates: "Where I am well off, there is my country."[22] Bloom emphasizes communal efforts and communal rewards much like those envisioned in the essay, "A Portrait," where Joyce speaks of a "confederate will"; the text gives us no reason to reject Bloom's position and accept Stephen's.

Joyce, at least at some points in his life, shared Bloom's socialism—not Stephen's Aesthetic detachment. That none of the men (Joyce, Stephen, Bloom) is an effective political leader links them, but Stephen's rejection of work and concern for others separates him from Joyce. Joyce is present in each of his characters, but his sympathies rest more with Bloom than with Stephen.

While Stephen's metaphor for the artist, "priest of eternal imagination," with its consonant symbolist theories of art and rejection of politics, separates him from his creator, whose realism involves symbolism but is never replaced by it and whose novels reveal social and political concerns and assumptions, the images that cluster around women more subtly delineate the creator's relationship to the created. Stephen's mother and his relationship to her seem to me crucial to our understanding of *A Portrait* and *Ulysses.* How Stephen sees all women—real and imaginary—draws him as close to his Aesthetic ancestors as any other image pattern in *A Portrait;* he shares a destructive and fascinated view of women with many writers of the Aesthetic persuasion. Joyce appears to have shared elements of their ambivalence and Stephen's. That Joyce never escaped this stereotyping of women is, as Suzette Henke has indicated, demonstrable.[23] But there are distinctions to be made among Stephen's, Joyce's, and Bloom's dealings with women, and those distinctions bring us closer to understanding how Joyce viewed Stephen.

Creatures and creator seem attracted to and repulsed by a maternal and devouring female who is human—May Dedalus, Molly Bloom, and Nora Barnacle—yet also mythic and historical—Ireland, the Cathleen, the old woman, the "sow that eats her farrow"—as well as fictional—Joyce's Polly Moran in "The Boarding House," Stephen's temptress, Bloom's imaginary Middle Eastern women. Joyce's letters to Nora, published in *The Selected Letters,* clearly connect Nora with this figure. Molly Bloom, as mother and matter, dominates her husband and, some argue, emasculates him. Yet Bloom, like Stephen and Joyce, is enormously drawn to this mother-wife-destroyer. That both Joyce's major male protagonists feel these emotions in itself suggests Joyce's psychological attitude.[24] And escape, a reiterated concern in almost all of Joyce's work from *Dubliners* through *Finnegans Wake* (where ALP finds her final dissolution an escape), was for Stephen and Joyce in part escape from mother Ireland—as they both fled to Paris. The woman-temptress of Stephen's villanelle, who is called the *"lure of the fallen seraphim,"* is only the most obvious of the destructive women that inhabit the pages of Joyce's works. Bloom's Bello is a grotesque version, imagined or created under the influence of Circe, another destructive and powerful woman. But Stephen's and Bloom's and Joyce's concern with the devouring female leads them to diverse courses of action.

For my present purposes, May Dedalus is most crucial, in part because she is dramatically the origin of Stephen's conditioned and stereotyped responses to women. His inability to understand his mother is presented as a symptom of his dissociation from his own emotions in *A Portrait.* When he breaks with the Church by refusing to do his Easter duty, he breaks with his mother, too. The break is sufficiently traumatic for Stephen to prompt a discussion with Cranly on the subject of his rebellion and that discussion ends with Stephen's decision to leave Ireland: "Away then: it is time to go" (*P,* 245). The congruence of the three breaks—with Church, mother, and home-land—reinforces the maternal and similar roles of each, mother, mother Church, motherland. Cranly, attempting to persuade Stephen not to leave the Church and not to cause his mother added pain but instead to "set her mind at rest" (*P,* 241), insists on one reality, what a mother feels about her children.

Opposed to this "real" feeling, this certainty, Cranly remarks on male ideas: "Every jackass going the roads thinks he has ideas" (*P*, 242). Cranly identifies men with ideas (and those are, for him, relatively unimportant) and women with emotional truth. And so did Joyce. Stanislaus Joyce recorded that the young James Joyce thought there were only two realities in the world, the love of a woman for her child and "man's love of lies." In life, Stanislaus, not James, refused to make the Easter duty (*MBK*, 91, 103–6). Through biography, then, we can see one distinction between Joyce and Stephen.

Even within the novel, Joyce associated women with emotional truth and Stephen eventually agrees. In the diary, Stephen records his mother's prayer.

> She prays now . . . that I may learn in my own life and away from home and friends what the heart is and what it feels. Amen. So be it. [*P*, 252]

May Dedalus and (at least partly) Stephen believe that he does not understand what the heart is and what it feels, that he does not understand emotional realities. While Cranly, from Stephen's point of view, knows the "sufferings of women" (*P*, 245), Stephen does not. Nor does he know his own heart. His isolation, his withdrawal, his tendency to observe and comment instead of actively doing within a community disastrously limit his perception of the world.

Joyce may, of course, be wrong in ascribing to mothers more understanding of emotional realities, but in his fictional world, we accept that analysis as dramatically true. Whether we wish to make that attribution, Joyce apparently did. For Joyce, the rejection of the mother in favor of the sterile temptress of the femme fatale tradition cuts Stephen off from the rough material of his art and from the process of creation, a process Joyce likened to pregnancy twice in *A Portrait*. There Stephen claims, in his discussion with Lynch, to need new experience before describing the creation of art:

> When we come to the phenomena of artistic conception, artistic gestation and artistic reproduction I require a new terminology and a new personal experience. [*P*, 209]

What Stephen cannot tell us is how the artist creates; the difference between the static, scholarly, relatively abstract words used to describe the effect of art on the observer ("art induces, or ought to induce," etc.) and the vocabulary here (conception, gestation, reproduction) suggests at once how infertile Stephen's theory is. The metaphor may, as various people have argued in various contexts, be inaccurate; artistic production is not like childbearing, but Joyce used it.

The one completed poem we see in *A Portrait* results from a process described in sexual, fertile, and maternal words: "In the virgin womb of the imagination the word was made flesh. Gabriel the seraph had come to the virgin's chamber" (*P*, 217). In that poem, Stephen describes and distorts the one relationship within which he comes closest to understanding "what the heart is and what it feels." His rough material is sexual (however frustrated) and emotional, not static and detached and scholarly. And the raw material depends upon a woman. As the novel ends, Stephen dismisses even this woman/material, turning off his emotions with a refrigerating apparatus.

Although women can, within Joyce's own universe, destroy men (and threaten at least to do so frequently), such escapes as Stephen's are negative: how one creates art and poetry with so little notion of the feelings and motives and concerns of other human beings (and the self) is a mystery. Stephen's chosen profession requires that he be able to understand, to sympathize, to identify with others. We see his inability to do that most clearly in his relationships to women—and as those relationships mimic the relationships suggested and described in the imagery of the Aesthetes, Joyce judges Aestheticism as well as Stephen. The imagery focuses the primary emotional limitations of those men who found so little audience and so much unhappiness. Stephen's poem itself, as a product of Aestheticism, merely reinforces both problems— few can understand it and what one understands is Stephen's unhappiness. It is bad or, at least, limited art. Aestheticism is consonant with sterile isolation, personally and artistically.

This maternal image, central to *A Portrait*, then focuses Stephen's primary emotional limitation and connects it to community (Ireland and the Church) and to art (the villanelle, the esthetics). But another quirk is apparent. If these women whom one wishes to escape are all illusory, figments of the imagination, then a trip to Paris, or the moon, would not facilitate escape. Even the death of his mother cannot release Stephen; he desires and fears the ghoul-like mother who reaches out to him threatening God's wrath in "Circe" and who throughout *Ulysses* seems to menace him.

Joyce's own escape from the mythic and geographical devouring nation occurred twice: in the first escape, Joyce left Dublin for Paris by himself, only to return as Stephen did; the second time, Joyce took Nora Barnacle with him. Despite the image of devouring and maternal Nora in Joyce's letters, despite the marital problems those letters indicate, despite the destructive potential of such characters as Molly Bloom and ALP, Joyce's problems with women did not lead him out of relationship; they did not destroy his ability to live with Nora, have children, write novels. Nor, despite accounts of Joyce's formality with friends, is there any indication in the biograpy that he did not have friends; he did not lead an isolated life. Stephen's relationship to his mother does not cohere with another relationship to a woman, nor to writing (the sterile artist of *Ulysses* has produced only one poem, an imitation of one of Hyde's *Love Songs of Connaught*). In 1904, the year of Stephen's fictional day, Joyce had published in *The Irish Homestead* stories that later formed part of *Dubliners,* and the day itself ironically commemorates Joyce's meeting with Nora Barnacle. All three men are pulled back to their devouring mother/woman—for Bloom returns to his mother/wife, Molly Bloom. For Bloom, Molly is not simply destructive: she is the central character in his most vivid, mutual, and positive memory—the courtship on Howth, and Molly, unlike E. C., remembers that episode with the same warmth as Bloom. For Stephen, however, this figure drawn both from the myths of Ireland and from the cultural apprehension of women manifest in nineteenth-century literature destroys his ability to have any satisfactory relationship with a woman. For Joyce, who felt the pressures and the destructive potential of women as clearly, the figure did not finally destroy his ability to relate to others or the ability to objectify the dangers inherent in such a view.

Escape from this figure—literary and historical and geographical and personal—is complex. If the escape coheres with a rejection of all relationships, as it does in Stephen's case, it produces guilt and paralysis. If escape coheres with an ability (or the good fortune) to make and sustain relationships as it apparently did in Joyce's case, then the escape is healthy. To insist upon remaining with the mother (whether the literal mother or the political mother or the mythic mother) is a refusal to move into adulthood, it is regressive. It is significant, I think, that so many Dubliners are caught in childhood or adolescence indicated by social, economic, and psychological patterns in Joyce's works.

As I have noted, in those novels, very few Dubliners work—not just because they are lazy. Those who do work are trapped in relatively menial, unproductive jobs. Unemployment is a social problem, but it can also have a psychological dimension. Whether we wish to associate work with the genital stage of development as Erik Erikson would, or with a more standard Western notion that adulthood involves and requires the ability to support oneself and to make a contribution to one's society, the scarcity of labor of any kind prevents Dubliners from moving into adulthood, and they remain as the Citizen does, the children of Mother Ireland (who does not indeed feed them well), and, at the same time, the only recognizably adult thing they do is bear children into the same morass. Their sexuality, that is, is adult only in the biological sense. Freudian insights are limiting, I think, if they do not seem to go beyond pointing out infantile and repressed difficulties present in all people; what is important in Joyce's works and thus important for us as readers is not that Bloom and Stephen are both oedipal (or in fact that Joyce was), but given that we are all to a certain extent the victims of our childhood fantasies and interests, what we each do—in spite of or because of or with those fantasies and difficulties.[25] I have argued elsewhere that Joyce is concerned not with the psychological quirkiness of his characters, but with what they do (what gestures they make), how they live given this *human condition*. Bloom, unlike Stephen, Lionel Johnson, Dorian Gray, or Ernest Dowson, works and loves—however odd some of his loves may be to an observer; in the world of human action, in the world of moments (rather than the world of the Paterian moment), Bloom functions. And so, apparently, did Joyce.

Joyce offered in *A Portrait* only one image of escape: Daedalus, the hawklike man. Unlike the women Stephen creates in his imagination, and unlike the priestly role of the artist he adopts, Daedalus does not repeatedly appear in the writing of Aesthetes. Although Pater had written of Daedalus, although Daedalus does appear in the works of Ruskin, he is not a stock metaphor of Aestheticism as the femme fatale and the artist-priest are. Furthermore, Pater's writing about Daedalus associated him with realism and religion, not symbolism.[26] Stephen chooses both the name *Daedalus* and a new father—and the myth embodies the primary tension of the novel. At the end of chapter 4, Stephen thinks he sees something, moves from a series of questions about what it is to an assertion that it is the hawklike man, the harbinger of his destiny, the symbol of his artistry and flight. We are moved, I think, in sympathy with Stephen in this rhythm:

> Now, at the name of the fabulous artificer, he seemed to hear the noise of dim waves and to see a winged form flying above the waves and slowly climbing the air. [*P*, 169]

He moves from his own name, and his thoughts about his name, to a perception that validates his inner beliefs.

> What did it mean? Was it a quaint device opening a page of some medieval book of prophecies and symbols, a hawklike man flying sunward above the sea, a prophecy of the end he had been born to serve . . . a symbol of the artist. [*P*, 169]

The answer could be "No." The series of questions presupposes the answer Stephen arrives at. Because this narrative is filtered through Stephen's mind, he does not ask, Is it a gull? Is it a sunspot in my eye? Stephen has created his own epiphany, not the external world. In fact, the words of the novel do not even assure us that there is anything in the sky—"he seemed to hear . . . and to see" (*P*, 169). In counterpoint, as I have noted before, the boys' yells mark Stephen as Icarus, not Daedalus. Pride, Stephen's besetting sin, produces Icarus's fall. While the Daedalus myth does inform the novel, the novel initiates and insists upon the importance of choosing one's father advantageously, a topic of overt concern in *Ulysses*, and suggests that Stephen in this choice may have chosen unwisely.

Just as Daedalus is imprisoned in a labyrinth of his own making, so Stephen creates his own imprisoning nets. At the same time, it is imperative that he, like Daedalus, use those same skills, artistry, to escape his self-created labyrinth. But whether Stephen can manage to escape, can manage to make his artistry liberating as well as imprisoning, simply is not clear within the text of *A Portrait*. The myth tells us ambiguous things about Stephen—the potential for destruction is at least as emphatic as the potential for liberation. It is not insignificant that this metaphor is not insistently part of the baggage of Aestheticism; it is the major, if ambiguous, source of hope for Stephen. Joyce does not deny art a liberating function. Properly used, by the mature artist—a Daedalus—the powers and skills can produce flight. Improperly used by the apprentice—an Icarus—the skills will produce drowning. Stephen does not know this fact.

These concerns about art and life discriminate Joyce from Stephen. In *Ulysses*, Joyce more overtly moved away from Stephen, and yet to argue that that movement indicates a substantive change in Joyce's attitudes seems foolish, for the second novel was begun almost immediately after *A Portrait* was finished; we do not know of a period in which Joyce could have radically altered his sense of artistry, although certainly an evolutionary or gradual change is possible.

While writing *Ulysses*, Joyce remarked to Budgen that Stephen no longer interested him as much as Bloom because Stephen "had a shape that can't be changed."[27] The conversation would have been worth hearing, for the facts of the novel seem to contradict as well as confirm Joyce's statement. Stephen's artistic theories are not static in *Ulysses;* the first chapter reestablishes his position in the tradition of the Aesthetes and then "Scylla and Charybdis" offers us a different and only partly Aesthetic analysis of Shakespeare. On the more human level, Stephen moves from almost total rejection of communality in *A Portrait* to seeing that a schoolboy is very much as he was when a child: an assertion not of uniqueness, his cry in the earlier novel, but of similarity and involvement. Stephen moves from refusing to allow anyone to touch him to acquiesing in Bloom's suggestion "Lean on me," although Stephen is vaguely uncomfortable: "—Yes, Stephen said uncertainly, because he thought he felt a strange kind of flesh of a different man approach him, sinewless and wobbly and all that" (*U*, 660). But as "they made tracks arm-in-arm across Beresford place" (*U*, 661), Stephen clearly allows Bloom a physical contact that he has rejected from other men in the novel.

Nevertheless, Joyce is certainly more interested in Bloom. As he pointed out to Budgen, Bloom is a complete man—many-sided and constantly in relationship (as husband, father, son, cuckold) as well as associated with different realms of life than Stephen is.[28] He is drawn to and curious about the world in ways we would describe as scientific and he adopts vocabulary and assumptions from contemporary science (topics to which I wish to return later). He is an agnostic or perhaps an atheist, rejecting communion as a drug (Marx's "opiate of the masses"?). He is a husband and yet a cuckold, father and yet no father. He is an adman. He is, as Peake has demonstrated, a citizen.[29] That is, one can be more interested in Bloom because there are more diverse motives, forces, thoughts, responses going on in a man who is not exclusively an artist. He is, from Joyce's point of view, "a complete man as well—a good man."[30] In Joyce's Paris notebook, when he discussed comedy and tragedy, he claimed that comedy produced joy, "the feeling which the possession of some good excites in us." Insofar as Bloom is the good man, and insofar as *Ulysses* allows us to "possess" that good, the novel is comic and excites joy. Because Stephen is not the complete man, Joyce saw him not as the good man—and hence not as likely to produce comedy—or joy. Perhaps no portrait of an artist is so likely to produce joy as a portrait of a good man.

Perhaps Stephen becomes a young man as artist in *Ulysses;* that Joyce can move away from focusing obsessively on art and the artist suggests that he has changed between the time he conceived *A Portrait* and the beginning of his work on *Ulysses,* and that his own psychological history allowed him to focus not on the self—either the mature or the young artist—but upon men and women less like himself than Stephen is. The solipsism noted in reference to Stephen is concomitantly a description of any artist who finds the most fascinating subject in the universe to be the artist whether his fictional artist is like or unlike him. The ability to move beyond one's personal concerns to those of the greater community (whether that be Dublin or Europe or the world) is presumably one of the abilities we associate with maturity. *Dubliners* attests to Joyce's ability to find others fascinating long before he wrote *A Portrait;* nonetheless, *Ulysses* suggests a movement away from self into a concern for more complete and complicated figures such as Leopold Bloom—a movement Joyce seems to point to in the conversation Budgen recorded.

The move away from focusing on the artist is a broadening of vision. By continuing to focus upon the roles and qualities of the artist, and by seeing Leopold Bloom as a kind of artist, and by claiming that Joyce continued in *Ulysses* to be writing about art as well as about political and social conditions and religion and a myriad of other human relationships, I appear to contradict myself. Yet the role of the artist remained one question for the modern Dubliner, just as the issue of an annual income was a question, or the fidelity of wives. In my analysis of *Ulysses,* then, I am much more overtly focusing only on one issue that Joyce raised in the novel, and do not wish to imply that my reading precludes other approaches. What I do wish to argue is that for Joyce questions about the artist remained crucial; the passage in *Finnegans*

Wake that reveals a kind of anality in the artist Shem, who makes ink from his own excrement, attests to Joyce's lifelong conflicts and concerns about art.[31] So, it seems germane to inquire what, if anything, Stephen Dedalus, Leopold Bloom, Molly Bloom, and the contrastive or supportive form and textures of the novel can contribute to our understanding of the ways in which this twentieth-century artist managed to find and use his own language and create his own form for communicating his idiosyncratic vision of the world.

Thus, in the next chapter, I examine the events that traumatized the young artist, Stephen, and the congruence of his artistic theories with his experience of life. Later I will turn to Leopold and Molly Bloom.

Notes

1. Georg Lukács, *The Meaning of Contemporary Realism*, trans. John and Necke Mander (London: Merlin, 1962): "The *typical* is not to be confused with the *average* . . . , nor with the *eccentric*. . . . A character is typical, in this technical sense, when his innermost being is determined by objective forces at work in society" (p. 122).

2. J. Mitchell Morse, "The Unobtrusive Rhetoric of *Ulysses*," *James Joyce Quarterly* 13 (Winter 1976): 206.

3. Richard Ellmann, *James Joyce* (New York: Oxford University Press, 1959), pp. 105–6.

4. W. B. Yeats, *Collected Poems* (New York: The Macmillan Company, 1956). All quotations from Yeats's poetry are from this edition.

5. Ellmann, *James Joyce*, p. 104.

6. Frank Budgen, *James Joyce and the Making of "Ulysses"* (Bloomington, Ind.: Indiana University Press, 1934), p. 105.

7. Lukács, *Contemporary Realism:* "A gifted writer, however extreme his theoretical modernism, will in practice have to compromise with the demands of historicity and of social environment. Joyce uses Dublin, Kafka and Musil the Hapsburg Monarchy, as the locus of their masterpieces" (p. 21). Most of the time, however, Lukács finds Joyce entirely a modernist.

8. Stanislaus Joyce, *The Complete Dublin Diary*, ed. George H. Healy (Ithaca, N.Y., and London: Cornell University Press, 1971), p. 2: "'He is not an artist he says. He is interesting himself in politics—in which he says [he has] original ideas. He says he does not care for art or music though he admits he can judge them. He lives on the excitement of incident.'"

9. See *Oeuvres Complètes de Gustave Flaubert*, 21 vols. (Paris: L. Conard, 1923–54), 11:61–62; Francis Steegmuller, *The Letters of Gustave Flaubert, 1830–1887* (Cambridge, Mass.: Belknap Press of Harvard University Press, 1980), p. 230.

10. Karl Jung, "Psychology and Literature," *The Spirit in Man, Art, and Literature, Collected Works*, eds. Sir Herbert Read, et al., 20 vols. (Princeton, N.J.: Bollingen Series 20, Princeton University Press, 1966), 15:101.

11. Irene Hendry Chayes, "Joyce's Epiphanies," *Sewanee Review* 54 (July 1946): 449–67. This essay is frequently reprinted.

12. See discussion, chapter 3.

13. Homer Obed Brown, *The Early Fiction of James Joyce: The Biography of a Form* (Cleveland, Ohio: Case Western Press, 1972), pp. 26–27.

14. Ibid., p. 50.

15. Pater, "Conclusion," *The Renaissance*, pp. 237–39.

16. Richard Ellmann, *The Consciousness of James Joyce* (Toronto: Oxford University Press, 1977).

17. David Krause, *Sean O'Casey: The Man and His Work* (New York: Macmillan Co.,

1975), pp. 3, 4–5. Other statistics Krause cites are equally germane: in January 1900, Dublin's mortality rate was 46.0 per 1000; at the same time the mortality rate in English cities was 18.0 or 19.0. The first section of Krause's book on O'Casey can easily serve as a useful context for O'Casey's junior by two years. Despite the Joyce family's comparative prosperity, Joyce could not have remained ignorant of the starvation, infant mortality, terrible housing, and economic disaster that rendered Dublin not less dreary than the picture in *Dubliners* but drearier. Infants died more frequently in Dublin than in Calcutta during the plagues!

18. Edward Norman, *A History of Modern Ireland* (Coral Gables, Fla.: University of Miami Press, 1971), pp. 222–27.

19. Robert Scholes and Richard M. Kain (eds.) reprint the original essay in *The Workshop of Daedalus: James Joyce and the Raw Materials for "A Portrait of the Artist as a Young Man"* (Evanston, Ill.: Northwestern Press, 1965), pp. 67–68.

20. "The Symbolism of Poetry," see discussion, chapter 2.

21. Ellmann, *The Consciousness of James Joyce*, p. 84. Robert Martin Adams, *Surface and Symbol: The Consistency of James Joyce's "Ulysses"* (New York: Oxford University Press, 1962), claims Bloom cites "in perfect seriousness, the selfish and unpatriotic man's motto" (p. 102). I see no selfishness implied in the context: "All must work, have to, together."

22. Weldon Thornton, *Allusions in "Ulysses"* (Chapel Hill, N.C.: University of North Carolina Press, 1968), p. 447: "Bloom is probably trying to think of 'Uni bene, ibi patria' ('Where I am well off, there is my country'), but there may also be overtones of the similar 'Patria est ubicunque est bene' ('My country is wherever I find happiness')."

23. Suzette Henke, *Joyce's Moraculous Sindbook: A Study of "Ulysses"* (Columbus, Ohio: Ohio State University Press, 1978), see chapter 11, pp. 233–50.

24. Such patterns in Joyce resemble what Charles Mauron has called personal myth; see "L'Inconscient dans l'oeuvre et la vie de Racine," *Annales de la Faculté des Lettre d'Aix-en-Provence* (1957); *Introduction to the Psychoanalysis of Mallarmé*, trans. Archibald Henderson, Jr., and Will L. McLendon (Berkeley, Calif.: University of California Press, 1963), pp. 217–49.

25. Mark Shechner, *Joyce in Nighttown* (Berkeley, Calif.: University of California Press, 1974); Sheldon Brivic, "James Joyce: From Stephen to Bloom," *Psychoanalysis and Literary Process,* ed. Frederick C. Crews (Cambridge, Mass.: Winthrop Press, 1970), pp. 118–62; Chester Anderson, "On the Sublime and its Anal-Urethal Sources in Pope, Eliot, and Joyce," *Modern Irish Literature: Essays in Honor of William York Tindall*, ed. Raymond J. Porter and James D. Brophy (New York: Iona College and Twayne Press, 1972), pp. 235–49: these three critics and all the contributors to the *James Joyce Quarterly* Special Issue on *Joyce and Modern Psychology* 13 (Spring 1976) can both represent work on Joyce from avowedly psychoanalytic critics and indicate the range of scholarly discussions about Joyce's own psyche.

26. Walter Pater, *Greek Studies* (London: Macmillan & Co., 1910), pp. 237–38.

27. Budgen, *The Making of "Ulysses,"* p. 105.

28. Ibid., pp. 15–16, 64, 276.

29. C. H. Peake, *James Joyce: The Citizen and the Artist* (Stanford, Calif.: Stanford University Press, 1977).

30. Budgen, *The Making of "Ulysses,"* p. 17. Joyce listed among the attributes of Ulysses son, father, husband, lover, companion in arms, war dodger, "first gentleman in Europe," inventor (pp. 16–17). Budgen repeatedly discusses Bloom as the all-round man.

31. Shem the penman section, especially, and I quote only a small portion, p. 185:

> Then, pious Eneas, conformant to the fulminant firman which enjoins on the trmylose terrian that, when the call comes, he shall produce nichthemerically from his unheavenly body a no uncertain quantity of obscene matter not protected by copriright in the United Stars of Ourania or bedeed and bedood and bedang and bedung to him, with this double dye, brought to blood heat, gallic acid on iron ore, through the bowels of his misery, flashly, faithly, nastily, appropriately, this Esuan Menschavik and the first till last alshemist wrote over every square inch of the only foolscap available, his own body.

6
Trauma and Response

At the beginning of *Ulysses,* Stephen's aesthetic and personal vision of the world of life and art has been destroyed by time and in the early chapters of the novel is further subverted through parody. The novel in part records his attempt to reunify his life and to find a new aesthetic theory to replace the loss. Traumas inherent in kinetic life, the effects of time, and the mere existence of people who are not controlled by him force Stephen to restructure his life and to reexamine his artistic theories.

Each of Stephen's central symbols—artist/priest, woman, Daedalus—disintegrates in the face of life. Joyce begins the first chapter with Buck Mulligan's parody of the Mass, an act particularly significant because now in *Ulysses* Mulligan, not Stephen, performs the role of the priest. The role Stephen designed for himself in *A Portrait* is at the outset of *Ulysses* assigned to another, a man Stephen labels "usurper." Stephen's role as transubstantiator of life into art and consequently his aesthetic framework have been undercut. The signs of dissolution are many: his perception of women is changed in the traumatic aftermath of his mother's death; Mulligan's engendering bird in "The Ballad of Joking Jesus" replaces the hawklike man, flying artist, Daedalus as a supernatural father; Stephen, more overtly than in *A Portrait,* is threatened by and concerned with his inability to control time and history. Nor have his specifically artistic projects worked out, as his memories of his trip to Paris and his encounter with Synge demonstrate. Finally, in *A Portrait,* Stephen felt he had experienced artistic fertility as the word was made flesh in "the virgin womb of the imagination"; now in *Ulysses,* that word and its artistic import are lost. His repeated demand that he be given the word indicates his failure to produce art—or to control the words that would compose it.

Stephen's sensitivity to his mother's death is revealed first in a confrontation with Mulligan, who has offended Stephen by saying to his aunt, *"it's only Dedalus whose mother is beastly dead"* (*U,* 8). Stephen claims that the offense lies in the word *only* modifying himself, but despite his arrogance—which lends credence to the assertion—that claim is hard to credit since the topic and images of his mother's death continue to haunt him throughout the day. In the riddle that Stephen asks at Mr. Deasy's school and in subsequent references to it, Stephen covertly introduces his sense of guilt concerning his mother.

> *The cock crew*
> *The sky was blue:*
> *The bells in heaven*
> *Were striking eleven.*
> *Tis time for this poor soul*
> *To go to heaven.*
>
> [*U*, 26]

The answer to the riddle, provided by Stephen, is "The fox burying his grandmother under a hollybush" (*U*, 27). At first glance, both the riddle and its answer are sheer nonsense. By jumping ahead to "Circe," we can solve our riddle. There Stephen asks

> Why striking eleven? Proparoxyton. Moment before the next Lessing says. Thirsty fox. *(He laughs loudly).* Burying his grandmother. Probably he killed her. [*U*, 559]

Part of another scene concerns the same fox:

> (. . . *A stout fox drawn from covert, brush pointed, having buried his grandmother, runs swift for the open, brighteyed, seeking badger earth . . .)* [*U*, 572]

Stephen, who is being chased by Simon, is imagistically associated with the fox. Still later, Stephen confirms our suspicion that he feels guilty. Mulligan says, "Kinch killed her dogsbody bitchbody" (*U*, 580) in response to the appearance of May's ghost. Stephen initially responds to his mother, "Lemur, who are you?" and then

> They say I killed you, mother. He offended your memory. Cancer did it, not I. Destiny. [*U*, 580]

The only other character in *Ulysses* who kills a female relative is the fox who kills his grandmother. But given that Stephen proposes a consubstantial relationship among Shakespeare and his son Hamnet and character Hamlet, it is not difficult to see the connection between Stephen and the fox and May Dedalus and the grandmother. So Stephen's guilt, as irrational as it may be, is not merely over his refusal to pray for his mother at her death: it is a murderer's guilt.

We do not have to read the entire novel, however, for in the first chapter, Joyce provided sufficient hints to suggest Stephen's guilt. Contemplating the man's drowning nine days before, Stephen thinks:

> I want his life still to be his, mine to be mine. A drowning man. His human eyes scream to me out of horror of his death. I . . . With him together down . . . I could not save her. Waters: bitter death: lost. [*U*, 46]

The shift of pronoun from his to her is certainly a shift from thinking about whether he (Stephen) would have the courage necessary to save a man from drowning to a consideration of his responsibility for his mother's death. The waters and bitterness recall the bitter green bile of May's bowl. He could not save May. But it seems that his failure to pray for his mother has become for him a symptom of murder rather than a filial and religious failure. Furthermore, the passage quoted above occurs on the same page as another reference to the riddle: "Something he buried there, his grandmother" (*U*, 46). The juxtaposition, in a novel where narrative point of view is controlled to indicate the mental processes through which man adapts his world to himself and himself to his world, is significant because through it Joyce associated the riddle and his mother in Stephen's mind and hence in the patterns of the novel. The association prompts the reader to equate Stephen with the murdering and pursued fox.

May Dedalus has never been, in Stephen's mind, a mere flesh and blood mother. She, like the rest of Stephen's life, is part of a symbol pattern. May is the first of all for Stephen the figure of the woman. She is the first woman he sees, and she becomes the basis for his view of women. Furthermore, it is May Dedalus who sounds most overtly the ominous note at the end of *A Portrait*: "She prays . . . that I may learn in my own life and away from home and friends what the heart is and what it feels. Amen. So be it" (*P*, 252). His mother has warned Stephen of one of the dangers of Aestheticism. To live Aesthetically is to deny natural or what some have called unnatural affections; in any case, to deny emotional responses to life and art. Stephen's art and hence his life are to produce stasis; they excite neither desire nor loathing; the viewer is simply arrested; he neither acts nor is acted upon except in an intellectual sphere. May knows perhaps what Lord Henry in *The Picture of Dorian Gray* knows: "'If a man treats life artistically, his brain is his heart'" (*DG*, 388). And that is exactly what Stephen wishes to do at the end of *A Portrait of the Artist*, to treat life artistically.

The connection between Wilde's and Joyce's novels is more significant, however, because both protagonists are responsible for the death of their creators. That point needs a bit of exploring, for Stephen is only psychologically responsible for his mother's death; that is, he asserts and assumes his responsibility as well as fighting the idea. Dorian in fact kills his creator. Dorian becomes a portrait—eternally young—and that portrait was created by Basil, whom he murders. The confusion and ignorance that surround Dorian's parentage serve the purpose of making Basil and perhaps Lord Henry the true fathers or creators of the young man. He has no parents, and their absence makes the imagistic association of fatherhood and art easier and more obvious. Epifanio San Juan remarks on the pattern in Dorian Gray's life:

> When he kills Hallward, he denies the creator of his beauty; for the painter is solely responsible for his preternatural beauty and his vanity. Just as Adam denies his Creator, so Dorian commits the "sin" of pride.[1]

The parallel of course is not exact, for Stephen's creators are presumably both May and Simon Dedalus. But Stephen questions his own paternity in questioning the idea of paternity:

> —A father, Stephen said, battling against hopelessness, is a necessary evil. . . . Fatherhood, in the sense of conscious begetting, is unknown to man. It is a mystical estate. . . . Paternity may be a legal fiction. Who is the father of any son that any son should love him or he any son? [*U*, 207]

In Stephen's mind, May does create Stephen. Stephen's fixation on May as his only creator is suggested by his preoccupation with woman as the Virgin. Stephen in his role as Christ has only one human parent. Through the intervention of a mystical father, a Daedalus or a dove, with whom he equates himself, he is created. When Stephen associates the sense of mystical creation with the creation of a child, he is echoing himself: In *A Portrait* he speaks of creation as mystery. "The mystery of esthetic like that of material creation is accomplished" (*P*, 215). And the aesthetic creation of the villanelle is a mystery, told in terms of the annunciation complete with Gabriel, visions, enchantment, and finally the birth. At any rate, May carried him in her body, as Cranly said in *A Portrait*:

> Your mother brings you into the world, carries you first in her body. What do we know about what she feels? But whatever she feels, it, at least, must be real. It must be. [*P*, 242]

Stephen reiterates Cranly's position—and Joyce's—in *Ulysses*: "*Amor matris*, subjective and objective genitive, may be the only true thing in life" (*U*, 207). Stephen, in "murdering" his mother, has murdered his creator, his only sure link to history, as surely as Dorian has when he kills Basil. And in both novels, it is this real or symbolic murder that removes even the possibility of confession from both protagonists. Dorian for the first time does not confide in Lord Henry, though he toys with the idea and occasionally wishes he could; Stephen, who "always confesses" to Cranly, no longer has any confidant. Bloom, who learns many things about Stephen in "Circe," as they share visions and experience in that way details from each other's day, may fill the gap left by Cranly.

Both murders isolate the protagonists more completely from human society and life. They become persons without pasts, without history, or persons wishing to escape from their history. And neither of them can escape. Stephen's nightmare is his personal and racial history; Dorian's nightmare is equally personal and more obviously artistic. Without parents, he is created by an artist whom he murders. The midwife of his labors, Lord Henry, is no more the creator, in his mind, than Simon is the father from Stephen's point of view in essential or consubstantial senses. In Wilde's novel, Dorian expiates his sin, thus reconciling with the creator, by killing the "real" portrait and hence himself. Stephen, if reconciliation is possible for him, does it indirectly. His at-one-ment with Bloom in "Circe," "Eumaeus," and "Ithaca" may reestablish his unity with human life broken, in part, by his mother's death. For both protagonists, there is some kind of death involved: Dorian literally dies; Stephen hears the bells chiming a death knell as he leaves Bloom's house.

Similarly, in *Marius the Epicurean,* the death of Marius's mother both signals that Marius is separated from his own history and, because of its position in the plot, suggests the dangers of emotional separation from the mother. Marius's mother dies after an argument:

> She died away from home, but sent for him at the last, with a painful effort on her part, but to his great gratitude, pondering, as he always believed, that he might chance otherwise to look back all his life long upon a single fault with something like remorse, and find the burden a great one. For it happened that, through some sudden, incomprehensible petulance there had been an angry gesture, and a slighting word, at the very moment of her departure, actually for the last time. Remembering this he would ever afterwards pray to be saved from offences against his own affections; the thought of that marred parting having peculiar bitterness for one who set so much store, both by principle and habit, on the sentiment of home. [*M,* 24–25]

Marius, fortunately, discovers in time his offense to his mother and is spared the agenbite of inwit that Stephen suffers. Stephen's mother dies at home, but he is far from home and is sent for. And it is his single fault, his childish refusal to pray for her that overtly causes him remorse. What Marius learns from his mother's death is also interesting in terms of Stephen's maturation.

> But the death of his mother turned seriousness of feeling into a matter of the intelligence: it made him a questioner; and, by bringing into full evidence to him the force of his affections and the probable importance of their place in his future, developed in him generally the more human and earthly elements of character. A singularly virile consciousness of the realities of life pronounced itself in him; still however as in the main a

poetic apprehension, though united already with something of personal ambition and the instinct of self-assertion. [*M*, 26]

One of the reasons that May's ghost has such a tremendous effect upon Stephen is that he hasn't recognized the place in his own emotions of filial affection. May's death denies him the chance for reconciliation and for paying the filial debt incurred at birth. His guilt is not poetic, try as he may to turn it into riddles; it is a real and hence disturbing intrusion upon the insulated world of art in which he seeks to recreate life. Preferring to create the life, the symbols and images, out of which he will recreate, Stephen does not want the chaos, the chance, the coincidence of real life to destroy the symbolism.

But life does destroy symbol. His mother dies and Stephen returns to Dublin only to discover that he cannot control his life or his emotions. Not only has the initial woman of Stephen's life—his mother— "deserted" him and by that act subverted one of his major symbols, but other aspects of the symbolic woman Stephen created in *A Portrait* also disintegrate. In chapter 5 of *A Portrait* Stephen discovers in certain women the image of Ireland: one such woman is the young woman who calls Davin to her bed; another is E.C. In the later novel, these women are replaced, in Stephen's mind, by an old milkwoman; she is toothless and weak and she recognizes Mulligan, not Stephen, as her savior. It is Mulligan who will create the new race, either through his comic stud service or, more probably, through his medical practice. While Stephen had wished to affect the women of Ireland so that they would breed a less ignoble race, Mulligan proposes, as a kind of parody, a more literal breeding. What distresses Stephen is that the old woman, like E.C. in the earlier novel, looks to someone else: here the old woman looks to Mulligan:

> She bows her head to a voice that speaks to her loudly, her bonesetter, her medicineman: me she slights. To the voice that will shrive and oil for the grave all there is of her but her woman's unclean loins, of man's flesh made not in God's likeness, the serpent's prey. [*U*, 14]

Her "shrunken paps" (*U*, 13), her concern with bodily instead of spiritual needs contrast with Stephen's imagined temptress. But there are many similarities. For instance, in *A Portrait*, E.C. has in the same way "betrayed" Stephen by her response to the priest:

> His anger against her found vent in coarse railing at her paramour, whose name and voice and features offended his baffled pride: a priested peasant, with a brother a policeman in Dublin and a brother a potboy in Moycullen. To him she would unveil her soul's shy nakedness, to one who was but schooled in the discharging of a formal rite rather than to him, a priest

of eternal imagination, transmuting the daily bread of experience into the
radiant body of everliving life. [*P*, 221]

Mulligan takes the priest's role in usurping Stephen's proper relationship to the woman. Again the woman will reveal herself to the usurper
not to Stephen. What Stephen proposes to do with E.C.'s soul, had he
received it and its care, would be destructive to E.C. Like Rubek in
Ibsen's *When We Dead Awaken*, Stephen would transform the soul into
art but in consequence kill the soul as well.[2]

The milkwoman represents one dramatization of Stephen's
difficulties with women. Even more clearly we see the disruption of
Stephen's symbolic women in his response to the cocklepickers.
Stephen first thinks that they are midwives:

> Number one swung lourdily her midwife's bag, the other's gamp poked in
> the beach. From the liberties, out for the day. Mrs Florence MacCabe,
> relict of the late Patk MacCabe, deeply lamented, of Bride Street. One of
> her sisterhood lugged me squealing into life. Creation from nothing.
> What has she in the bag? A misbirth with a trailing navelcord, hushed in
> ruddy wool. [*U*, 37–38]

Stephen again creates what he wishes to see; and he sees what he wishes
to project from his own troubles and concerns. Again he worries about
his own birth. But the vision of the stillbirth may also be a vision of his
own stillbirth of artistic creation: Stephen has not produced his art. It,
like the child he imagines, is a "misbirth." In *A Portrait*, the creation of
the villanelle is a spiritual-sexual conception and birth, rendered in the
terms of the Annunciation and Incarnation of Christ. Furthermore,
Stephen identifies himself with the midwives-cocklepickers (and with
Swinburne): "Like me, like Algy, coming down to our mighty mother"
(*U*, 37).

The midwives lead him to contemplate his own birth and parentage, still rejecting his unsubstantial father:

> Wombed in sin darkness I was too, made not begotten. By them, the
> man with my voice and my eyes and a ghostwoman with ashes on her
> breath. They clasped and sundered, did the coupler's will. From before
> the ages He willed me and now may not will me away or ever. . . . Is that
> then the divine substance wherein Father and Son are consubstantial? [*U*,
> 38]

Stephen's revery over his father, his mother, his trip to Paris, his relationship to his mother and her death, his status as a "changeling" (a
word later used to describe Bloom's son, Rudy), and finally his concern
with drowning and his own courage, continues for ten pages. Then we
discover and Stephen realizes that his midwives are "Cocklepickers" (*U*,

46). These cocklepickers and the visions Stephen creates out of their presence are parallel to the beatific vision of the girl on the beach at the end of chapter 4 of *A Portrait*. The beach is the same; the sea is the same; and Stephen is still trying to shape the vision; but in *Ulysses*, his vision doesn't work as well. It is narratively broken by "reality"; the women are clearly or realistically labeled; they are cocklepickers. The ineluctable modality of the visible refuses to conform to Stephen's vision. The emphasis on midwives and on Stephen's artistic concerns is crucial because, as we can remember from *A Portrait*, Stephen has yet to work out a theory that accounts for the creation of art: he simply has a theory of its apprehension and forms. During a passage whose fertile images clashed with the generally dry and scholastic discussion of aesthetics in *A Portrait*, he tells Lynch:

> So far as this side of esthetic philosophy extends Aquinas will carry me all along the line. When we come to the phenomena of artistic conception, artistic gestation and artistic reproduction I require a new terminology and a new personal experience. [P, 209]

Joyce's concern with production and reproduction is manifested both in Stephen's symbols (e.g., women become midwives and mothers) and in the elaborate joke about reproduction-gestation in the structure of "Oxen of the Sun." That chapter, with its pattern of gestation and growth that finally gives birth to the Word, is a parody of artistic reproduction, at least as Stephen conceives of it. Stephen indeed needs a new experience and a new terminology. His mistake in identifying the cocklepickers is a symptom of premature closure: he looks once and identifies his vision, revealing more of himself than of the women. In some ways, that is, Stephen hasn't changed much between the novels. In his beatific vision on the beach in *A Portrait*, he moved from wondering about Daedalian figures to a certainty that whatever was in the sky, it was Daedalus, and a symbol of his destiny. In *Ulysses*, he appears at least to be questioning the perception. As Marius's mother's death makes him a questioner, May's death begins to make Stephen one too. To question the theories about art that he had developed in *A Portrait* is inevitably to alter them. They were built on the sand of the beach, not on rock.

Throughout the first three chapters of *Ulysses*, Stephen and Mulligan quote Swinburne and Stephen silently remembers lines from Swinburne's poetry—another indication that Stephen's aesthetic concerns are not completely changed between novels. The most obvious of Swinburne's poems is "The Triumph of Time." Mulligan begins the quotations by associating the snotgreen of Stephen's handkerchief with a "new art colour for our Irish poets" and subsequently by associating that with Swinburne:

—God, he said quietly. Isn't the sea what Algy calls it: a grey sweet mother? The snotgreen sea. The scrotumtightening sea. . . . She is our great sweet mother. . . . Our mighty mother. [*U*, 5]

Immediately Mulligan tells Stephen that his aunt "thinks you killed your mother" and rebukes Stephen for his failure to pray. Stephen makes the connection between the sea in Swinburne's poem and his mother even clearer or muddier:

Pain, that was not yet the pain of love, fretted his heart. Silently, in a dream she had come to him after her death, her wasted body within its loose brown grave-clothes giving off an odour of wax and rosewood, her breath, that had bent upon him, mute, reproachful, a faint odour of wetted ashes. Across the threadbare cuffedge he saw the sea hailed as a great mother by the wellfed voice beside him. The ring of bay and skyline held a dull green mass of liquid. A bowl of white china had stood beside her deathbed holding the green sluggish bile which she had torn up from her rotting liver by fits of loud groaning vomiting. [*U*, 5]

Swinburne's poem is addressed to a woman who has deserted her lover for another man. Mulligan's—and then Stephen's—association of May with the sea in which the man seeks comfort links her tangentially to Stephen's would-be lover, because the woman who has deserted Stephen for another is Ireland, his mother, and the muse figure who is to inspire him to create the uncreated conscience. Thematically, Stephen's position and the position of the speaker in Swinburne's poem are also similar: both feel that they have lost a patterned and reassuring life in losing their women; both feel deserted; both see the sea as a symbol of flux, change, time, history, and yet, also, eternity. Stephen's mother is associated with the sea as a symbol of time, history, and eternity because she is, for him, the causal agent forcing him to see that he cannot control time or direct change. In chapter 5 of *A Portrait*, the clocks are symptomatically broken as Stephen's sense of communal time fails. Stephen creates time in that chapter through his emotions—for instance, he expands the interval between waking and sleeping as he creates the villanelle. Similarly, his esthetic theory claims that art arrests the mind of the viewer, holding it static, outside of that shared and everyday sense of time. In these ways, he tries to escape the world's time, which is fluid and kinetic, and move into a static and eternal realm of art. There time is either nonexistent or the "immeasurable background" against which we see art. By making his mother into a symbol, Stephen had attempted to move her into that realm where time does not affect people; his mother shatters that world, insulated against the ravages of time, by dying—that is, by behaving as a human being and not a symbol.

That change, a change occurring in and marking the passing of time, is something that Stephen can neither control nor ignore. Although this change in Stephen's life appears to him to be simply destructive, it is not. It is part of the permanent, because essential nature of life. In a similar way, Swinburne's poem affirms this essential nature of change as well as revealing the persona's despair over it. The poem may need quoting in part:

> The sweet sea, mother of loves and hours,
> Shudders and shines as the grey winds gleam,
>   Turning her smile to a fugitive pair.
>
> Mother of loves that are swift to fade;
>   Mother of mutable winds and hours.
> A barren mother, a mother-maid,
>   Cold and clean as her faint salt flowers.
>
>   [ll. 62–68]
>
> . . . .
> I will go back to the great sweet mother,
>   Mother and lover of men, the sea.
> I will go down to her, I and none other,
>   Close with her, kiss her and mix her with me;
> Cling to her, strive with her, hold her fast:
>
>   [ll. 257–61]
>
> . . . .
> O fair green-girdled mother of mine.
>
>   [l. 265][3]

Despite the many negative and cold images Swinburne associates with the sea, the sea is also the comforter and, despite its coldness and barrenness, the "mother of loves" and the "mother and lover of men." To associate this sea with May Dedalus is to express ambivalence about her—whether those ambivalent associations are Mulligan's or Stephen's is unclear, although Stephen is certainly ambivalent. His mother's death has destroyed some of the patterns of meaning he created in his life; and yet he seems to move psychologically toward his mother, not away from her. Part of that movement is, as he describes it, a movement in favor of artistic fertility. Part of the movement, too, appears to be oedipal—rejected by one woman, Swinburne's persona seeks another, who is a "mother and lover of men." By analogy, Stephen seems to seek his mother, too; what he feels is ambiguous; it is "not yet the pain of love."

The allusions to Swinburne's poem, while they link Stephen once again with the Aesthetes and demonstrate the traumatic nature of Stephen's life, do not seem in Stephen's revery to be parodic as Mulligan's parody of the Mass at the beginning of the novel is. Allusions to Oscar Wilde are, in contrast, satiric, and their victim is Stephen Dedalus. The usurper, Buck Mulligan, takes from Oscar Wilde the weapons of irony, paradox, and parody to attack Stephen; as Stephen's esthetics parallel some of Wilde's, that attack is, like other actions of Mulligan, a usurpation, at least in Stephen's mind. Mulligan quotes Wilde: "The rage of Caliban at not seeing his face in a mirror" and immediately uses it to attack Stephen, or at least to associate him with Oscar Wilde. "If Wilde were only alive to see you" (*U*, 6). Stephen makes it clear that he does know Wilde when he replies, "It is a symbol of Irish art. The cracked lookingglass of a servant" (*U*, 5).⁴ Having usurped Stephen's priestly function as he parodies the Mass, Mulligan now usurps Stephen's use of Oscar Wilde. And the parody, the attack is effective: Stephen doesn't, like Caliban, wish to see his face in a mirror, but at the same time, he is enraged, like Caliban, if he doesn't see himself reflected.

That cracked looking glass has, at the beginning of the chapter, reflected Buck Mulligan as priest, not Stephen. In that, too, Mulligan is, as Stephen labels him at the end of the chapter, a usurper. Worse yet, from Stephen's point of view, Mulligan does not take the priestly role seriously. Although readers may find humor in Stephen's use of the Mass, his parody of the Annunciation, and his talk about the priesthood of the imagination in *A Portrait*, it is clear that Stephen finds nothing humorous in these uses. Buck, on the other hand, uses and abuses and parodies the Church and, by doing so, parodies Stephen's seriousness about his art, lampoons the symbols in which Stephen conceives of his art and vocation, and indicates a great deal more freedom from the nets of the Church than Stephen has shown in his gloriously proclaimed flight. Stephen is so controlled by the Church and its metaphors and its rituals that even in the act of rebellion he can only mimic the Church. Just as he says to his classmates, so we may say to him: "If we must have a Jesus, let us have a legitimate Jesus" (*P*, 198). The parody of the mirror operates as the parody of the Mass operates. Buck uses the same rough literary material, an acquaintance with Wilde and Pater, to mock Stephen as Caliban.

Just as Mulligan takes literary and religious allusions and metaphors away from Stephen through parody, so he has the same effect upon the image of the bird-Daedalus, the artificer. By the end of *A Portrait* the bird has come to evoke or represent art, the artist, and the proper father. In the beginning of *Ulysses*, another bird stands as the proper father, but Mulligan certainly changes its meaning in "The Ballad of Joking Jesus":

> —*I'm the queerest young fellow that ever you heard.*
> *My mother's a jew, my father's a bird.*
> *With Joseph the joiner I cannot agree,*
> *So here's to disciples and Calvary.*
>
> [*U*, 19]

This song parodies Stephen's agony in *Ulysses* over his father figure, but it also undercuts the Daedalian father-artist Stephen created for himself in *A Portrait*. Stephen wishes to see himself not only as Christ, but also as the son of Daedalus, the hawklike man, and thus his father is, imaginatively, a bird. Mulligan's irreverent parody suggests the limitations of Stephen's vision and helps to destroy it. Mulligan is even described in this chapter as having "winglike hands" (*U*, 19) and "birdlike cries" (*U*, 19), and as being like "one about to rise in the air" (*U*, 19). The usurpation appears complete, and it is significant that Mulligan usurps Stephen's position by using the same words, symbols, and patterns. Symbols, Stephen is discovering, do not mean the same thing to everyone nor in every situation. Despite what Yeats has to say about the sacred symbols out of *spiritus mundi*, the idea that symbols have fixed, precise meanings works no better for Stephen than it has for Yeats's poems.[5] The point is that the significance of the metaphors drawn from Church and bird is no longer the significance of metaphor. The tenor and vehicle have collapsed for Stephen. So to usurp or take over the words, as Mulligan does, is to usurp the only reality Stephen wishes to recognize. Stephen confuses metaphor and symbol with "that which they were emblems for" as a function of the way he generally confuses art with life.

All of these disruptions to the esthetic theory that Stephen had developed for himself in *A Portrait of the Artist* are possible because his esthetic and his definition of reality are built upon magic words, not ideas. If the artist in Stephen's cosmology could stand without its foundations—the priest of eternal imagination, Daedalus, the isolation and egocentrictiy of Aestheticism, and the allusions to Aesthetes—then Mulligan and the events of Stephen's life could not undermine the world Stephen constructed for himself. However, his concept of the artist depends upon the magic word *priest;* the word is totally associated with the concept, so to usurp, by changing the meaning of the word as Mulligan does, is to subvert the concept of the artist, to kick out its underpinnings. The parodic use of the Mass has the same function. If, in Stephen's construct of the world, the transubstantiation of the artist into art were merely a metaphor for artistic creation to be used and then discarded, Mulligan's usurpation could not exist. He would simply be using or creating another metaphor. But Stephen had hoped that metaphor and symbol were in fact reality: to usurp the words, the linguistic representation of the metaphor, is to usurp Stephen's "reality," or to destroy it. Similarly, the bird image that Stephen had constructed in *A Portrait* was, by the end of that novel, no longer an image for the artificer-artist, but the being himself. Daedalus is God; the artist is Christ; to use those words to refer to something else destroys the linguistic pattern through which Stephen governs, or had hoped to govern, his world.

This point is difficult to make. Stephen behaves as though his magic words have only one meaning, his. He had complained in *A Portrait* of words that he had not made or accepted; his magic words are words he has made. He rejects what he has called the marketplace meaning of words, wanting words to carry only his meaning in all contexts. His life and his art depend, to a large extent, on these privately created words. As Mulligan uses the same words, allusions from the same literary figures, the same images that Stephen has used, he dramatizes Stephen's failure while at the same time he helps to create that failure. In all these ways, Mulligan is, for Stephen and his partisans, a "usurper."

To blame Mulligan is, however, to shift responsibility. The changes in Stephen's life are changes that occur because of time and the human condition. Stephen fights the effects of time throughout *Ulysses*. In "Scylla and Charybdis," he tries to control definitions, including his somewhat comic assertion that "horseness is the whatness of allhorse" (*U*, 186), an assertion that claims a Platonic stability for the word. But Stephen knows that time is now a potent force that he cannot control. He knows that he changes in time as well as maintaining some permanent characteristics:

> —As we, or mother Dana, weave and unweave our bodies, Stephen said, from day to day, their molecules shuttled to and fro, so does the artist weave and unweave his image. . . . the mole on my right breast is where it was when I was born, though all my body has been woven of new stuff time after time. . . . In the intense instant of imagination . . . that which I was is that which I am and that which in possibility I may come to be. [*U*, 194]

Even in his new awareness of the effects of time—and its inevitable corollaries change and flux—Stephen has not in fact given up altogether the achronological nature of his theories in *A Portrait*, although we can see both it and a deterministic perception of time in this passage. Furthermore, this passage is a rather direct allusion to Walter Pater, a progenitor of the Aesthetes and a man who, at least in the "Conclusion" to *The Renaissance*, demonstrated a fear of change and time and mortality similar to Stephen's. Stephen alludes to a passage in which Pater comments that in the modern world "to regard all things and principles of things as inconstant modes or fashions has more and more become the tendency" and that, finally, what we discover is movement: "It is with this movement, with the passage and dissolution of impressions, images, sensations, that analysis leaves off—that *perpetual weaving and unweaving of ourselves.*"[6] As the artist weaves and unweaves himself, he is in Stephen's world weaving and unweaving his image, because his image is his body and self. Clearly it is the flux, the uncontrolled change that Stephen (and, perhaps, Pater) cannot tolerate and that he turns into a vision of permanence by showing that change changes nothing. History, the movement in time, is the nightmare from which Stephen tries to escape. Since he must weave and unweave himself, never quite the same yet never totally different, Stephen cannot escape his history. This sense of flux, even within some kind of permanence, is almost alien to Stephen in *A Portrait:* it is a sign of his growth that he recognizes it as reality. No longer are the villains in his reveries nets with their stability and visibility; the villains are the shifting and weaving of the self as the self travels through time.

Stephen's sense of his historical position has provided his symbols of the artist, whether those symbols come from Greek myth or nineteenth-century poetry. His sense of modernity resembles T. S. Eliot's sense of the modern in "Tradition and the Individual Talent," but it is probably more importantly based upon Wilde's belief that critics and artists must have a sense of history. Wilde wrote that critics

> shall be able to realise, not merely our own lives, but the collective life of the race, and so to make ourselves absolutely modern, in the true meaning of the word modernity. For he to whom the present is the only thing that is present, knows nothing of the age in which he lives. To realise the nineteenth century, one must realise every century that has preceded it and that has contributed to its making. To know anything about oneself, one must know all about others. [5: 189–90]

In one sense it is Stephen who provides, through historical allusions and references in his stream of consciousness, the first half of Wilde's requirement for man, and it is Bloom, in his imaginative sympathy for others, who provides the other half of modernity. Stephen's historical sense is also akin to Dorian Gray's:

> There were times when it appeared to Dorian Gray that the whole of history was merely the record of his own life, not as he had lived it in act and circumstance, but as his imagination had created it for him, as it had been in his brain and in his passions. . . . It seemed to him that in some mysterious way their lives had been his own. [*DG*, 263]

If we look at this passage carefully and compare it to Stephen's sense of history, we notice that Stephen, like Dorian, is extraordinarily solipsistic in his sense of the past. Although he uses materials from the past, they are reconstructed in his imagination. Leopold Bloom represents more clearly in *Ulysses* the weight of the past, the experience of peoples in the past. In "Ithaca," Stephen listens to Bloom chant in Hebrew and discusses with him ancient writing. What Stephen hears in Bloom's voice, "a profound ancient male unfamiliar melody," is "the accumulation of the past" (*U*, 689). Bloom represents two ways of understanding that are new to Stephen: a compassionate understanding of what contemporaries feel and a compassionate understanding of the human, rather than literary past. In the union between Bloom and Stephen in "Circe," "Eumaeus," and "Ithaca," Joyce dramatized the whole person—rooted in history and in the contemporary human condition. Stephen's isolation from others, a product of his fictional life and artistic choices, and a corollary of his mother's death, is assuaged by his meeting with Bloom. The sense of imaginative connection with past peoples, represented by Stephen's literary allusions, is at least in part only another way of dramatizing his isolation from the present and from the human beings of the past.

Connecting with people like him, his distant kinsmen, had been one of Stephen's motives for going to Paris at the end of *A Portrait.* Yet, in the early chapters of *Ulysses,* we discover that that venture has failed, too. His meeting with Synge, evoked in an exchange between Mulligan and Stephen, is reported in "Scylla and Charybdis":

> —The tramper Synge is looking for you, he said, to murder you. He heard you pissed on his halldoor in Glasthule. He's out in pampooties to murder you.
> —Me! Stephen exclaimed. That was your contribution to literature. . . .
> Harsh gargoyle face that warred against me over our mess of hash of lights in rue Saint-André-des-Arts. In words of words for words, palabras. Oisin with Patrick. Faunman he met in Clamart woods, brandishing a winebottle, *C'est vendredi saint!* Murthering Irish. His image, wandering, he met. I mine. I met a fool i' the forest. [*U,* 200]

Stephen's meeting with Synge, we gather, was not congenial. Yet Stephen has, by his own report, met people like him, "I mine." But that person was not just Stephen or Synge, but "a fool i' the forest." Later in the chapter Stephen quotes from Maeterlinck:

> *If Socrates leave his house today he will find the sage seated on his doorstep. If Judas go forth tonight it is to Judas his steps will tend.* Every life is many days, day after day. We walk through ourselves, meeting robbers, ghosts, giants, old men, young men, wives, widows, brothers-in-love. But always meeting ourselves. [*U,* 213]

Stephen meets himself in Synge, discovers similarities between them that he rejects, and fails in his artistic mission to "encounter experience" or to create "the uncreated conscience" or to write any literature. The failure of that trip is part of the trauma that destroys Stephen's comfortable world. Like Pater's Marius, who goes to Rome on his poetic mission and discovers the plague, man's brutality to man, and his own inadequacies, Stephen discovers nothing healthy or artistically productive in his journey to Paris; he travels from "virgin Dublin" to "corrupt Paris" (*U,* 188).

The failure of the trip to Paris is revealed by Stephen when in a revery in "Scylla and Charybdis" he thinks:

> Fabulous artificer, the hawklike man. You flew. Whereto? New-haven-Dieppe, steerage passenger. Paris and back. Lapwing. Icarus. *Pater, ait.* Seabedabbled, fallen, weltering. Lapwing you are. Lapwing he. [*U*, 210]

This journey and Stephen's experience of it, then, has destroyed for him another major symbol of his artistry. Elements of the myth that he rejected or ignored in *A Portrait* are now dominant: as Icarus, he has fallen into the sea, has become "seabedabbled." Furthermore, as George L. Geckle has shown, Stephen's use of the word *lapwing* to denote himself is not accidental. Stephen understands the significance of that reference; a lapwing is a bird that frequents cemeteries, builds its nest in dung, is associated with chewing on corpses, and is totally a reversal of Stephen's association of himself with birds in *A Portrait*.[7] It is important that the symbol—a bird—is constant in this shift of self-perception. Stephen retains the linguistic sign; the things signified change, the sign remains the same. That is, either Stephen is undercutting his own prior view that words and symbols have fixed meanings or he is undercutting his own prior view that he knows what those meanings are.

There is one final symptom of Stephen's trauma between the events of *A Portrait* and the beginning of *Ulysses* that I wish to comment upon: Stephen's demand, in *Ulysses*, that he be given the word. When he defines *claritas* in *A Portrait*, he employs an unspoken analogue in Aquinas so that the *claritas* Stephen refers to is Aquinas's idea of the quality of God, the first *claritas*. For Aquinas, the Son, the Word, is the physical, formed revelation of *claritas*. Hughes T. Bredin, discussing Stephen's esthetics, elaborated on Aquinas's idea: Aquinas

> attributes *claritas* to the Second Person of the Trinity. The Son possesses clarity, "in that He is the Word, which is the light and splendour of the Intellect." . . . And analogously, it can be inferred that form, "flowing from" the first clarity [God], possesses clarity in that it is intelligible. Since it is the nature of form to *be* intelligible, form in a sense *is* clarity. *Claritas*, then, seems to be the manifestness, or iconicity, of form.[8]

This explanation of Stephen's use of the word *claritas* is absolutely consistent with his identification of himself as priest and his use of other religious terms as metaphors for art. As the artist is like God, he must create forms with *claritas*, or forms that are *claritas*. To "lose" the word, the *claritas*, for a priest of eternal imagination is, then, a serious and destructive loss. When Stephen asks his mother's ghost for the word in *Ulysses*, a very complicated request is involved. The Word, once the

incarnation represented by the villanelle, is lost and must be redis-
covered. Stephen is asking for the artistic form of his life that May's
death has destroyed, he is asking for the incarnation, he is asking about
his destiny, and he is making a sexual demand. Stephen associates May–
Mary Dedalus with the Virgin Mary partly because he doesn't want his
father to be her sexual mate; her sex partner is to be God, the begetter
and begotten, and, within Stephen's framework, Stephen the artist is
most like God.

   During the sexual dance preceding the appearance of May, Stephen
first dances with each of the prostitutes, but does not complete the
dance; that is, he does not complete the sexual encounter.[9] Then he
dances with his own ashplant, which has been an artistic symbol and
achieves phallic connotations here; dancing with the ashplant thus implies artistic and sexual masturbation. Finally his mother appears to
him, announcing herself as May Goulding—the unmarried mother of
Stephen—and he makes his sexual, artistic demand of her. But his rejection of Simon as father is the rejection of a man who cuckolded Stephen
by his own conception; Stephen stands in relationship to May as, in
some ways, Bloom stands in relationship to Molly. When Stephen
refers to May as Mary in the later chapters of the novel (*U*, 670, 682,
695), he makes more obvious the association in his mind between his
mother and the Virgin. Furthermore, his demand is for a "word known
to all men," which suggests Christ, who appears as the form so that all
men might believe, or know, the Word. Stephen's need is for a means of
communication, a form known to all men, an understandable and intel-
ligible word.

   In all these ways, then, we see at the beginning of *Ulysses* how
destroyed Stephen's life is. His carefully created sense of vocation and
destiny, his artistically shaped and controlled world, the very images
through which he has understood himself have been destroyed by time,
change, parody—by life. Given this condition, Stephen must regroup,
construct new ways of understanding himself as artist, as son, as human
being. Part of that process involves finding a new way of understanding
the role and behavior of the artist.

   Stephen's first attempt to reconstruct an aesthetic theory is found
in his discussion of Shakespeare. Here again, Stephen is following in the
footsteps of the Aesthetic tradition of the English nineteenth century.
The difference between this discussion and discussions about aesthetics
in *A Portrait* is in part a difference between the two novels: in *Ulysses*,
Joyce does not use Stephen's mind as the exclusive filter. We can see
more clearly in *Ulysses* Stephen's indebtedness to the tradition and particularly to Wilde through the comments of Stephen's listeners in "Scylla and Charybdis." Stephen's theory is introduced with thoughts that
evoke the matrix of symbolism surrounding the figure of the artist in the
Aesthetic tradition and in Stephen's mind:

> Formless spiritual. Father, Word and Holy Breath. Allfather, the
> heavenly man. Hiesos Kristos, magician of the beautiful, the Logos who
> suffers in us at every moment. This verily is that. I am the fire upon the
> altar. I am the sacrificial butter. [*U*, 185]

Stephen's sense of the artist as sacrificed and sacrificing, and hence as
associated with Christ or the Word, and his perception of words as
magical spells developed in *A Portrait* are still present here.[10] The artist
is still the martyr, still the fire and the butter being burned. The images
used to evoke the artist have changed little from the images at the end of
A Portrait. Stephen is still going to use his "dagger definitions" (*U*, 186)
much as his esthetic discussion had largely depended upon definitions.
He attempts to control his audience, just as he attempted to control
Lynch in the earlier novel, by making "them accomplices," which is to
make them into fellow murderers as well (*U*, 188). The beginning of the
narrative in which Stephen spins out his theory is in the form of a
meditation, complete with composition of place, etc.—the form used
by the priest in *A Portrait* to create a sense of Hell so effectively.
Stephen is still using the rituals and forms of the Church in his art. The
player speaks:

> To a son he speaks, the son of his soul, the prince, young Hamlet and to
> the son of his body, Hamnet Shakespeare, who has died in Stratford that
> his namesake may live for ever.
> —Is it possible that that player Shakespeare, a ghost by absence, and
> in the vesture of buried Denmark, a ghost by death, speaking his own
> words to his own son's name (had Hamnet Shakespeare lived he would
> have been prince Hamlet's twin) is it possible, I want to know, or prob-
> able that he did not draw or foresee the logical conclusion of those prem-
> ises: you are the dispossessed son: I am the murdered father: your mother
> is the guilty queen. Ann Shakespeare, born Hathaway? [*U*, 188–89]

Stephen cannot emotionally remain focused on his critical theory for
long. Because the theory is a psychological necessity for him—and
because it is built on his own traumatic experience[11]—he weaves in and
out of the theory, drawing parallels to his own experience. He associates, for instance, Shakespeare's indebtedness with his own, then
drops Shakespeare to claim that another he, since all molecules change,
borrowed the money (an echo of the passage from Pater quoted above).
He outlines his history, finally acknowledging that Conmee in fact
"saved [him] from pandies" (*U*, 190), a realization that he was not the
betrayed martyr way back at Clongowes. The discussion of Ann Hathaway, who bore Shakespeare's children and "laid pennies on his eyes . . .
when he lay on his deathbed," similarly leads immediately to a memory
of May's deathbed:

> Mother's deathbed. Candle. The sheeted mirror. Who brought me

into this world lies there, bronzelidded, under few cheap flowers. *Liliata rutilantium.* [*U*, 190]

May did for Stephen part of what Ann did for Shakespeare: Ann "saw him into . . . the world" (*U*, 190). That vision of bringing or seeing into the world, which May certainly did for Stephen, is associated with Ann Hathaway. May, then, seems to have betrayed Stephen in some skewed, oedipal fashion. In "Proteus," Stephen not only asks for "that word known to all men" but wishes to be touched and thinks of kissing— "mouth to her womb" in connection with his mother (*U*, 47–49). It is as though in Stephen's mind May should have given birth to Stephen's children. In the following discusion, Stephen claims that Shakespeare was chosen by Ann:

> By cock, she was to blame. She put the comether on him, sweet and twentysix. The greyeyed goddess who bends over the boy Adonis, stooping to conquer, as prologue to the swelling act, is a boldfaced Stratford wench who tumbles in a cornfield a lover younger than herself. [*U*, 191]

The exposition is interrupted by a discussion and catalogue of most of the literary figures of Dublin in 1904: Yeats, AE, Starkey, Miss Mitchell, Moore and Martyn, Sigerson, James Stephens. They are, perhaps most significantly, writing literature, unlike Stephen.

Stephen's explanation of Shakespeare is based upon a reading of the plays that attempts to explain the dramas through elements of Shakespeare's life. The obvious problem with such a reading is that neither Stephen nor modern critics know enough about Shakespeare's life to hazard intelligent hypotheses about that life, let alone its relationship to the art. In the peculiarities of Stephen's theory lies Joyce's comment on psychoanalytical criticism. Stephen maintains that Shakespeare has been defeated and betrayed by Ann until his "belief in himself has been untimely killed" (*U*, 196). And so Shakespeare writes *Hamlet,* allowing King Hamlet to know the manner of his own death:

> But those who are done to death in sleep cannot know the manner of their quell unless their Creator endow their souls with that knowledge in the life to come. The poisoning and the beast with two backs that urged it king Hamlet's ghost could not know of were he not endowed with knowledge by his creator. That is why the speech (his lean unlovely English) is always turned elsewhere, backward. Ravisher and ravished, what he would but would not, go with him from Lucrece's bluecircled ivory globes to Imogen's breast, bare, with its mole cinquespotted. He goes back, weary of the creation he has piled up to hide him from himself, an old dog licking an old sore. But, because loss is his gain, he passes on towards eternity in undiminished personality, untaught by the wisdom he has written or by the laws he has revealed. His beaver is up. He is a ghost, a

shadow now, the wind by Elsinore's rocks or what you will, the sea's voice, a voice heard only in the heart of him who is the substance of his shadow, the son consubstantial with the father. [*U*, 196–97]

Shakespeare and his son and his characters are, from Stephen's point of view, consubstantial and the real motive behind the play lies in Shakespeare's family life. In this passage Shakespeare becomes the sea which was associated in the first chapter of *Ulysses* with May Dedalus and Swinburne and in *A Portrait* with dramatic art, the highest art. Shakespeare is the sea's voice; in *A Portrait*, the dramatic energy of art is imaged as a sea as

> the vitality which has flowed and eddied around each person fills every person with such vital force that he or she assumes a proper and intangible esthetic life. The personality of the artist, at first a cry or a cadence or a mood and then a fluid and lambent narrative, finally refines itself out of existence, impersonalises itself. . . . The esthetic image in the dramatic form is life purified in and reprojected from the human imagination. . . . The personality of the artist passes into the narration itself, flowing round and round the persons and the action like a vital sea. [*P*, 215]

Does Shakespeare, denied his conscious and active role in material creation simply because he is a man, find the similar creative impulse fulfilled in art? He loses his personality, becomes a ghost, only to create the art form and correspond with the consubstantial son.

After Mulligan enters the library and some banter occurs, Mr. Best provides an analogue to Stephen's procedure and theory:

> —The most brilliant of all is that story of Wilde's, Mr Best said, lifting his brilliant notebook. That *Portrait of Mr W. H.* where he proves that the sonnets were written by a Willie Hughes, a man of all hues.

His listeners catch his mistake:

> —For Willie Hughes, is it not? the quaker librarian asked.
> Or Hughie Wills. Mr William Himself. W. H.: who am I?
> —I mean, for Willie Hughes, Mr Best said, amending his gloss easily. Of course it's all paradox, don't you know, Hughes and hews and hues the colour, but it's so typical the way he works it out. It's the very essence of Wilde, don't you know. The light touch. [*U*, 198]

Mr. Best's error indicates how difficult it is to describe this piece by Wilde. Part of the difficulty stems from the fact that the cast of characters change their positions regarding the composition of the sonnets. The theory that is proposed by one character and initially rejected but later accepted by another is that Shakespeare wrote the sonnets for a young boy actor whose beauty appears to match that of Dorian Gray. That is, the story appears to argue that Shakespeare's sonnets are the expression of a homosexual love. Several difficulties attach to the theory: there is no record of the existence of this boy actor, although lists of actors exist; one of the adherents of the theory forges a portrait of the boy in order to convince another character; people seem willing to die for the theory (one may in fact, the other dies of consumption); and, finally, the minute an antagonist is convinced of a protagonist's theory, the protagonist rejects it.[12] Where Wilde stands in all of this speculation is impossible to determine. But the methodology, speculation from some few facts of Shakespeare's life to the work, is clearly Stephen's own methodology. He starts with the fact that Shakespeare leaves only his "secondbest bed" to his wife—and from that evidence adduces the theory of betraying wives and brothers. Further, similarities between the way Stephen reasons and the ways Wilde's characters reason and behave warn us that Stephen is quite capable of inventing evidence to warrant his aesthetic theory. He is still trying to escape the world of communal fact and knowledge. He still, like the characters in Wilde's story, wants only the semblance of reality, transmuted into a satisfying lie.

Stephen himself connects Shakespeare and Wilde. Earlier, he speaks of Shakespeare as "a lord of language" (*U,* 196). Edmund L. Epstein correctly identifies this as a quotation from Wilde's *De Profundis* "published in 1905, but Joyce commited other anachronisms in *Ulysses.*"[13] The quotation comes from a section in which Wilde relates his reaction to his mother's death: "Her death was terrible to me; but I once a lord of language, have no words in which to express my anguish and shame." What makes this source for the allusion (rather than Tennyson[14]) so compelling is the conjunction of dead mothers and an inability to produce art, to have the word. Secondly, Stephen's allusion to poison and King Hamlet's death may also relate to Wilde's "Pen and Poison."[15] Stephen continues to associate himself with the Aesthetic tradition.

Shakespeare leads Stephen to contemplate his own theory of fatherhood, which is his theory of creation, both material and artistic, and is a mystery.

> Well: if the father who has not a son be not a father can the son who has not a father be a son? When Rutlandbaconsouthamptonshakespeare or another poet of the same name in the comedy of errors wrote *Hamlet* he was not the father of his own son merely but, being no more a son, he was and felt himself the father of all his race, the father of his own grandfather, the father of his unborn grandson who, by the same token, never was born for nature, as Mr Magee understands her, abhors perfection. [*U,* 208]

The point is that Shakespeare, denied a son, produces the play and hence becomes the father of his race through some mysterious method. The mystery of aesthetic creation produces the timeless Shakespeare. Part of Shakespeare's attraction for Stephen is of course this timeless quality, because Shakespeare has escaped the nightmare of his history. Mulligan parodies Stephen by claiming that the theory means "Himself his own father. . . . I am big with child. I have an unborn child in my brain. Pallas Athena! A play! The play's the thing!" (*U*, 208). What Mulligan's words imply is accurate: the word made flesh becomes the artistic creation. Like Stephen's villanelle, Shakespeare's plays become what one critic calls the masculine substitute for the certainty of creation a woman feels in childbirth.[16] Stephen sees Shakespeare, too, as his own father because Stephen wishes to be the father of himself. Self-creation would reject Simon as father and violator of May's virginity. But Stephen's dilemma is also indicated in this passage. He cannot locate himself in the flux that he sees as threatening because he can be neither a son nor a father. Having no father whom he accepts, he cannot be a son, and having no son, he cannot be a father.

Bloom is in a similar, although more literal position. He has no son—Rudy died early; he has no father—Virag committed suicide. He cannot, in Stephen's view, be either a son or a father. The different applications of the same statement reveal the basic difference between Bloom and Stephen, while the fact that we can apply the same statement to both reveals their similarities. The statement can be literally applied to Bloom; the statement is only symbolic for Stephen who emotionally, psychologically, and symbolically has no father and, because he has produced no art, no son.

Stephen's theory about Shakespeare discovers a consistent theme that resonates to conflicts in Shakespeare's own life—that is, Stephen suggests that writers construct plays by working out over and over again their own psychological situations. The theme Stephen chooses to see in Shakespeare's plays resonates more obviously to Stephen's own life. In a long passage Stephen attempts to show that Shakespeare's one obsession with the betraying woman and usurping brother informs the whole of Shakespeare's canon:

> Because the theme of the false or the usurping or the adulterous brother or all three in one is to Shakespeare, what the poor is not, always with him. The note of banishment, banishment from the heart, banishment from home, sounds uninterruptedly from *The Two Gentlemen of Verona* onward till Prospero breaks his staff, buries it certain fathoms in the earth and drowns his book. It doubles itself in the middle of his life, reflects itself in another, repeats itself, protasis, epitasis, catastasis, catastrophe. It repeats itself again when he is near the grave, when his married daughter Susan, chip of the old block, is accused of adultery. But it was the original sin that darkened his understanding, weakened his will and left in him a

strong inclination to evil. The words are those of my lords bishops of
Maynooth: an original sin and, like original sin, committed by another in
whose sin he too has sinned. It is between the lines of his last written
words, it is petrified on his tombstone under which her four bones are not
to be laid. Age has not withered it. Beauty and peace have not done it
away. It is in infinite variety everywhere in the world he has created, in
Much Ado about Nothing, twice in *As you like It*, in *The Tempest*, in
Hamlet, in *Measure for Measure*, and in all the other plays which I have
not read. [*U*, 212]

The beginning of the passage finds Stephen again equating his position
with that of Shakespeare. The images of exile and banishment resonate
to Stephen's theory about himself; and the staff of Prospero is surely an
analogue for Stephen's magic staff, artistic perception, and onanistic
phallic symbol. Shakespeare, according to Stephen, is thus enslaved to
his own history, which he never escapes, but like an ordinary person
"must work off bad karma first" (*U*, 185) because he participated in the
original sin. Like the characters of Yeats's *Purgatory*, he "returns after a
life of absence to that spot of earth where he was born, where he has
always been, man and boy, a silent witness and there, his journey of life
ended, he plants his mulberrytree in the earth. Then dies" (*U*, 213).
Hamlet's pattern and, according to Stephen, Shakespeare's are the same.
   But what Stephen really reveals is not Shakespeare, but himself and
his attempt to come to terms with his life. Indeed, his comment that this
pattern exists in "all the other plays which I have not read" surely
suggests that he, too, is aware of the limits of his explanation for Shakespeare's drama. It is the rejection of his mother's wish, his "murdering
her," and his unacceptable affection for her, that force him back to the
place where he was born, Dublin, to plant his mulberry tree—which
may suggest something about art.

   And, what though murdered and betrayed, bewept by all frail tender
   hearts for, Dane or Dubliner, sorrow for the dead is the only husband
   from whom they refuse to be divorced. If you like the epilogue look long
   on it: prosperous Prospero, the good man rewarded, Lizzie, grandpa's
   lump of love, and nuncle Richie, the bad man taken off by poetic justice to
   the place where the bad niggers go. Strong curtain. [*U*, 213]

Stephen's sorrow, his husband, is what torments him and is the fact
from which he cannot be divorced. Yet, it is as a poet that Stephen
hopes to have his revenge—to conquer Buck, Simon, and all the other
betrayers of the artist Stephen—just as Shakespeare had his revenge in
his plays. Shakespeare, like Stephen, is, in this view, more interested in
the possible than the actual: "He found in the world without as actual
what was in his world within as possible" (*U*, 213). And Shakespeare
thus creates the outer reality from his inner possibility.

Here Stephen's theory appears to take a new twist. He equates all men with each other by suggesting that we always meet ourselves in the outer world; but the suggestion is also that the reason we meet only ourselves is that we are prepared to meet only ourselves. There is a Shakespeare "doubtless all in all in all of us" because Shakespeare is that "androgynous angel" (*U*, 213) who is like God both wife and husband and who creates from himself and out of himself. The parody of this vision of "glorified man" is of course Bloom's virginal pregnancy and birthing of *"eight male yellow and white children"* (*U*, 494). What for Stephen is a mystical act of creation from an abstraction, the "androgynous angel," for Bloom is a literal creation of offspring from himself. Shakespeare becomes everyman through his shared limitations and assets as a concrete human being.

Stephen ends his theory by denying belief in it (*U*, 214). Mr. Best identifies Wilde as the source or inspiration of the whole theory by suggesting that Stephen "ought to make it a dialogue, don't you know, like the Platonic dialogues Wilde wrote" (*U*, 214). The final irony of the chapter is that the established usurper, Mulligan, produces a play—*"Everyman His own Wife or A Honeymoon in the Hand"* (*U*, 216), which parodies Stephen's theory and his artistic pretensions. Stephen determines that he must escape the library and Mulligan, but he does so with the kind of literary omens that plague his life.

> Part. The moment is now. Where then? If Socrates leave his house today, if Judas go forth tonight. Why? That lies in space which I in time must come to, ineluctably.
> My will: his will that fronts me. Seas between. [*U*, 217]

Bloom passes between Stephen and Mulligan, and Stephen remembers both an incident in *A Portrait* and a dream. The juxtaposition of the incident with the dream as omens suggests a shift in the pattern of meaning in the two novels.

> Here I watched the birds for augury. Ængus of the birds. They go, they come. Last night I flew. Easily flew. Men wondered. Street of harlots after. A creamfruit he held to me. In. You will see. [*U*, 217]

The omens Stephen "saw" in *A Portrait* turned out to be false or not omens at all. In that novel Stephen shaped the experience and insisted upon his interpretation of it. The dream sequence is an uncontrollable imaging in his unconscious; and it is the dream Stephen remembers on the Strand and the dream that Bloom has also had. The juxtaposition of the two kinds of omens—one created and interpreted by Stephen, the other experienced by Bloom and Stephen and hesitantly interpreted by both of them, is a shift from a predetermined perception of the world to a recognition of the coincidental and uncontrollable nature of flux within the mind.

David L. McCarroll's article on these dreams[17] reveals their significance for Stephen and Bloom. McCarroll points out that both Stephen and Bloom remember their dream first on the Strand and that significant elements of the two dreams are identical. Stephen remembers the "Street of harlots. . . . Haroun al Raschid. . . . That man led me, spoke" (*U,* 47), the creamfruit, melon, red carpet, and the invitation, "In. Come" (*U,* 47). Bloom remembers his dream in "Nausicaa": "Come in. All is prepared. I dreamt" (*U,* 370). Haroun al Raschid stems from Bloom's interest in the Near East, the "plump mellow yellow smellow melons" of Molly (*U,* 734) underlie the "creamfruit" of the dream; and the meeting of Bloom and Stephen in "Circe," Bloom's subsequent invitation to return to Eccles Street, and the "offer" of Molly make this dream a significant adumbration of the relationship between the two men. The fact that Stephen remembers his dream for the second time as Bloom passes between Stephen and Mulligan tightens the symbolic meaning of it.

The two dreams and Bloom's position in them add to the messianic or deliverer motif that is being fashioned around him. Mulligan has already mockingly associated Bloom with Christ through an allusion to Swinburne's "Hymn to Prosperine": "His pale Galilean eyes" (*U,* 201). The Jewishness of Bloom, commented upon by Buck (*U,* 200–201, 217), reinforces Bloom's position as a new messiah, for as Bloom tells the Citizen, Christ was "a jew and his father was a jew. Your God" (*U,* 342).

The chapter ends with a parody of the villanelle of *A Portrait:*

> *Laud we the gods*
> *And let our crooked smokes climb to their nostrils*
> *From our bless'd altars.*

[*U,* 218]

Joyce, in this chapter, has dramatized a shift in Stephen's perception of the artist. That shift is suggested to us through the analogous Shakespeare criticsm of Oscar Wilde. The essay "Mr W. H." was and is read as a revelation of Wilde's ambivalent sexuality. The analogue thus suggests to Joyce's readers that Stephen's theory has more to do with self-revelation than with an illumination of Shakespeare. Stephen has changed: he is not so confident, he is beginning to understand the forms of parody employed by some of his Aesthetic ancestors—particularly Wilde—in ways in which he did not understand them in *A Portrait.* But the echoes in this chapter of Pater, Swinburne, and Wilde clearly suggest Stephen's continuing inclination toward that tradition and practice of art. And though Shakespeare begins to replace the artist-priest-God and the Daedalian father, Shakespeare as described by Stephen is much like those figures.

If "Scylla and Charybdis" sets up Shakespeare as Stephen's newest symbol for the artist, Joyce, in part, parodied many of Stephen's symbols and ideas in "Oxen of the Sun" and "Circe." In the first of these two chapters, the narrative mimics styles of writing from the Church litany to modern slang and mimics nine-month gestation that ends with the birth of the Word, "Burke's." Like Stephen's attempts at creation, the chapter begins with a liturgical invocation, here to the Godhead in the tripartite form favored by the Church. Unlike Stephen's earlier and private version of gestation and birth in the Incarnation metaphors surrounding the creation of the villanelle, this incarnation produces for Stephen an insignificant pub. The literal analogue of the birth of the word is the birth of Mina Purefoy's child. Bloom, characteristically, is more interested and engaged in that literal birth than Stephen is. The chapter makes the contrast overt:

> It had better be stated here and now at the outset that the perverted transcendentalism to which Mr S. Dedalus' (Div. Scep.) contentions would appear to prove him pretty badly addicted runs directly counter to accepted scientific methods. Science, it cannot be too often repeated, deals with tangible phenomena. The man of science like the man in the street has to face hardheaded facts that cannot be blinked and explain them as best he can. There may be, it is true, some questions which science cannot answer—at present—such as the first problem submitted by Mr L. Bloom (Pubb. Canv.) regarding the future determination of sex. [*U*, 418]

Bloom tries to apply some kind of principles of observation to the solving of problems. He inquires about infant mortality (his own pressing problem after Rudy's death) and Mulligan proceeds to suggest environmental causes for such problems. Mr. J. Crotthers determines that rotten working conditions are the answer. The narrative voice suggests the most overtly Darwinian-Spencerian argument:

> Nature, we may rest assured, has her own good and cogent reasons for whatever she does and in all probability such deaths are due to some law of anticipation by which organisms in which morbous germs have taken up their residence tend to disappear at an increasingly earlier stage of development, an arrangement, which, though productive of pain to some of our feelings (notably the maternal), is nevertheless, some of us think, in the long run beneficial to the race in general in securing thereby the survival of the fittest. [*U*, 419][18]

Stephen's response makes little sense, but what he says to Bloom, and the descriptions of him, make more. "This morbidminded esthete and embryo philosopher" tells Bloom that

> once a woman has let the cat into the bag (an esthetic allusion, presumably, to one of the most complicated and marvellous of all nature's processes, the act of sexual congress) she must let it out again or give it life, as he phrased it, to save her own. [*U*, 420]

Stephen's point—ironic in its wrongheadedness—is that creation becomes a necessity to the female following intercourse just as artistic creation is a necessity. Yet Stephen's apparent failure to produce art lies at the center of his quandary and is not, any more than conception for a woman, inevitable. The alternative, to "let it out," as a method of saving "her own" life makes little sense. Joyce, calling Stephen a "morbidminded esthete," associates him with Aestheticism and suggests how such notions about art cohere with peculiar notions about life.

At the moment of birth, the medical students and Stephen determine on the word—"upon the utterance of the Word. Burke's" (*U*, 422–23). Bloom, in contrast, "stays with nurse a thought to send a kind word to happy mother" (*U*, 423) and only then follows the drinkers. In a parody of Carlyle's style and vision, the narrative voice equates, as Stephen does, the act of procreation with the act of God's creation—in opposition to a scientific sense of life.

> By heaven, Theodore Purefoy, thou has done a doughty deed and no botch! Thou art, I vow, the remarkablest progenitor barring none in this chaffering allincluding most farraginous chronicle. Astounding! In her lay a Godframed Godgiven preformed possibility which thou hast fructified with thy modicum of man's work. Cleave to her! Serve! Toil on, labour like a very bandog and let scholarment and all Malthusiasts go hang. Thou art all their daddies. . . . Art drooping under thy load. . . . Head up! For every newbegotten thou shalt gather thy homer of ripe wheat. [*U*, 423]

Theodore, in this parody, becomes like Shakespeare the creator of the most, like Shakespeare the fulfiller of possibility, the egg present in the female. This passage reasserts man's position in the creativity of the material world, but certainly doesn't deny the spiritual or superhuman aspect of creation, the mystical creation of the artist. Another parody of creation is indicated by the order of the chapters: "Oxen" gives birth to "Circe," a parody of life as art, here specifically of life as drama.

"Circe" dramatizes another attempt at structuring the universe through art, just as "Oxen" attempted to structure the universe and history through language, the material of poetic art. Mulligan, in "Scylla and Charybdis," had pointed the way to the fulfillment of Stephen's theory when he said, "The play's the thing" (*U*, 208). In "Circe" life becomes art, revealed in a parody of a play form. But that art is like life, somewhat chaotic and glued to the realities of empirical existence: the events of the chapter in which Stephen and Bloom participate are prompted by actual happenings, sounds, or objects that they perceive. The chaos of their individual souls is shaped ultimately by the artist-Joyce because he created whatever souls they have, but they perform and write their own drama out of their own experience and patterns of meaning. And they share the events of each other's days, becoming more closely associated until the vision of Shakespeare in the mirror announces their consubstantial unity. That unity creates, at least momentarily, the consubstantial son for Bloom and the consubstantial father for Stephen, and through the conjunction of Shakespeare and aesthetics, Stephen's aesthetic position as well as his psychological condition is revealed and related to Bloom as father-artificer-Shakespeare in the shared image in the mirror.

Just as Stephen in *A Portrait* shared with his creator some notions about art and many experiences, so Stephen in "Scylla and Charybdis," as he tries to reconstruct his world, shares with Joyce theories about Shakespeare. In the notes for Joyce's lectures on Shakespeare, he appears to have concentrated on the Elizabethan context for the plays and uses the three critics whom Stephen does; material from John Dover Wilson's *Life in Shakespeare's England* allowed Joyce to reconstruct what he saw as the social and realistic settings for his subject.[19] Given the facts we know about Joyce's comments, we may inquire what kind of statement Joyce could be making about Stephen's theory of art in *Ulysses*. That theory, a kind of psychological explanation for art, claims that Shakespeare—and one supposes by extension all artists—continued to write obsessively about the traumas and experiences of his own life. Joyce apparently asserted in his lectures and Stephen certainly asserts in *Ulysses* the importance of personal biography to any understanding of a poet's work, and uses information that both New Critics and the advocates of *poésie pure* reject. We do not have notes from all of Joyce's lectures, and thus cannot with any certainty claim that he did not propose theories much like Stephen's; what we can investigate is what in Joyce's notes does not appear in Stephen's mouth and whether or not the theory of creation proposed by Stephen seems to "fit" Joyce's practice.

That Joyce never exorcised certain traumas has been suggested before; his women, right through ALP, continue to share some of the attributes of the femme fatale; his own rather bizarre notion or sense of betrayal continued to affect negatively his life, including his advocacy of John Sullivan—a tenor Joyce believed to be betrayed and ignored.[20] Despite his rejection of the Freudians, Joyce appears to have shared with them a belief in fixated ideas and their roots in childhood.[21] And his own art suggests that Stephen is not wrong in ascribing to the artist the repetition of ideas that have their genesis in personal and emotional experience. What critics can continue to inquire is whether or not we wish to focus on the artist rather than on the art; but at least for Joyce, we have letters, novels, and lectures to indicate that Stephen's theory in "Scylla and Charybdis" is not far from Joyce's own belief and practice.

Not far, perhaps, but not quite the same either. As a novelist rather than a critic, Joyce, unlike Stephen, produces art that claims personal experience and emotion are as dependent upon communal, social, political, and economic realities as they are upon isolated, individual response; as a critic, Joyce used material collected from Wilson's study—concerned as it was with social configurations—that does not appear in Stephen's theory. Thus to understand Shakespeare, Joyce felt that his audience and indeed he himself needed some information about the realities of Elizabethan England. To understand Eveline's decision at the end of her story in *Dubliners* requires that we understand the economic conditions and the social pressures sketched in the first two pages of the story—as well as understanding the emotional pressures of memory and her mother's request. To understand Bloom's situation, we must understand not just his particular family but also the anti-Semitism represented by Mr. Deasy and the Citizen in *Ulysses*. For Joyce to write effectively as he himself realized after Archer's criticism of the lost, first play, he had to remain tied to Ireland and the conditions he knew.[22] Stephen, in contrast, remains tied to two sources of information—ideas present in previous literature and ideas one can make up or find out about the author in question, without much visible concern for an author's cultural experiences that are neither literary nor idiosyncratic.

Furthermore, despite the fact that Stephen echoes some of Joyce's own theories about Shakespeare, he does do one thing in his discussion that Joyce makes very clear: he distorts or manufactures "fact." William Schutte points out several instances of this practice; one will serve to demonstrate his contention, and mine.

> While he [Stephen] is presenting his theory, Stephen himself admits to one deliberate distortion of the evidence available. . . . His admission is silent. Joyce's readers learn about it; Stephen's auditors do not. He has been speaking of the firedrake which arose at about the time of Shakespeare's birth. He has pictured for the librarians the young Shakespeare watching it "lowlying on the horizon, eastward of the bear, as he walked by the slumberous summer fields at midnight, returning from Shottery and from her arms" (207). Abruptly he warns himself not to tell his listeners that Shakespeare "was nine years old when it was quenched." As it stands, the sentence is Joyce's warning to the reader that he will do well to check all of Stephen's statements before he accepts them. . . . Stephen's silent admission that he has here distorted the facts as he knows them

serves to cast doubt over all his "facts." Had Joyce not intended it to do so, he would hardly have introduced into the narrative the sentence in which Stephen makes the admission.[23]

Stephen's theory thus points to another danger in criticism and art: the critic may perceive consistency only by warping fact to suit the preconceived theory or by asserting that a pattern exists, as Stephen does, in unread plays. And the critic, like the author, is likely to perceive the world in terms of his own needs, as Stephen does here.

Thus, Stephen is here as he was earlier, like his creator and unlike him. Joyce dramatizes some of those differences in the character of Leopold Bloom and in his juxtaposition of Stephen and Bloom. In Bloom, who has the "touch of the artist" about him, we find another kind of art, kinetic and affective, commercial, and in some ways more successful than Stephen's art. It is a kind of art that Joyce was, ambivalently, attracted to. Apparently quite different from Stephen's art, Bloom's art as well as Stephen's and Joyce's art—all art—resonates to the traumas and concerns of the artist and of the audience.

Notes

1. Epifanio San Juan, *The Art of Oscar Wilde* (Princeton, N.J.: Princeton University Press, 1967), p. 52.
2. Sidney Feshbach, "A Dramatic First Step: A Source of Joyce's Interest in the Idea of Daedalus," *James Joyce Quarterly* 8 (1971): 202.
3. "The Triumph of Time," *Complete Works of Algernon Charles Swinburne*, ed. Sir Edmund Gosse, C. B. and Thomas James Wise, 20 vols. (New York: Russell and Russell, 1968), 1:169–81.
4. Cf. Wilde, "The Decay of Lying," 5:38: "I can quite understand your objection to art being treated as a mirror. You think it would reduce genius to the position of a cracked looking-glass"; "The nineteenth century dislike of Realism is the rage of Caliban seeing his own face in a glass. The nineteenth century dislike of Romanticism is the rage of Caliban not seeing his own face in a glass" ("Preface" to *Dorian Gray*).
5. Yeats believed that every symbol evokes specific and universal response:

> All sounds, all colours, all forms, either because of their preordained energies or because of long association, *evoke indefinable and yet precise emotions*, or, as I prefer to think, call down among us certain disembodied powers, whose footsteps over our hearts we call emotions. ["The Symbolism of Poetry," *Essays and Introductions*, pp. 156–57, emphasis mine.]

Judging from the amount of argument created by Yeats's symbols, and his later development as a poet, symbols were not quite the magical powers that he believed.
6. Pater, "Conclusion," *Studies in the History of the Renaissance* (London: Macmillan and Co., 1910), pp. 236–37.
7. See "Stephen Dedalus as Lapwing: A Symbolic Center of *Ulysses*," *James Joyce Quarterly* 6 (1968): 104–14. Mr. Geckle demonstrates Stephen's knowledge of this image and its meaning through an explication of the surrounding text in *Ulysses*.
8. Hughes T. Bredin, "Applied Aquinas: James Joyce's Aesthetics," *Éire-Ireland* 3 (1968): 65.

9. Alan Dundes, "Re: Joyce—No In at the Womb," *Modern Fiction Studies* 8 (1962): 144.

10. Chester Anderson, "The Sacrificial Butter," *Accent* 12 (1952): 3–13, discusses at some length the parallels between Christ and Stephen in the last chapter of *A Portrait*.

11. William M. Schutte, *Joyce and Shakespeare: A Study in the Meaning of "Ulysses"* (New Haven, Conn.: Yale University Press, 1957), makes much the same point about the "causes" of Stephen's theory. "In this effort to get at the truth he has gradually settled on the career of William Shakespeare as one which may provide a key to the understanding of his own condition" (p. 85); most of Schutte's chapter 4 discusses the ways in which the Shakespeare theory responds to Stephen's emotional needs. Schutte and I disagree, however, on exactly what those emotional needs are and on Joyce's relationship to the theory. Nonetheless, my discussion is indebted to Schutte.

12. Oscar Wilde, "The Portrait of Mr W. H.," *The Complete Works*, 12 vols. (Garden City, N.Y.: Doubleday, Page & Co., 1923), 6:181–303.

13. "Cruxes in *Ulysses:* Notes Toward an Edition and Annotation," *James Joyce Review* 1 (1957): 32.

14. Thornton agrees with Epstein, but cites also Tennyson's "To Virgil." Weldon Thornton, *Allusions in "Ulysses"* (Chapel Hill, N.C.: University of North Carolina Press, 1968), p. 181.

15. Oscar Wilde, "Pen, Pencil, and Poison," *The Complete Works*, 5:67–106.

16. Dundes makes the same point in relationship to Stephen's creative impulse: "The male form of creativity is the spoken and written word" ("Re: Joyce," p. 137).

17. David L. McCarroll, "Stephen's Dream—and Bloom's," *James Joyce Quarterly* 6 (1969): 174–76.

18. Although this passage is probably not a direct allusion to any specific writer, the ideas are Darwinian; they might indeed be from Spencer's *The Study of Sociology* (which Joyce owned). Spencer apparently appalled readers and critics by his tough-minded refusal to compromise with sentiment or to espouse notions of intrinsic human worth.

19. For the notes for Joyce's lectures, see William H. Quillian, "Shakespeare in Trieste: Joyce's 1912 *Hamlet* Lectures," *James Joyce Quarterly* 12 (1974–75): 7–63. Quillian builds on Schutte's analysis of the sources for Stephen's theory in "Scylla and Charybdis."

20. Richard Ellmann, *James Joyce* (New York: Oxford University Press, 1959), pp. 632ff.

21. The first version of *A Portrait* makes the point (see *Workshop*), as does Joyce in some of his letters.

22. See *Letters*, 2:8ff; Ellmann's discussion, *James Joyce*, pp. 82–83.

23. Schutte, *Joyce and Shakespeare*, p. 53.

7

Advertisement and Realism: Leopold Bloom

That Stephen and Bloom are antithetical characters has been a common-place in commentaries about *Ulysses* at least since Frank Budgen's *James Joyce and the Making of "Ulysses"* in 1934. Joyce was apparently drawn to such antitheses: Shem and Shaun, false and true fathers, virgins (Eveline, for instance) and temptresses (Polly, for instance), Gabriel Conroy and Michael Furey—these and other pairs populate all his fiction. At the same time, Joyce seems to make some of the antithetical characters "share" certain experiences and then to "record" how differently each acts. Characterizing people through these contrasting responses, Joyce encourages us to make finer distinctions among his characters than their labels might indicate. To begin my discussion of Leopold Bloom, I would like to comment upon the "Nausicaa" chapter, using a hint dropped by Richard Ellmann in *James Joyce* more than twenty years ago. Ellmann pointed out that Joyce "plays Stephen's youthful point of view against Bloom's mature point of view, often confronting them with the same places and ideas" through "repetition of incidents from *A Portrait*, often with parodic changes. Stephen's vision of the girl at the seashore, with its stages or excitement carefully delineated, is parodied in *Nausicaa* by Bloom's orgasmic but equally detached contemplation of Gerty McDowell."[1]

Ellmann is right that Bloom's vision of a girl on the beach is parallel to and parodic of Stephen's vision, but an additional, although perhaps less obvious, source of parody lies in parallels between Gerty and Stephen. Gerty provides a contrast to Stephen's girl, but just as importantly her perception and her ways of perceiving provide both a foil to Bloom and a parodic parallel to Stephen's perception and ways of perceiving. Bloom, the mundane, realistic, empirical, is contrasted with Gerty, the romantic, "spiritual," literary, just as Bloom and Stephen contrast in their habitual methods of seeing.

Unlike Stephen's angel from the fair courts of life, who assists

Stephen in intellectual orgasm and commitment to a static and arresting art, Gerty assists Bloom in real orgasm and a commitment to the physical desire that Stephen labels as improper to art. Of course, Bloom isn't interested in such an abstract, symbolist art. Gerty has interesting underwear.

Gerty parallels Stephen's prim behavior in *A Portrait* during this experience and the conjunction is not very flattering to him. She dreams of an impossible knight who comes to recognize her true but hidden worth, charm her, and take her away from the mundane existence of Dublin, just as Stephen's girl opens the gates of life and experience to him. The chapter in *Ulysses* contains an approximation of Gerty's thoughts about what is happening between herself and Bloom. The description of her as she would describe herself ties her to Stephen's woman:

> The waxen pallor of her face was almost spiritual in its ivorylike purity though her rosebud mouth was a genuine Cupid's bow, Greekly perfect. Her hands were of finely veined alabaster with tapering fingers and as white as lemon juice and queen of ointments could make them though it was not true that she used to wear kid gloves in bed. [*U*, 348]

Stephen's woman, too, has ivorylike purity, a quality Stephen first notices in Eileen's hands and later associates with the girl on the beach whose "thighs, fuller and softhued as ivory, were bared" (*P*, 171). Gerty's thighs will be bared before the chapter ends. Like many of Stephen's visions of women, Gerty combines the sensualty and spirituality of Pre-Raphaelite women. Her lips are full—a "rosebud mouth . . . a genuine Cupid's bow." Gerty's hands, like the hands of the female figure Stephen sees in the earlier novel, have "tapering fingers" that remind us of ivory as in *"House of Ivory."* Gerty's eyes, too, remind us of Stephen's woman:

> Mayhap it was this, the love that might have been, that lent to her softly-featured face at whiles a look, tense with suppressed meaning, that imparted . . . a charm few could resist. Why have women such eyes of witchery? Gerty's were of the bluest Irish blue, set off by lustrous lashes and dark expressive brows. [*U*, 348–49]

Like the eyes of Stephen's woman, these hold the observer's eyes and are mysteriously expressive. The ironic thing is, of course, that this section is really from Gerty's point of view just as the chapter in *A Portrait* is from Stephen's point of view; each of them creates a woman he or she wants to create. "Gerty's crowning glory was her wealth of wonderful hair. It was dark brown with a natural wave in it" (*U*, 349). Gerty is, in short, the Pre-Raphaelite woman and the woman Stephen creates in part from the materials of that tradition—fingers, eyes, hair,

the colors blue and ivory, the combination of sensuality and spirituality—but she is also a parody of that tradition, especially as it was
translated into the popular imagination. Gerty is even a "ministering
angel" as Stephen's woman is. The images and symbols are all there. She
looks at Bloom and finds the "saddest" eyes; she sees him as a Byronic
figure of failed love. He is foreign, has "superbly expressive" eyes, and
is "in deep mourning, she could see that, and the story of a haunting
sorrow was written on his face" (*U*, 357).

What is so damning to Stephen in this rendition is that Gerty does
exactly what he had done: she sees what she wishes to see and doesn't
really care about Bloom's reality—at least she cares no more than
Stephen had cared about the girl on the beach. Stephen had dreamed of
quietly meeting "in the real world the unsubstantial image which his
soul so constantly beheld . . . and in that moment of supreme tenderness
he would be transfigured. . . . Weakness and timidity and inexperience
would fall from him in that magic moment" (*P*, 65). The woman on the
beach fulfills this dream. Gerty sees Bloom:

> Here was that of which she had *so often dreamed.* It was he who mattered
> and there was joy on her face because she wanted him because she felt so
> instinctively that he was like no-one else. The very heart of the girlwoman
> went out to him, her *dreamhusband,* because *she knew on the instant it
> was him.* [*U*, 358, italics mine]

> Gerty's lips parted swiftly to frame the word but *she fought back the sob
> that rose to her throat,* so slim, so flawless, so beautifully moulded it
> seemed one an artist might have dreamed of. She had loved him better
> than he knew. [*U*, 362, italics mine]

> Heart of mine! She would follow her dream of love, the dictates of her
> own heart that told her he was her all in all, the only man in all the world
> for her for love was the master guide. Nothing else mattered. *Come what
> might she would be wild, untrammelled, free.* [*U*, 365, italics mine]

Stephen, who discovers at last the vision that has been waiting for him,
"as if they had known each other," is like Gerty who sees this man as
her predestined husband. Bloom's strength and tenderness are like the
tender moment in which Stephen would be transfigured. Like Gerty,
Stephen avoids breaking the "holy silence of his ecstasy" (*P*, 172;
U, 362), like Gerty, Stephen is "wild," free of his grave clothes (*P*, 170–
72; *U*, 365). Like Gerty, whose flame rising to her face creates "a
burning scarlet" "till the lovely colour of her face became a glorious
rose" (*U*, 360), Stephen's woman has "a faint flame" that "trembled on
her cheek" (*P*, 171), and "His cheeks were aflame" (*P*, 172). Like
Gerty's vision of Bloom, Stephen's vision is supposed to pass "into his
soul forever" (*P*, 172). Both find something they have been seeking, and

both essentially create that something. So we find an analogy to
Stephen's beatific vision in the sentimental dreams of a young girl.
Stephen is not Gerty, nor is he quite so sentimental. But Gerty's posi-
tion here, as a foil to Bloom, sharpens our perceptions of Stephen's and
Bloom's relationship.

Bloom's reaction is different. He watches Gerty swinging her legs
as Stephen had watched his girl "gently stirring the water with her foot
hither and thither" (*P*, 171). In the silence, like Stephen's holy silence,
following the orgasm, Gerty and Bloom relish their encounter. Bloom's
perception of the event is radically different from Gerty's and from
what Stephen had seen in his encounter. Bloom watches her and the first
piece of information we get from him is that "she's lame! O!" (*U*, 367).
He considers, in his down-to-earth way, what prompted Gerty to
tempt him. Bloom contemplates the naturalness of the activity and
assumes that she knew what he was doing and was intentionally leading
him on. He contemplates whether she'll get "piles" from sitting on the
rock. He thinks about how perfume is transmitted, of Molly and Milly;
and, in contrast to Gerty's vow of eternal devotion, of the transitory
nature of the relationship. "We'll never meet again. But it was lovely"
(*U*, 382). Bloom thinks immediately of his own life, his daughter and
wife, of the physical act just completed; in short, of all the actual or
pseudoscientific acts in which he has been involved. There is nothing
romantic about Bloom's "For this relief much thanks" (*U*, 372). It is a
physical necessity. And he assumes that all young women like Gerty
will simply marry and raise children: "Sad however because it lasts only
a few years till they settle down to potwalloping and papa's pants will
soon fit Willy" (*U*, 373).

Stephen achieves orgasm through intellectual and emotional stimulation; Gerty's satisfaction is totally emotional and sentimental; Bloom
physically manipulates himself. Therein lies a symbol of their differences. Stephen and Gerty contemplate figures from romances and
heroic poems; Bloom contemplates Molly, smells, menstrual cycles, the
erotic function of underwear, the naturalness of physical relief. Then
Bloom contemplates the scientific difficulties Gerty might be imposing
upon herself: "Dew falling. Bad for you, dear, to sit on that stone.
Brings on white fluxions. Never have little baby then less he was big
strong fight his way up through. Might get piles myself" (*U*, 376).

Bloom, like Stephen, contemplates the flux of life and its cyclical
nature. But where Stephen uses the symbol of the sea that he finds in
poetry—not the sea itself but the sea as presented in Swinburne's
poem—Bloom contemplates the change of lovers on Howth (*U*, 377).
Bloom comments, "Think you're escaping and run into yourself" or
"Longest way round is the shortest way home" (*U*, 377); Stephen uses a
literary allusion to Maeterlinck. When Bloom does remember a literary
analogy, it is to Rip Van Winkle, not to a symbolist or Aesthete. The

magnificent, sensual, parted full lips of Stephen's woman become a subject for improvement when Bloom suggests saying *prunes* and *prisms* everyday (*U*, 371). And even the obvious failure to leave a message on the sands, which Stephen wishes to do in order to stop the encroachment of the sea and time, does not perturb Bloom. Instead of an ash-plant, Bloom has the more literal "wooden pen" (*U*, 382).

As Bloom contemplates change within time, he witnesses the kind of flux that Stephen sees as creating his "nightmare of history." Bloom's history, composed of as many elements that might create nightmare as Stephen's is—his son's death, his father's suicide, Molly's impending or accomplished adultery, his own rejection by his society because he is a Jew—does not lead him to believe either that he is captured in a nightmare or that the history of his life or man's is leading to Mr. Deasy's "manifestation of God." In fact, for Bloom, history is apparently un-mappable: sometimes he appears to believe in cyclical or repetitive history, sometimes in a progressive theory of man's history, sometimes even in a providential theory, and frequently only in a theory of random change. Here in "Nausicaa" he espouses cycles: "History repeats itself" and "All that old hill has seen. Names change: that's all. Lovers: yum yum" (*U*, 377). But then Bloom is never so consistent as Stephen because he does not have a preconceived, rigid pattern into which he inserts details of his life.

In Bloom, Joyce has created a character who simply sees differently and normally sees more of what is actual than what is possible. He investigates what makes him think of certain things at specific times. He checks his associations against what his senses report. Bloom is attached to the here and now, not just to the past or future. Because of these differences in the ways Bloom sees and the associations he makes, any art that he might produce would, of necessity, be very different from the art of a Stephen Dedalus. Indeed, to think of Bloom as an artist is not one's first instinct.

Yet, Joyce was reportedly pleased when a critic pointed out that Bloom, too, was an artist. When Joyce discussed the mythic model for Bloom, Homer's Ulysses, with Budgen, he noted that Ulysses was an inventor, a kind of artist.[2] His profession is called the "gentle art of advertisement" in "Aeolus," but is there excluded from "literature," by Professor McHugh. Twice in *Ulysses* Bloom is called a bit of an artist—albeit once by himself (*U*, 235, 653). Furthermore, as William H. Schutte has suggested, Bloom uses and contemplates language in many of the ways that Stephen does.[3] Leopold's own summation of advertising describes as accurately as anything else his kind of art: "to arrest involuntary attention, to interest, to convince, to decide" (*U*, 683). In short, Bloom is a kinetic artist whose intentions are directly or indirectly propagandistic, although he rejects propaganda that encourages bloodshed or hatred (*U*, 657).

His contributions to literature are minimal. His first effort, which can be compared to Stephen's first and destroyed verse to E.C. in *A Portrait,* is characteristically written to gain money and to advertise the self.

> *An ambition to squint*
> *At my verses in print*
> *Makes me hope that for these you'll find room.*
> *If you so condescend*
> *Then please place at the end*
> *The name of yours truly, L. Bloom.*

[*U*, 678]

Before we judge Bloom's motives too harshly, perhaps we should re-member that Stephen Dedalus offers his work for sale in "Scylla and Charybdis." More important is that Bloom's motives for producing his "art" are straightforward: he does not attempt to substitute a satisfying, because manipulated, art for an unsatisfying, isolated life. The second recorded specimen is an "acrostic upon the abbreviation of his first name," and the voice of the narrator of "Ithaca" labels Bloom as a kinetic poet—thus opposing him to Stephen, the static artist and "mor-bidminded esthete" (*U*, 420). To Molly, Bloom sends the following love poem:

> *Poets oft have sung in rhyme*
> *Of music sweet their praise divine.*
> *Let them hymn it nine times nine.*
> *Dearer far than song or wine,*
> *You are mine. The world is mine.*

[*U*, 678]

Even allowing for Stephen's superior education in literature, these two examples make clear that in comparison Bloom is not intended to be a poet. On the other hand, while Stephen wonders in *A Portrait* about sending E. C. the villanelle, Bloom does send his verse to Molly. Even so early in his career the adman has some knowledge of his audience. He has one intent; his language allows him to express that intent, and at least to judge from his subsequent wedding, he is successful with his verse—an adjective that one cannot apply to Stephen (nor does he apply it to himself). As clearly as E. C. fails to understand Stephen, so clearly the villanelle would merely confuse, frighten, and repel her (assuming she could understand herself as a devouring temptress). That Stephen's villanelle has an intended audience beyond himself is arguable; like the priest without congregation, Stephen is so isolated that he is an artist without audience.

The early efforts at verse are not the only parallels to Stephen's

literary acts worth examining. In the course of *Ulysses,* Leopold contemplates kinds of epiphanies, discusses the uses of literature, and constructs a prose poem about a temptress, Molly Bloom. Through
presenting Bloom's contemplations and productions, Joyce juxtaposed
Stephen and his art with a different kind of artist and a different kind of
art.

In "Calypso," Bloom reads, while defecating, a "prize tidbit"
"written by Mr Philip Beaufoy," who gets paid "at the rate of one
guinea a column," or, as Bloom calculates it for us, "Three pounds
thirteen and six" (*U,* 68–69). This reading leads Bloom to speculate on
his own literary ambitions.

> Might manage a sketch. By Mr and Mrs L. M. Bloom. Invent a story
> for some proverb which? Time I used to try jotting down on my cuff what
> she said dressing. Dislike dressing together. [*U,* 69]

What's curious about Bloom's fantasy is that he mimics Stephen's
epiphanies, and Joyce's, which were generally stolen from one or
another friend and written down surreptitiously.[4]

Later in "Nausicaa," Bloom comes back to this prize tidbit after his
encounter with Gerty. The chapter's style reminds us of the narcissism
involved in Bloom's literary fantasies—in its earliest manifestation, the
desire to see his verses in print. Here Bloom thinks of following a man:

> Walk after him now make him awkward like those newsboys me today.
> Still you learn something. See ourselves as others see us. So long as
> women don't mock what matter? That's the way to find out. Ask yourself
> who is he now. *The Mystery Man on the Beach,* prize tidbit story by Mr
> Leopold Bloom. Payment at the rate of one guinea per column. [*U,* 375–
> 76]

Bloom, that is, speculates about writing in order to create a story that
will then explain a gentleman on the beach. In "Eumaeus," having left
the cabman's shelter, he wonders whether he might not produce a
sketch, drawn realistically ("taken down in writing," "*My Experiences,
let us say, in a Cabman's Shelter*") (*U,* 647). In each case, Bloom moves
from some acutely observed event or character to the notion of writing;
his slices of life would probably (if we are to judge from his poems) be
banal, clichéd, and relatively useless as "high" art. But, then, they might
also, like his poem, accomplish their purpose: to get Bloom the money.
Despite the blatant differences between Stephen's oval-shaped leaves
and Bloom's prize tidbits, each is attempting to find meaning in apparently mundane events. One wants fame—"copies to be sent if you died
to all the great libraries of the world" (*U,* 40), a notion Joyce himself
entertained—the other, money. One imagines realistic art, the other
attempts to peer into essences.

Bloom's claims to artistry, clearly, are not like those Stephen makes. Bloom believes that art is merely one kind of work—as his discussion with Stephen about politics indicates. Art is, perhaps, merely the arrangement of detail and the embedding of significance in the details of one's life. In that definition of art, Bloom produces one real prose poem: his memory of a day on Howth with Molly Tweedy. Like all of Bloom's memories, this one is shaped in part by his current situation and so feeding metaphors predominate; unlike many of his memories, it is not interrupted and achieves a kind of closure. Eating in Davy Byrnes, Bloom remembers:

> Crushing in the winepress grapes of Burgundy. Sun's heat it is. Seems to a secret touch telling me memory. Touched his sense moistened remembered. Hidden under wild ferns on Howth. Below us bay sleeping sky. No sound. The sky. The bay purple by the Lion's head. Green by Drumleck. Yellowgreen towards Sutton. Fields of undersea, the lines faint brown in grass, buried cities. Pillowed on my coat she had her hair, earwigs in the heather scrub my hand under her nape, you'll toss me all. O wonder! Coolsoft with ointments her hand touched me, caressed: her eyes upon me did not turn away. Ravished over her I lay, full lips full open, kissed her mouth. Yum. Softly she gave me in my mouth the seedcake warm and chewed. Mawkish pulp her mouth had mumbled sweet and sour with spittle. Joy: I ate it: Joy. Young life, her lips that gave me pouting. Soft, warm, sticky gumjelly lips. Flowers her eyes were, take me, willing eyes. Pebbles fell. She lay still. A goat. No-one. High on Ben Howth rhododendrons a nannygoat walking surefooted, dropping currents. Screened under ferns she laughed warmfolded. Wildly I lay on her, kissed her; eyes, her lips, her stretched neck, beating, woman's breasts full in her blouse of nun's veiling, fat nipples upright. Hot I tongued her. She kissed me. I was kissed. All yielding she tossed my hair. Kissed, she kissed me. [*U*, 175–76]

It is Bloom's favorite recollection—and one of Molly's too. Bloom's memory, touched off by two flies mating, encompasses his relationship to that mighty woman who so torments Stephen. While Molly is remembered here in part as a mother feeding a child, she does not devour Bloom. Startlingly different is the woman's relationship to the man. In Stephen's versions, Ann Hathaway seduces her lover in a cornfield and wounds him—or Stephen's muse figure lures him already fallen, though weary of ardent ways—or the muse withdraws her eyes and departs. In a parallel scene, Stephen's "angel of mortal beauty" gives no external sign of responding to him at all. The sterility and manipulation and isolation of Stephen's version contrasts movingly with the fertility and mutuality of Bloom's: "All yielding she tossed my hair. Kissed, she kissed me." That is not to say that Leopold's relationship with Molly would be a psychologist's description of married bliss. What is crucially different is that while Stephen's visions of women concern either a ghost (his mother) or real women converted immediately into things they are not (angels of mortal beauty, lure of the fallen seraphim, midwives, etc.), Bloom's visions of women—Gerty and Molly and Milly—are views of existing women and always concern some mutually perceived relationship. Bloom is accurate about his "angel of mortal beauty"; she does call him to err. Stephen is not. Molly's soliloquy makes it clear that Bloom is essentially accurate; just as Gerty's half of "Nausicaa" makes it clear that she consciously responds to Bloom and engages in a parallel fantasy with him.

Joyce uses these different prose poems and the situations they record to point out differences between Stephen and Bloom as they represent different kinds of art. Bloom's realistic and accurate art, however low-brow we may think it, is possible because he perceives things and people outside himself more accurately than Stephen, grants others a separate existence, and writes for an audience. Stephen's refusal (inability?) to write for any audience is one symptom of his inability to form reciprocal relationships. Bloom can contact other human beings—in private life and in his profession. The two areas of human activity, art and love, reflect upon each other; the person who cannot contact another human being in life will not be able to contact other human beings in an audience. Joyce dramatized the consistency in Stephen Dedalus's life; insofar as Stephen is a type of the Aesthete, Joyce analyzed or suggested that a similar coherence between life and art was implicit in Aestheticism. Bloom's realistic art and his human ties dramatically counter Stephen's and present an alternative.

Just as Joyce dramatized in Stephen the human motivations that helped to produce the Aesthete and the consequences of that kind of isolated artistry, so in Bloom he dramatized another extreme of art. Bloom's personality and experience make him more capable of any art that communicates to others, that establishes relationship. His scientific, social, political, and religious views and actions are consonant with this kind of art. While the reader and Joyce admire Bloom as human being more than Stephen, he, like Stephen, is an extreme: moneymaking propaganda and ads are not, finally, Joyce's mode any more than onanistic Aestheticism is. Joyce associates ideas about other aspects of life with realistic and naturalistic art—ideas that constitute the obverse of Stephen's ideas—in his characterization of Bloom.

Bloom's attraction to pornograhic art, an art productive of kinesis, is antithetical to Stephen's attraction to symbolist art, and art productive of stasis. His interest in the monetary rewards of writing smacks of a philistine attitude uncongenial to Stephen. When Bloom uses the *Matcham's Masterstroke* as toilet paper, he equates art with money and the useful arts. But what looks like another view in contrast to Stephen's about the uses of art really is not so very different from Stephen's views:

> . . . he reflected on the pleasures derived from literature of instruction
> rather than of amusement [*Sweets of Sin*] as he himself had applied to the
> works of William Shakespeare more than once for the solution of difficult
> problems in imaginary or real life. [*U*, 677]

Shakespeare, the victim of Stephen's theory of the creative process, is
for Bloom, too, a source of solutions. Bloom apparently used Shakespeare in much the way some Christians use the Bible—but that analogy
is accurate both for those Christians who open the Bible at random and
find solutions to problems and for those Christians who attempt to use
the ethical precepts of the Bible as guides to their lives. Bloom's imaginary life appears to be as significant for him as his "real" life, and
literature is, for many of us, a method of thinking about problems of
imaginative life. As far away from Stephen's use of literature as Bloom's
appears to be, that distance is an illusion. Stephen's theories about
Shakespeare, like the theories of stasis and radiance in *A Portrait*, pro-
ceed just as surely out of what Bloom would call "difficult problems in
imaginary or real life" as Bloom's use of literature does. Stephen comes
to Shakespeare intent upon making sense out of his own relationships to
his mother and father—and to literature as a consequence of those
human relationships; he uses literature—especially Shakespeare and
Shakespeare's plays—to solve these difficult problems. Bloom has sub-
limated this causal connection between personal problems and art less;
he overtly expects literature to be about people's emotions and their
lives.

Part of Bloom's attitude about literature is that it should provide a
living for a young man who has talent. Bloom's own talent, perhaps
only tangentially literary, is for advertisement and he at least makes and
has, generally, made enough money at that profession to support his
family, despite periods during which Molly has had to work. He sees in
his own kind of writing "infinite possibilities hitherto unexploited" (*U*,
683).

> . . . the modern art of advertisement if condensed in triliteral monoideal
> symbols, vertically of maximum visibility (divined), horizontally of maxi-
> mum legibility (deciphered) and of magnetising efficacy to arrest involun-
> tary attention, to interest, to convince, to decide. [*U*, 683]

This patently kinetic or, as Stephen might label it, improper art is
described in terms that parallel Stephen's art: triliteral monoideal symbols are like Stephen's symbol of the temptress-virgin-mother, Bloom's
interest in arresting the mind echoes Stephen's announcement that art
must arrest the mind of the spectator, and though for different reasons,
each emphasizes the viewer of art rather than the art object. Bloom too
plays with words, juggles them, contemplates their sounds and patterns
(*U*, 684). And he indicates to Stephen that originality is not the finest

measure of the artist or the guarantee of success. Stephen's art, original because he wishes to express only himself and his soul, is implicitly judged by Bloom's attitude:

> Which example did he adduce to induce Stephen to deduce that originality, though producing its own reward, does not invariably conduce to success?
>
> His own ideated and rejected project of an illuminated showcart, drawn by a beast of burden, in which two smartly dressed girls were to be seated engaged in writing. [*U*, 684]

Bloom's idea is basically funny—but not as a consequence nonserious. His point is well taken. The self-reward of private art is the only reward it offers. Total originality cannot conduce to success. Art, in order to have an audience, must contain what Stephen has attempted to reject— the banal, the common, and the communal, those old truths of "what the heart is and what it feels" (*P*, 252)—and must entertain others—not simply the producer of the art.

Leopold Bloom as an adman communicates to an audience; if his desire to make his audience buy something makes him less an artist than Stephen, his ability to make his audience understand his intentions and perceive his "message" makes him more of an artist than Stephen. Bloom works from what his audience knows to what it does not know; he uses Irish political associations to construct an ad, for instance. Realistic, topical, mundane information that appeals to the mind and eyes of the consumer is necessary for his art; those same elements can help the literary artist communicate to his own audience. Bloom's affective art could help start a revolution or awaken a people. Yet Joyce also suggests that Bloom's art is not always successful.

Bloom's more realistic and affective art can be taken as poles away from Stephen's art, and we can discern differences in the political notions of the two characters that follow the kinds of patterns their personal lives follow. Political ideas are not, in this discussion, limited to questions of state organization, but rather, issues of community and man in society. Bloom may not wish to start a revolution—to change the social institutions of society by force—but he shares with Stephen a certain despair about the condition of Ireland and about how that condition affects the human beings who attempt to live there. Unlike Stephen, however, his indictment of present society is reasonably specific. Stephen worries about Ireland devouring her heroes; that is, about the destructive potential of patriotism. Bloom worries about starving people. During "Sirens," Bloom contemplates the "Minuet of Don Giovanni" and thinks of the contrast between "Court dresses of all descriptions in castle chambers dancing" (*U*, 282), and "Misery. Peasants outside. Green starving faces eating dockleaves. Nice that is" (*U*, 282). Patriotism, too, starves peasants, as Bloom indicates in his distortion of a patriotic song: "The harp that once did starve us all" (*U*, 168). The culture of the upper classes dancing the minuet and the warlike patriotism of the Irish alike do "starve us all."

Bloom, as he diagnoses the problems of Ireland, generally focuses upon class structure and economics. He believes, for instance, that the rich determine who will be protected by the police; his explanation for the assignments of the "guardians of the law" in "quiet parts of the city" is that "the obvious reason being they were paid to protect the upper classes" (*U*, 615). Even worse, Bloom sees not just neglect, but malice in the arrangement, thinking that arming the constables is "tantamount to inciting them against civilians should by any chance they fall out over anything" (*U*, 615). Using words and diction associated with anarchists, Bloom labels competition in society as an evil that makes men like animals.[5] When Corley touches Stephen for money, Bloom allows it because "everyone according to his needs and everyone according to his deeds"—a contradiction. He sees with unhappiness that Corley's begging is no different from all other economic relationships:

> Probably he was one of his hangerson but for the matter of that it was merely a question of one preying on his nextdoor neighbour all round, in every deep, so to put it, a deeper depth and for the matter of that if the man in the street chanced to be in the dock himself penal servitude, with or without the option of a fine, would be a very *rara avis* altogether. [*U*, 619]

Bloom's own carefulness with money makes him less likely to offer Corley the halfcrown, although he has donated money for the Dignam family; but his sense of justice and of the injustice of the society in which he lives makes him see that beggars are not more disreputable than the others who prey on their neighbors "all round" in other ways. This kind of perception about the economic system of Ireland (and Europe, for that matter) leads him to believe that all the causes of man's unhappiness can be found in the faulty base of society.

He doesn't simply demand jobs for the jobless; he ventures to suggest a standard wage for all workers; and he sees economics as the basis for race hatred and for the Anglo-Irish conflict. In "Eumaeus," the alleged Skin-the-goat introduces the topic:

> [He] was airing his grievances in a forcible-feeble philippic anent the natural resources of Ireland, or something of that sort, which he described in his lengthy dissertation as the richest country bar none on the face of God's earth, far and away superior to England, with coal in large quantities, six million pounds' worth of pork exported every year, ten millions between butter and eggs, and all the riches drained out of it by England levying taxes on the poor people that paid through the nose always, and gobbling up the best meat in the market, and a lot more surplus steam in the same vein. [*U*, 640]

Skin-the-goat has, as one might expect, mixed fact with fancy; Ireland's coal is minimal or nonexistent. But his evaluation of her exports, though exaggerated, does point to one anomaly: Ireland should not have had starving masses in 1904. As an agricultural land, Ireland produced enough and more than enough to feed her people; yet, through rents and taxes and absentee landlords, souls such as Dilly Dedalus ate very badly. Bloom attributes to the money question all these quarrels and more:

> All those wretched quarrels, in his humble opinion, stirring up bad blood—bump of combativeness or gland of some kind, erroneously supposed to be about a punctilio of honour and a flag—were very largely a question of the money question which was at the back of everything, greed and jealousy, people never knowing when to stop. [*U,* 643]

His attempt to find some "scientific" explanation for such behavior is one indication of how much Bloom is the everyman, enamored of science and evolution, but uncertain about or inaccurate with both.

Bloom's revolutionary credentials date back to his youth. At about Stephen's age he became interested in "the evicted tenants' question" (*U,* 656). Although he never quite agreed with the Land League, he had been "in thorough sympathy with peasant possession" (*U,* 657). Yet, despite the fact that he had once gone "a step further than Michael Davitt" (*U,* 657), he later was "cured of" these opinions. Bloom's position here is odd. Why should Bloom, who advocates a redistribution of income, have rejected these youthful views? How did he go "a step further"? In a collection of anarchists' views that Joyce owned during the writing of *Ulysses,* Eltzbacher's *Anarchism,* Benjamin Tucker claimed that the problem with the Land League was that it did not go far enough: " 'The Irish Land League failed because the peasants were acting, not intelligently in obedience to their wisdom, but blindly in obedience to leaders who betrayed them at the critical moment. Had the people realised the power they were exercising and understood the economic situation, they would not have resumed the payment of rent at Parnell's bidding, and today they might have been free.' "[6] Perhaps Tucker's comments indicate a way in which Bloom might have gone a step further, a step further that Joyce probably knew. But Bloom is not agrarian and the Land League was; his notions about socialism and societal organization are so evidently urban that I would speculate that his rejection is based on that distinction.

In the same passage Bloom rejects "the casualties invariably resulting from propaganda and displays of mutual animosity and the misery and suffering it entailed as a foregone conclusion on fine young fellows, chiefly, destruction of the fittest" (*U,* 657). Here we may have Bloom's real objection to most political movements; like the doctrines of Tolstoy and Godwin in Eltzbacher's collection, Bloom's political doctrine is more concerned with avoiding the "destruction of the fittest" and with avoiding suffering in political life than with any particular political program. Like Tolstoy, Bloom seems, finally, to believe in "love."[7] Despite Bloom's scientific bias, he sees that man-made conflicts are, unlike the conflicts in the natural world, likely to end in the destruction of the best. So he must reject the kind of direct action proposed by the Land League and other "revolutionary" groups.

His association with Sinn Fein after his youthful support of Michael Davitt accords with this rejection. John Wyse Noland and later Cunningham attribute to Bloom the name "Sinn Fein": "John Wyse saying it was Bloom gave the idea for Sinn Fein to Griffith to put in his paper all kinds of jerrymandering, packed juries and swindling the taxes off of the Government and appointing consuls all over the world to walk about selling Irish industries" (*U*, 335–36). Bloom, despite his cooling ardor for revolution, has evidently continued to work for the cause. And work in his own, pacifistic way; as an advertiser, his duty to make people want a product can have political ramifications. As an adman, he can suggest how to use the popular press to further political ends. If the peoples of the world begin to buy Irish products, both the economic and political condition of Ireland will improve. Cunningham, a few pages later, reinforces Nolan's claims: "—That's so, says Martin. Or so they allege" (*U*, 337). Adams dismisses Bloom's association with Sinn Fein as out of character for the anti-Semite Griffith and for the self-effacing Leopold Bloom.[8] Perhaps we are dealing with one of those inconsistencies in the text. Nonetheless, that Bloom would perceive the economic need to peddle Irish goods does not strike me as out of character for a commercial man. Nor would Joyce see the commercial suggestions as ludicrous. In letters to Stanislaus, he advocated similar measures:

> But, so far as my knowledge of Irish affairs goes, he [Griffith] was the first person in Ireland to revive the separatist idea on modern lines nine years ago. . . . A great deal of his programme perhaps is absurd but at least it tries to inaugurate some commercial life for Ireland and to tell you the truth once or twice in Trieste I felt myself humiliated when I heard the little Galatti girl sneering at my impoverished country. You may remember that on my arrival in Trieste I actually "took some steps" to secure an agency for Foxford tweeds there. [*Letters*, 2: 167]

In a later letter Joyce commented, "The Irish proletariat has yet to be created. A feudal peasantry exists" (*Letters*, 2: 187). Perhaps Joyce saw these views as absurd later, but Bloom's advocacy of commercial liberation and economic progress does not immediately label him as having a ludicrous view of nationalism. Joyce, it seems, was not above the commercial and nationalist ventures of the Irish—and this at a time when he was writing of Stephen Dedalus, the would-be poet who refuses to sign peace petitions or have anything to do with the commercial life of his nation.

The commercial metaphor is crucial to an understanding of Bloom's political bias: "A revolution must come on the due instalments plan" (*U*, 643). Installment plans, with their implication of contracts entered into by two or more parties as well as with the overt meaning of gradual or incremental progress, avoid bloodshed and insist upon contractual relationships, mutuality and negotiation. That metaphor is consonant with all of Bloom's views of the world and of people. His announcement in "Cyclops" that he is talking about the opposite of hatred—what "is really life," "love" (*U*, 333), denies the use of arms against political enemies, just as he would reject the use of arms against Blazes Boylan. Bloom himself associates the two kinds of "warfare": too much politics smacks of the same motives that produce murders of passion, "off the same bat as those love vendettas of the south" (*U*, 642). Injustice, the enemy of Leopold Bloom and what he considers all liberation, precludes acting toward the neighbor with love, as Nolan points out to the Citizen, "isn't that what we're told? Love your neighbours" (*U*, 333). In short, Bloom's philosophy, if we can call his odd assortment of ideas a philosophy, is ludicrous only to a doctrinaire politician. His ideal of the redistribution of income is prompted by the belief that it would promote "friendlier intercourse between man and man" (*U*, 644). There is no use in "force, hatred, history, all that. That's not life for men and women, insult and hatred" (*U*, 333).

What do all of these political and personal attitudes have to do with art? Bloom's realistic and kinetic art are much more capable of drawing attention to and analyzing social conditions because as an acute observer he sees more than Stephen does. For instance, in "Lotos-Eaters" he understands and points out the soporific nature of religious faith: "Stupefies them first," "Blind faith. Safe in the arms of kingdom come. Lulls all pain" (*U*, 80–81). His descriptions of life—his proposed art—not only would earn money but also solve problems: who is the gentleman on the beach, how do we look to another? Most importantly by communicating in more than one way, with the banal elements of life, he achieves contact with his audience. Naturalism—a pseudoscientific investigation into the roots of societal conditions—and realism—the careful description of external life—allow Bloom to understand people and Dublin. Bloom can understand others because he can understand himself and project imaginatively on to others: he understands Gerty, he can deal with the constables that represent the state. And he can communicate, even if only partially, that knowledge to an audience, as well as manipulate his audience—whether it is Molly Tweedy or the consumers of Dublin or Arthur Griffith. His political emphasis on community coheres with his modes of perception—mundane, realistic, common, gradual—and they all cohere with realism as a literary form rather than with Aestheticism. Zola, who imagined the world getting better bit by bit as artists investigated it and revealed it, would have understood Bloom's installment plan.[9] The early Yeats, who believed all progress was miraculous and sudden,[10] and Stephen Dedalus, who seeks alchemical transmutation, would not.

Joyce's dedication to realistic art, at least realistic detail, is clear not just from his letters to relatives and friends checking on mundane matters about the high-tide mark on the Liffey or the drop around 7 Eccles Street and not just from his letters that are critical of nonrealistic detail in the works of others, but also in the very textures of his fiction. Ironically, Joyce fulfills Wilde's negative description of the realistic writers who, from Vivian's point of view, produce rotten art because they always write about the people and places they know and because they substitute for an interesting creation (a lie) the dullness and repetitiveness of nature. In "The Decay of Lying," Vivian damns them:

> . . . the modern novelist presents us with dull facts under the guise of fiction. The Blue-Book is rapidly becoming his ideal both for method and manner. He has his tedious *"document humain."* . . . He is to be found at the Librairie Nationale, or at the British Museum, shamelessly reading up on his subject. He has not even the courage of other people's ideas, but insists on going directly to life for everything, and ultimately, between encyclopædias and personal experience, he comes to the ground, having drawn his types from the family circle or from the weekly washerwoman, and having acquired an amount of useful information from which never, even in his most meditative moments, can he thoroughly free himself.
>
> The loss that results to literature in general from this false ideal of our time can hardly be over-estimated. [5: 12–13]

And so, Vivian describes Joyce's blue book, an investigation and an installment in a political plan, drawn realistically from people and places in Joyce's family and hometown.

At the same time, Bloom's pseudoscientific notions suggest that Joyce saw naturalism as only pseudoscience. Despite his attraction to science, remembered by his brother,[11] Joyce dramatized that the ways of seeing which the kinetic artist advocates are not exactly objective and that they are, at times, as muddled as the Aesthete's. And, although Bloom shares a sexual fantasy with Gerty, the encounter is, like all of Stephen's (except with whores), also onanistic.

Bloom, as counterpoint to Stephen, offers the possibility of relationships between the artist and his society, between the artist and his audience, and between art and politics. He asserts the value of everyday experience, of apparently insignificant thoughts, of the common man: all things that the Aesthetes rejected; all things that the naturalists-realists valued.

Notes

1. Richard Ellmann, *James Joyce* (New York: Oxford University Press, 1959), pp. 369, 370n. More recently, Fritz Senn, in "Nausicaa," *James Joyce's "Ulysses": Critical Esays*, ed. Clive Hart and David Hayman (Berkeley, Calif.: University of California Press, 1974), pp. 277–311, has discussed and listed parallels between Leopold and Stephen, many of which I also use in this chapter. See especially pp. 285–86 of his essay.

2. Frank Budgen, *James Joyce and The Making of "Ulysses"* (Bloomington, Ind.: Indiana University Press, 1934), p. 64.

3. William H. Schutte, "Leopold Bloom: A Touch of the Artist," in *"Ulysses": Fifty Years*, ed. Thomas Staley (Bloomington, Ind.: Indiana University Press, 1974), pp. 118–31.

4. Gogarty complains of this practice, although Stanislaus denies Joyce did it. However acquired, Joyce did use his friends in his epiphanies.

5. A claim made in the section on Peter Kropotkin in Paul Eltzbacher, *Anarchism: Exponents of the Anarchist Philosphy*, ed. James J. Martin, trans. Stephen Byington (New York: Chips, n.d.), pp. 96–97. This volume is a reprint of a volume Joyce owned—see Richard Ellmann *The Consciousness of James Joyce* (Toronto: Oxford University Press, 1977).

6. Benjamin Tucker, in *Anarchism*, p. 142.

7. See Godwin's section (pp. 24–40) and Tolstoy's section (pp. 149–81) in *Anarchism*. Tolstoy's comments are, perhaps, most interesting, for his doctrine is much like Bloom's. See also Michael Bukunin, pp. 79–80, in *Anarchism*.

8. Robert Martin Adams, *Surface and Symbol: The Consistency of James Joyce's "Ulysses"* (New York: Oxford University Press, 1962), pp. 100–104. Cunningham, a Protestant, might find Griffith's program negative—hence his word "allege."

9. See Émile Zola's *The Experimental Novel and Other Essays*, trans. Belle M. Sherman (New York: Haskell House, 1964); in that theory, the novelist is a moralist who, through experiment, points the way to gradual improvement of society. Proudhon, who rejected all violence, seems also to see gradualism as the answer to social change (*Anarchism*, pp. 55–60). Bloom's metaphor is the metaphor of a businessman.

10. *Uncollected Prose of W. B. Yeats*, ed. John Frayne and Colton Johnson, 2 vols. (New York: Columbia University Press, 1970, 1976), 2:199; see discussion, chapter 3.

11. Stanislaus Joyce, *The Complete Dublin Diary*, ed. George H. Healy (Ithaca, N.Y., and London: Cornell University Press, 1971): "The word 'scientific' is always a word of praise in his mouth" (p. 54). Stanislaus Joyce more than once records Joyce's interest in and attraction to science.

8
Adman Meets Aesthete

The antithetical personalities of Bloom and Stephen—Jew-Greek, Jew-Catholic, materialist-spiritualist, scientist-poet—unite briefly in "Circe." Neither one of them in this longest chapter of the book controls his associations; both of them are more prone to move outside of their normal patterns of perception and behavior because, in part, the censor we call "control" operates less actively. As they gaze into a mirror, they "see" Shakespeare:

LYNCH

(Points.) The mirror up to nature. *(He laughs.)* Hu hu hu hu hu hu.
(Stephen and Bloom gaze in the mirror. The face of William Shakespeare, beardless, appears there, rigid in facial paralysis, crowned by the reflection of the reindeer antlered hatrack in the hall.)

SHAKESPEARE

(In dignified ventriloquy.) 'Tis the loud laugh bespeaks the vacant mind. *(To Bloom.)* Thou thoughtest as how thou wastest invisible. Gaze. *(He crows with a black capon's laugh.)* Iagogo! How my Oldfellow chokit his Thursdaymomun. Iagogogo! [*U*, 567]

This Shakespeare, crowned by the traditional headgear of cuckolds, reflects—or is a reflection of—Stephen's and Bloom's psyches. Within the novel, the only "evidence" that Shakespeare was a cuckold and deserves these antlers is that which Stephen offers in "Scylla and Charybdis"; this particular Shakespeare immediately connects with Stephen's emotional associations and analysis. Insofar as the theory Stephen develops about Shakespeare answers or resonates to his psychological condition, so too does this reflection. Yet, Bloom also has some similarities to this version of Shakespeare for he is literally cuckolded by Molly and Blazes's assignation. The Shakespeare that appears in the mirror as both gaze into it, then, reflects both personalities and unites them.

The antlers of the cuckold less obviously "belong" with Stephen than with Bloom. And yet, indirectly and largely subconsciously, Stephen imagines himself usurped in his relationship to his mother by Simon Dedalus. Although I cannot here trace all the passages that outline the nature of Stephen's relationship to May and Simon Dedalus, a relationship we can label "oedipal," I can point out some of them. Even the sense of guilt Stephen has about his mother's death, his sense of responsibility for her death, is aligned with oedipal relationships in Ernest Jones's study of *Hamlet,* a volume Joyce owned during the writing of *Ulysses.* In the first chapter of the novel, Stephen associates his mother with sexuality by quoting Swinburne. In "Proteus," as he contemplates midwives, his own engendering, and his mother's death, the illicit and unacknowledged nature of his relationship to May Dedalus becomes clearer. Thinking of his own conception, he reduces his parents to images: "the man with my voice and my eyes and a ghost-woman with ashes on her breath" (*U*, 38). His mother is already dead and his father is described as though Stephen were the father of Simon—a "man with my voice and my eyes." Stephen consistently imagines his father not to be his father, arguing in "Scylla and Charybdis" that paternity "may be a legal fiction" (*U*, 207). When Stephen encounters his mother in "Circe," she is given not her married name but her maiden name—she becomes the unwed mother of Stephen Dedalus, May Goulding. Such patterns of thought reject the natural father and the father's sexual relationship to the mother.

Stephen sees a dog and thinks of his riddle, a riddle we associated both with May Dedalus and with Stephen's relationship to her: "Something he buried there, his grandmother" (*U*, 46). He begins to consider women:

> Tides, myriad-islanded, within her, blood not mine, *oinopa ponton,* a winedark sea. Behold the handmaid of the moon. In sleep the wet sign calls her hour, bids her rise. Bridebed, childbed, bed of death, ghost-candled. *Omnis caro ad te veniet.* He comes, pale vampire, through storm his eyes, his bat sails bloodying the sea, mouth to her mouth's kiss. [*U*, 47–48]

Much of this passage echoes images and patterns Stephen has used before about women—for instance, the virginal imagery and the cadence of "Behold the handmaid of the moon." Stephen, having mentioned his "Hamlet hat" (*U*, 47), includes in this revery images more closely associated with his mother; the imagery of "bed of death, ghost-candled" is used in "Scylla and Charybdis" as the link between Ann Hathaway and May Dedalus: "Mother's deathbed. Candle" (*U*, 190). His mother is also one of the ways he links himself with Shakespeare, a man represented both in "Scylla and Charybdis" and in "Circe" as cuckolded.

In "Proteus," the generalized woman is maternal, prompted first by the midwives and then in Stephen's associations marked by her womb:

> His lips lipped and mouthed fleshless lips of air: mouth to her womb. Oomb, allwombing tomb. [*U*, 48]

The ghostwoman, May Dedalus, like this imaginative figure, has "fleshless lips"; Stephen's only connection with her is imaginary. On the next page, Stephen begins his demand for the word, and associates it with loneliness and "touch":

> Touch me. Soft eyes. Soft soft soft hand. I am lonely here. O, touch me soon, now. What is that word known to all men? I am quiet here alone. Sad too. Touch, touch me. [*U*, 49]

In popular slang, *touch* has specifically sexual meanings—as Molly uses it with Bloom, "give us a touch." In "Circe," May Goulding receives the request—"Tell me the word, mother, if you know now. The word known to all men" (*U*, 581)—more than a coincidence in this novel. Stephen moves from these two requests, one ostensibly literary and the other more obviously sexual, to the song he sang to his mother: "And no more turn aside and brood," Yeats's song of *"love's bitter mystery."* In "Circe," May Goulding almost accuses Stephen: "You sang that song to me. *Love's bitter mystery*" (*U*, 581). The long revery in "Proteus" moves finally back to a contemplation of the sea, a sea initially associated with Stephen's mother. In the sea Stephen perceives a cosmic cycle of life that parallels the cycles his thoughts began with— "Bridebed, childbed, bed of death."

The request for the word, the obvious sexuality of the passages, (Stephen's association of the birth of the word or artistic reproduction with sexual reproduction, his rejection of Simon, his punishment-fantasy in "Circe" all conspire to indicate Stephen's oedipal relationship to his mother.)

Stephen's various discussions of the fiction of paternity and of the act of intercourse lead to the conclusion that he wishes at least to be the son of the Virgin mother who creates himself—begotten, not made. But the position concerns the arts as well as psychology. Shakespeare's creativity and aesthetics, according to Stephen, stem from his cuckolded and betrayed position.(Stephen wants, like Bloom, to be creative, though Bloom simply wishes to have children and Stephen wishes to create art.)Like Shakespeare, Bloom has lost his only son. Nonetheless, both characters are figures who are usurped—Blazes, Simon, Mulligan, Mulvey, perhaps even the boyfriend of Milly are usurpers, betrayers, adulterers. The facial paralysis of rage that appears in the mirror mimics the rage of Caliban at seeing, or perhaps not seeing his face in the mirror. In mimicking Caliban, this Shakespeare reflects Stephen. (Bloom's paralytic rage concerns his ineffectiveness in his wife's and his daughter's situations: "Will happen, yes. Prevent. Useless: can't move") (*U*, 67).

SHAKESPEARE

> (*With paralytic rage.*) Weda seca whokilla farst.
> (*The face of Martin Cunningham, bearded, refeatures Shakespeare's beardless face . . .*) [*U*, 568]

Again, this Shakespeare reflects the thoughts of Bloom and Stephen: in "Hades," Bloom considered Martin Cunningham to look like Shakespeare (*U*, 96) and in "Scylla and Charybdis," Stephen says,

> All those women saw their men down and under: Mary, her goodman John, Ann, her poor dear Willun, when he went and died on her, raging that he was the first to go, Joan, her four brothers, Judith, her husband and all her sons, Susan, her husband too, while Susan's daughter, Elizabeth, to use granddaddy's words [e.g., William Shakespeare's], wed her second, having killed her first. [*U*, 202–3]

That is, Stephen has thought both of an enraged Shakespeare and of a less garbled version of "Weda seca whokilla farst." It takes both Bloom's and Stephen's psyches to produce the reflection. The figures of Martin and Mrs. Cunningham, figures associated with Bloom, lead Stephen to recall sexual perversity ("Queens lay with prize bulls" [*U*, 569]) and homosexuality, as well as Lynch, who remembers vampires and voyeurism, which Stephen and Bloom evidently find attractive.

But even more significantly, in this moment that unifies the psyches of Bloom and Stephen, Stephen remembers his dream:

> I dreamt of a watermelon. . . . It was here. Street of harlots. In Serpentine Avenue Beelzebub showed me her, a fubsy widow. Where's the red carpet spread? [*U*, 571]

Bloom evidently recognizes the dream, for at this point he approaches Stephen. Stephen rejects Bloom in fighting the father figure of Simon, who appears as a vulture (a hawklike man). We have, of course, already discovered that the symbol pattern in which Daedalus is the father ends in Stephen's being a "lapwing, seabedabbled." Simon is transformed into a hunter leading a pack of dogs after Stephen-fox, who, *"having buried his grandmother,"* is running for cover. Stephen's visions of Simon are the products of his self-judgment; he *deserves* to have Simon hunt him. But the noise in the street (*U*, 574) disrupts the fantasy and allows Stephen to return to the brothel.

Bloom has many of Stephen's attributes: both associate the Mother with the Church. Stephen's mother calls upon him to repent; while Bloom's mother responds to her son:

> O blessed Redeemer, what have they done to him! . . . Sacred Heart of Mary, where were you at all, at all? [*U*, 438]

Stephen's mother screams, "O Sacred Heart of Jesus, have mercy on him! Save him from hell, O divine Sacred Heart!" (*U*, 582). Bloom's vision of his mother precedes Molly's appearance, Stephen's vision of May is associated with "Who Goes with Fergus?" and hence with a forbidden sexual love. The emotional content of Stephen's female figure thus is seriously revealed as trauma in "Circe"[2]; Bloom's vision of his mother is not distanced and transformed into art, and it remains a significant emotional problem. Bloom has some of Stephen's psychological difficulties, but Bloom deals with them as problems, not as art. Similarly, Bloom sees his political problems as political and emotional, not as artistic imperatives.

The dance of the harlots, Stephen, Lynch, and Bloom which precedes the appearance of May's ghost begins with a description:

> (*Arabesquing wearily, they weave a pattern on the floor, weaving, unweaving, curtseying, twisting, simply swirling.*) [*U*, 577]

Several allusions are included in this description: one to "The Seaside Girls,"[3] one to Pater's description of the weaving and unweaving of the self in time,[4] and another to Oscar Wilde's poems "The Harlot's House" and "The Ballad of Reading Gaol."[5] In the first poem, Wilde dramatizes the failure of love through the harlot's relationship to a man. The people in the poem become automatons, skeletons, clockwork puppets, phantom lovers, and horrible marionettes, just as the people in "Circe" do, and as May Dedalus does when she appears. And the thematic significance of the dances is similar. Below are appropriate passages from Wilde's poem to compare with the text of "Circe":

> We caught the tread of dancing feet,
> We loitered down the moonlit street,
> And stopped beneath the Harlot's house.
>
> Inside, above the din and fray,
> We heard the loud musicians play
> The "Treues Liebes," of Strauss.
>
> Like strange mechanical grotesques,
> Making *fantastic arabesques*,
> The *shadows raced across the blind*.
>
> We watched the *ghostly dancers spin*

To sound of horn and violins,
Like black leaves wheeling in the wind.

[ll. 1–12, italics mine]

. . . .

Then turning to my love I said,
"The dead are dancing with the dead,
The dust is whirling with the dust."

But she, she heard the violin,
And left my side and entered in:
Love passed into the house of Lust.

Then suddenly the tune went false,
The dancers wearied of the waltz,
The *shadows ceased to wheel and whirl,*

And down the long and silent street,
The dawn with silver-sandalled feet,
Crept like a frightened girl.

[ll. 25–36, italics mine]

The dance in "Circe" with its *"mosaic of movements"* (*U*, 577), like the "mechanical grotesques" and "fantastic arabesques," forms *"Bright midges"* that *"dance on wall"* (*U*, 579) as the "shadows raced across the blind," or in "Circe" as *"they weave a pattern on the floor"* (*U*, 577). Like the dance in Wilde's poem, the dance in "Circe" is a dance of the living and the dead. The intrusion of May into Stephen's consciousness causes him, like the dancers in Wilde's poem, to stop. *"The couples fall aside"* and *"He stops dead"* (*U*, 579). Just as Stephen's love for his mother has turned into an oedipal fixation, so, in Wilde's poem, the persona's lover passes into a brothel. Stephen meets his mother's ghost in a brothel because his love for her is illicit and unacceptable. The similarities between the Wilde poem and Joyce's text suggest or reinforce the suggestion that Stephen's love includes lust, and associate Stephen and Aestheticism with homosexuality. The ghostly dancers of the poem which along with the violin lure the woman into the brothel are like the figure of May's ghost. The grotesque quality of both works stems partly from the failure of love and sexuality, imaged in *Ulysses* as Stephen dances with each of the whores, but finally returns to his onanistic ashplant, the self-created symbol of artistic creation.

Another poem by Wilde, "The Ballad of Reading Gaol" contains a similar dancing scene:

Alas! it is a fearful thing
To feel another's guilt!

[ll. 265–66]

. . . .

The troubled plumes of midnight shook
  Like the plumes upon a hearse:
And as bitter wine upon a sponge
  Was the savour of Remorse.

                    *   *   *

The gray cock crew, the red cock crew,
  But never came the day:
And crooked shapes of Terror crouched,
  In corners where we lay:
And each evil sprite that walks by night
  Before us seemed to play.

They glided past, they glided fast,
  Like travellers through a mist:
They mocked the moon in a rigadoon
  Of delicate turn and twist,
And with formal pace and loathsome grace
  The phantoms kept their tryst.

With mop and mow, we saw them go,
  Slim shadows hand in hand:
About, about, in ghostly rout
  They trod a saraband:
And the damned *grotesques made arabesques,*
  Like the wind upon the sand!

With the pirouettes of marionettes,
  They tripped on pointed tread:
But with flutes of Fear they filled the ear,
  As their grisly masque they led.

                          [ll. 279–304, italics mine]

The situation in the poem centers on the virtual refrain that "all men kill the thing they love" just as Stephen, who loves his mother, has "killed" her. The use of identical words or virtually identical words to describe the dance, the similarities in situation (both personas are imprisoned—physically or spiritually) through a murder of the thing they love; the remorse and the nightmare vision that the remorse and guilt create, all these suggest that Wilde's poem and its similarities to "Circe" are not mere coincidence. The real terror beyond remorse of Wilde's protagonist is isolation, the kind of isolation Stephen feels:

With midnight always in one's heart,
  And twilight in one's cell,
We turn the crank, or tear the rope,
  Each in his separate Hell,

> And the silence is more awful far
> Than the sound of a brazen bell.

> And never a human voice come near
> To speak a gentle word:
> And the eye that watches through the door
> Is pitiless and hard.
>
> [ll. 589–98]

The message of the poem, if it has one, is also contained in Stephen's predicament.

> And all men kill the thing they love,
> By all let this be heard,
> Some do it with a bitter look
> Some with a flattering word,
> The coward does it with a kiss,
> The brave man with a sword!
>
> [649–54]

Stephen has killed his mother, not with a sword, but with "a bitter look," or oedipally, with "a kiss." The dancing of the harlots and Stephen, then, with its echoes of two of Oscar Wilde's poems, suggests a context in which to understand Stephen's dilemma. Stephen, whose vision all of this is, provides us inadvertently with another sign of his literary masters, again pointing out his indebtedness to the Aesthetes and decadents of the close of the century.

At the close of the dance, Stephen's mother appears. May's ghost, mad, corrupt, half-decayed, rises from Stephen's sense of guilt over the murder, sexual deviation, and his failure to produce art—hence his failure to live his life satisfactorily. The exchange, presented as a three-way conversation among Stephen, May, and Buck Mulligan, is interesting in terms of aesthetic responses and analogues and in terms of Stephen's search for an acceptable theory of art.

BUCK MULLIGAN

She's beastly dead. The pity of it! Mulligan meets the afflicted mother. *(He upturns his eyes.)* Mercurial Malachi.

THE MOTHER

(With the subtle smile of death's madness.) I was once the beautiful May Goulding. I am dead.

STEPHEN

(Horrorstruck.) Lemur, who are you? What bogeyman's trick is this?

BUCK MULLIGAN

(Shakes his curling capbell.) The mockery of it! Kinch killed her dogs-body bitchbody. She kicked the bucket. *(Tears of molten butter fall from his eyes into the scone.)* Our great sweet mother! *Epi oinopa ponton.*

THE MOTHER

(Comes nearer, breathing upon him softly her breath of wetted ashes.) All must go through it, Stephen. More women than men in the world. You too. Time will come.

STEPHEN

(Choking with fright, remorse and horror.) They said I killed you, mother. He offended your memory. Cancer did it, not I. Destiny. [*U*, 580]

Thus far, Stephen has confirmed several suspicions the reader holds about him. That he feels guilt over his mother's death is clear; that he associates his mother with the sea (through the allusion to Swinburne's "The Triumph of Time") and hence associates himself with the rejected lover who turns to the sea for solace is clear; once again it is a quotation from a poet of the tradition that alerts us to Stephen's own condition. May Dedalus resembles the sphinx in Wilde's poem of the same name. The persona of that poem asks the sphinx, as Stephen asks May, impossible questions about art and history: sing of the labyrinth and "all your memories." The sphinx brings to the protagonist a vision of death like the ashen breath of May Dedalus: "And on my brows I feel the damp and dreadful dews of night and death" (l. 152). Like May the sphinx is a "songless, tongueless ghost of sin" (l. 163) which appears because the persona's "taper burning bright" (l. 164) invites it.[6] May is tongueless in that she cannot answer Stephen's question, and she clearly appears because of his sense of guilt. Finally, May's *"grinning claws," "her black-ened, withered right arm"* (*U*, 582) have the sinister overtones of the ivory claws and dark breast of the sphinx.

The use of May's maiden name (Goulding) suggest Stephen's desire to erase the existence of Simon, or at least Simon's relationship to the mother. The conversation continues:

THE MOTHER

(A green rill of bile trickling from a side of her mouth.) You sang that song to me. *Love's bitter mystery.* [*U*, 581]

The inclusion of a quotation from Yeats's "Who Goes with Fergus?" completes the association of Stephen with the Aesthetic tradition. Understanding the sources and contexts of Stephen's allusions is necessary to comprehending the scene's significance. Stephen's demand, coming after all the "Aesthetic" signals have been repeated, is an artistic, sexual one: "Tell me the word, mother, if you know now. The word known to all men" (*U*, 581). This request is quite complicated. Weldon Thornton tells us that, through an allusion to Homer's *Odyssey*, Stephen, like Ulysses, is asking what caused her death.[7] In Stephen's personal history, the word is associated, too, with the creative urge and the fundamental unit of literature. In addition, Stephen asks for the word because of his confusion of creation-sex-literature with his mother and his oedipal relationship to her. The word with its biblical echoes involves light, an image of artistic impregnation in *A Portrait*, and the self-begotten state of Christ, who is one of Stephen's analogues for the artist in the earlier novel. But Stephen is not even Icarus any more; he is no longer the young artist in his subconscious mind. Toward the end of the scene he responds: "The corpsechewer! Raw head and bloody bones!" (*U*, 581). Stephen's vision of himself as "lapwing," a bird that frequents cemeteries, is recalled with the echo of Stephen's earlier mental attack on his mother: "Ghoul! Chewer of corpses!" (*U*, 10). And Stephen's association of the bird with his own failed artistry in "Scylla and Charybdis" reminds us that the scene has implications for Stephen's art.[8] May again breathes on Stephen, much as the Holy Ghost breathes life into the world; but instead of life, May breathes the air of ashes and death. The solution to Stephen's personal and artistic problems cannot be found through his vision of his mother. Oedipal love, like self-centered and onanistic artistry, is sterile and produces death-in-life. Later in the novel, through Bloom, Joyce associates Aestheticism with homosexuality and with autoeroticism.

The maternal and female cannot provide the word, a means of artistic creation for the young artist. Bloom—with all he represents—and Stephen—with all he represents—must, together, look into the mirror to "produce" Shakespeare. Bloom is necessary for art. Yet Stephen appears to reject both the male and the female possibilities for art later in "Circe" when he runs away from Bloom and smashes the vision of his mother by smashing the chandelier. The smashing of the chandelier with his phallic ashplant is in some ways a sexual violation of his mother that can release him from his obsession, or at least begin the release. What he has left is Bloom. Bloom, as "Circe" reveals, shares the essence of many of Stephen's experiences. Bloom is not an artist, at least not in Stephen's sense of the artist. He represents the naturalistic, scientific, and realistic mode of art not because he practices it, but because his life suggests the aesthetics of that tradition as Stephen's life has suggested his pattern of aesthetics. It is not that Bloom works out any theory of art—to do so would almost contradict the sense of realism, the sense of not consciously shaping life—that the tradition, if carried to its extreme, as Stephen carries his tradition to an extreme, would demand. Bloom recognizes the younger man as a poet (*U*, 591), and somehow important and special because of it. And he recognizes

Stephen's vulnerability, which is consonant with and represented by the younger man's theories of art. The subconscious union in "Circe" ends with Bloom's vision of Rudy as Stephen lies on the pavement unconscious. In that scene Bloom repeats parts of the Masonic vow, swearing to keep in confidence all he knows of Stephen's mind and his emotional state.

"Eumaeus" and "Ithaca" are logical and rational discoveries of communality. In them Stephen is initiated into a world of communication, where he can talk to other human beings, establish some ties with them, and accept their differences from him, without violating his own uniqueness. The exile, cunning, and separatism proposed by Stephen and to a large extent fulfilled through his life, have proved unsatisfactory. He wants "the word known to all men," not the symbolic mirror of his inner mind, which no other human being can understand. Bloom unconsciously shows him how to communicate. Bloom, by accepting Stephen's limitations, by being willing to ignore or pass over the idiosyncracies of this young man, allows Stephen to communicate with him. Bloom, for instance, is favored with the rendition of "The Parable of the Plums" and other of Stephen's artistic creations. While Bloom doesn't understand Stephen, he accepts him and demonstrates a willingness to understand that provides hope.

Bloom attempts to engage Stephen in a conversation about poetry and we discover the extent to which Stephen is disillusioned with language and words:

> —A beautiful language [Italian]. I mean for singing purposes. Why do you not write your poetry in that language? *Bella Poetria!* it is so melodious and full. *Belladonna voglio. . . .*
> —Sounds are impostures, Stephen said after a pause of some little time. Like names, Cicero, Podmore, Napoleon, Mr Godbody, Jesus, Mr Doyle. Shakespeares were as common as Murphies. What's in a name?
> —Yes, to be sure, Mr Bloom unaffectedly concurred. Of course. Our name was changed too, he added, pushing the socalled roll across. [*U,* 622–23]

Stephen, who had seen in his surname the omen of his vocation, now questions that vocation by doubting the significance of names. Sounds, once as important as rhythm and meaning, are also suspect now, "impostures." Stephen doubts the efficacy of sounds and meaning and symbolic omens because they have not provided him with the structured life he sought. But he also seems to be doubting, in the same sense, the theory surrounding Shakeseare and Jesus, the creator of "the most" and the self-creator. Creativity in general appears in disrepute following the harrowing experience of "Circe."

Stephen associates himself with Irish nationalists and Yeats when he later suggests a situation similar to the one in *The Countess Cathleen:*

—In this country people sell much more than she ever had and do a roaring trade. Fear not them that sell the body but have not power to buy the soul. She is a bad merchant. She buys dear and sells cheap. [*U*, 633]

Bloom's literalistic response to Stephen is to question his belief in the soul, during which Bloom appears to agree with Huxley's "The Physical Basis of Life." "I believe in that myself because it has been explained by competent men as the convolutions of the grey matter" (*U*, 633).

But it is on the subject of Stephen's or any artist's relationship to society and Ireland that Bloom and Stephen most specifically disagree. In a passage discussed earlier,[9] Bloom suggests that everyone including artists must work. In doing so Bloom threatens Stephen's superiority because he reduces artistry and artisthood to the level of *work*. While Bloom sees himself as properly educated in perceiving the artist to be as important as the peasant or the worker with his hands, Stephen sees insult in making the peasant as important as the artist. Bloom sees newspapers, the modern universal medium, as the place to produce one's art; Stephen's aristocratic sense of the artist rejects such a democratic notion. To be an artist-for-hire is not congenial to Stephen. Yet Shakespeare, we might remember, played to the pit as well as the court.

Bloom's subsequent thoughts and worries about Stephen are interesting because Joyce dramatized through Bloom the point of view that the middle class held about the Aesthetes and decadents, Yeats's tragic generation, and because Bloom associates Stephen with that group, as the narrator does in "Oxen of the Sun." Bloom sees them as more threatening to Stephen's welfare than the reader does, perhaps, but that is because Bloom represents a group that rarely reads *Ulysses*. Through Bloom's eyes, however, we learn something of Joyce's own belief about art and something of how this novel is structured. Bloom remembers with "some consternation" that Stephen "had just come back from Paris" (*U*, 645). "He brought to mind instances of cultured fellows that promised so brilliantly, nipped in the bud of premature decay, and nobody to blame but themselves" (*U*, 645). Bloom sees hope for Stephen in "Sheer force of natural genius" (*U*, 646), but his concern for the effects of bohemian life in Paris suggests one way of viewing the artistic colony. Bloom associates the group with sexual deviation; it is interesting not because Bloom is absolutely right, but because he comes as close to Stephen's problems as he does.[10] Bloom, like Stephen, here associates sex and art. In contrast, Bloom's own proposed artistry is a realistic description of people one encounters in "*a Cabman's Shelter*" (*U*, 647). Bloom and Stephen, although agreeing subterraneously, have yet to find a common ground on which to communicate consciously as they have subconsciously in "Circe."

The first ground appears to be physical. As they leave the shelter, Bloom "passed his left arm in Stephen's right and led him on accordingly" (*U*, 660). Stephen, aware of the presence of the other man, does not, as he has done earlier, reject the physical contact. This posture is maintained as they find the first of their means of communication: a discussion of music.

> So they passed on to chatting about music, a form of art for which Bloom, as a pure amateur, possessed the greatest love, as they made tracks arm-in-arm across Beresford place. Wagnerian music, though confessedly grand in its way, was a bit too heavy for Bloom. . . . And talking of that, taking it for granted he knew all about the old favourites, he mentioned *par excellence* Lionel's air in *Martha*, *M'appari*, which, curiously enough, he heard, or overheard, to be more accurate, on yesterday . . . from the lips of Stephen's respected father.[*U*, 661]

Bloom can assume a common, cultural basis for communication in shared musical experience. And it is Molly's singing and Simon's singing that permit such a communication. Sources of Stephen's and Bloom's sexual difficulties paradoxically provide the source for communication.

> Stephen, in reply to a politely put query, said he didn't but launched out into praises of Shakespeare's songs, at least of in or about that period, the lutenist Dowland who lived in Fetter Lane near Gerard. [*U*, 661]

Stephen's penchant for Elizabethan love songs has been known to the reader from *A Portrait*. But in the earlier novel this interest has been a secret source of pleasure.

> His mind, when wearied of its search for the essence of beauty amid the spectral words of Aristotle or Aquinas, turned often for its pleasure to the dainty songs of the Elizabethans. His mind, in the vesture of a doubting monk, stood often in shadow under the windows of that age, to hear the grave and mocking music of the lutenists. . . .
> The lore which he was believed to pass his days brooding upon so that it had rapt him from the companionships of youth was only a garner of slender sentences from Aristotle's poetics and psychology.[*P*, 176]

The Elizabethan songs had been a private and secret source of pleasure, providing Stephen with something less esoteric and more earthly than that which he was supposed to be considering. The defensive barrier of his private aesthetics precluded the revelation of his interest. The change here in *Ulysses* is indicated by his revelation to Bloom of this interest. Stephen has earlier placed the old matrix of Church fathers between himself and Bloom (in the discussion of the soul above); here he avoids that block to communication. The adjustment suggests Stephen's need and desire to communicate, which in turn suggests he is no longer satisfied with his weapons of silence, cunning, and exile. Stephen's

hesitancy to admit his fondness for Elizabethan songs may even stem
from a comment in Wilde's "Decay of Lying":

> All that we desired to point out was, that the magnificent work of the
> Elizabethan and Jacobean artists contained within itself the seeds of its
> own dissolution, and that, if it drew some of its strength from using life as
> rough material, it drew all its weakness from using life as an artistic
> method. [5:30]

In short, the failure of distance from life and of refinement into art may
be what frightens Stephen who is forced back to aesthetics when he
hears "a laugh too low" in the age (*P*, 176).

Stephen has broken the self-imposed isolation that formed a
significant part of his and his tradition's sense of the artist. The conversation and communication, once started, branches into a variety of
subjects. As

> they walked, they at times stopped and walked again, continuing their
> *tête-à-tête* . . . about sirens, enemies of man's reason, mingled with a
> number of other topics of the same category, usurpers, historical cases of
> the kind. [*U*, 665]

That is, the conversation begins to branch out to include all the items
that are psychologically and emotionally and intellectually important to
both men. Doubtless, given their different approaches to life, they differ on these issues. But Stephen has found a responsive audience. The
conversations with Lynch and Cranly in *A Portrait* displayed two different and root causes for Stephen's failure to communicate: in Lynch's
case Stephen looked for no contribution, he lectured; in Cranly's case
Stephen attempted to reject the significant and important differences. In
Bloom's case, the tête-à-tête continues, regardless of differences of
opinion and approach. Stephen has learned something, at least he has
acquired a desire to communicate.

The beginning of "Ithaca" reiterates what we have seen at the end
of the previous chapter. The first question of this answer and question
chapter makes both their similarities and their differences clear:
"WHAT PARALLEL COURSES DID BLOOM AND STEPHEN
FOLLOW REturning?" (*U*, 666). The list of conversational topics is
not remarkable for the choices or selectivity involved, but rather for the
randomness of the items included:

> Music, literature, Ireland, Dublin, Paris, friendship, woman, pros-
> titution, diet, the influence of gaslight or the light of arc and glow-lamps
> on the growth of adjoining paraheliotropic trees, exposed corporation
> emergency dustbuckets, the Roman catholic church, eccelesiastical celi-
> bacy, the Irish nation, jesuit education, careers, the study of medicine, the

past day, the maleficent influence of the presabbath, Stephen's collapse. [*U,* 666]

Stephen's need to think only important artistic thoughts has disappeared in this novel; he even deigns to discuss things that he probably doesn't care about (paraheliotropic trees). Bloom, we know (*U,* 667), has discussed a variety of similar topics before, but Stephen hasn't; in short, the older man is not changing, the younger man is. Both discover in the other a love of music and Continental life. Bloom dissents from Stephen's and Wilde's "eternal affirmation of the spirit of man in literature"(*U,* 666). [11]

The famous imbibing of cocoa is an act of communion. It is an act of communion in which the esoteric and ritualistic elitism of the Catholic Church is absent. "Epp's massproduct," as "the creature cocoa" (*U,* 677) is called, is, in contrast to the consecrated wine of the altar, a universal, communal drink, not limited to priests of one sect; like its title, the cocoa is for the mass of people, not a select group. The significance is that the "audience" for the cocoa is the same audience that a popular artist should reach; the "audience" for wine is only the priest. Stephen's art and his concept of art are, for him, the artist alone. Like the priest, who is the only one who drinks the wine, Stephen is the only one who can understand and appreciate his art. The text makes the conjunction clearer as Bloom moves from the cocoa to a consideration of literature, and demonstrates that he, like Stephen, uses literature to solve "difficult problems in real or imaginary life":

> Had he found their solution?
> In spite of careful and repeated reading of certain classical passages, aided by a glossary, he had derived imperfect conviction from the text, the answers not bearing on all points. [*U,* 677]

Initially Bloom's resort to literature for answers to practical or possible problems may seem to be another point disengaging him from Stephen, as I have indicated earlier. [12] Yet Stephen turns to literature and literary symbols in *A Portrait* in order to deal with his life (e.g., *The Count of Monte Cristo,* Hauptmann's women) and to literary criticism and texts in *Ulysses* (the Shakespeare theory and reading of the plays as a way to deal with his own psychological condition). Stephen, of course, cloaks his pragmatic use of literature more effectively, using literature as an escape from disorder without announcing that use. But he and Bloom share this "impure" use of literature. Leopold does use poetry more kinetically—largely because he sees his problems as kinetic problems, not static ones. Stephen's static problems lead him to use literature differently. Each of them discovers that literature cannot in fact provide exact answers.

It is also true that Leopold's first attempts at poetry are much less satisfactory than Stephen's. The poem sent to Molly is drivel. But as in Stephen's villanelle, the major metaphor here is the hymn: Bloom's poem reads, *"Let them hymn it nine times nine"* (*U*, 678); Stephen's villanelle rises in *"one eucharistic hymn"* (*P*, 221).

In *A Portrait*, Stephen contemplates words as "the reflection of the glowing sensible world through the prism of a language manycoloured and richly storied" (*P*, 166–67); in *Ulysses*, Bloom recalls the same image but again with his characteristically different approach to life:

> Because in middle youth he had often sat observing through a rondel of bossed glass of a multicoloured pane the spectacle offered with continual changes of the thoroughfare without, pedestrians, quadrupeds, velocipedes, vehicles, passing slowly. [*U*, 681]

The point is that Bloom then and still prefers the changes of the external and kinetic to those in Stephen's world, where all change is negative because not static.

Stephen and Bloom then exchange what could be called their artistic productions. Bloom presents a sketch for an advertisement that did not work. Stephen, trying to communicate, constructs a scene for Bloom:

> What suggested scene was then constructed by Stephen?
> Solitary hotel in mountain pass. Autumn. Twilight. Fire lit. In dark corner young man seated. Young woman enters. Restless. Solitary. She sits. She goes to window. She stands. She sits. Twilight. She thinks. On solitary hotel paper she writes. She thinks. She writes. She sighs. Wheels and hoofs. She hurries out. He comes from his dark corner. He seizes solitary paper. He holds it toward fire. Twilight. He reads. Solitary.
> What?
> In sloping, upright and backhands: Queen's hotel, Queen's hotel, Queen's Ho. [*U*, 684]

Stephen communicates something to Bloom inadvertently as he chooses the hotel in which Bloom's father committed suicide. It is as though art here communicates without control, because the listener necessarily brings certain emotional and intellectual associations with him. Bloom attributes this to "Coincidence" (*U*, 685). But he finds relief from his own kinetic pain in the scene. Stephen next relates his *Parable of the Plums*, initially introduced in "Aeolus." The response by Bloom is typical of his world view:

> Did he see only a second coincidence in the second scene narrated to him, described by the narrator as *A Pisgah Sight of Palestine* or *The Parable of the Plums?*
> It, with the preceding scene and with others unnarrated but existent by implication, to which add essays on various subjects or moral

apothegms (e.g. *My Favourite Hero* or *Procrastination is the Thief of Time*) . . . seemed to him to contain . . . possibilities of financial, social, personal and sexual success, whether specially collected and selected as model pedagogic themes (of cent per cent merit) for the use of preparatory and junior grade students or contributed in printed form, following the precedent of Philip Beaufoy or Doctor Dick or Heblon's *Studies in Blue,* to a publication of certified circulation and solvency or employed verbally as intellectual stimulation for sympathetic auditors, tacitly appreciative of successful narrative and confidently augurative of successful achievement, during the increasingly longer nights gradually following the summer solstice on the day but three following. [*U,* 685]

Bloom sees artistic success in practical terms: sex, money, fame. Stephen's artistry and his sense of mission as an artist begin, through Bloom's exaggeration of bourgeois attitudes, to look more positive than they do in isolation. That is, so long as we have only Stephen's humorless attitudes about art, he looks impossible. When Joyce juxtaposes them with Bloom's commercial attitudes, the merits and positive values of Stephen's perception come into focus. Bloom is too pedestrian to be the artist; he mirrors Stephen's failings as a mirror reverses the image. One difference between them is the difference between comedy and tragedy. Bloom is a comic figure, even capable of seeing himself as comic. His perceptions of art are more overtly comic than Stephen's partly because Stephen attempts to control the ludicrous side of his theory through exalted language. The truth is somehow in between or, more accurately, the truth contains both.

Stephen still has some things to learn from the older man. Their next topic of conversation is also, from Stephen's point of view, essentially a literary issue: language. In comparing the Hebrew and Irish languages, Stephen and Bloom discover another kind of similarity. The description of the languages, their shared technical attributes, sounds, and visual representations, leads to a comparison of two pieces of literature: an Irish song and *The Song of Songs.* Both are love songs; both contain visions of undying devotion; both contain references to war and armaments. Stephen's song is sung by a girl who has sold her weaving equipment

> . . . to buy my love a sword of steel
> That in battle he might wield
> Johnny's gone for a soldier.
> Oh my darling, oh my love
> Gone the rainbow, gone the dove
> Every tear could turn a mill
> Johnny's gone for a soldier.

In the passages of *Song of Songs,* the male describes his beloved:

Thy lips are like a thread of scarlet,
and thy speech is comely:
thy temples are like a piece of
pomegranate within thy locks.
Thy neck is like the tower of David builded
for an armoury,
whereon there hang a thousand bucklers,
all shields of mighty men.

Initially the passages the two men relate appear to have only superficial resemblances. But each song contains a lament for the separation from the beloved. Bloom doesn't quote those passages because of a "defective mnemotechnic," but he does paraphrase so that we can assume the context of *Song of Songs*.

I opened to my beloved;
but my beloved had withdrawn himself, and was gone:
My soul failed when he spake:
I sought him, but I could not find him;
I called him, but he gave me no answer.
The watchmen that went about the city found me,
they smote me, they wounded me;
the keepers of the walls took my veil from me.
I charge you, O daughters of Jerusalem,
if ye find my beloved, that ye tell him,
that I am sick of love.

Furthermore, Bloom is quoting one of the sources for the Litany of the Blessed Virgin, a liturgical source for Stephen's original symbolic woman. The subject of bereavement and love, central to Bloom's and Stephen's personal dilemmas, is presented in both literary allusions. Stephen and Bloom have found similar themes (themes of course present in much of literature) in two similar languages; the conjunction again suggests the communal and universal relevance, or truths, of literature: human emotion. But it also suggests that we find something shared when and only when we want to.

Stephen's identification of Bloom with Christ in the subsequent passages and with the "accumulation of the past" is matched by Bloom's perception of Stephen as both the "predestination of a future" (note the assertion that one will exist) and as the resolution or catastrophe in the structural sense; these associations suggest once again the importance of Bloom to Stephen and Stephen to Bloom. To the extent that Stephen sees Bloom as the past, he is Stephen's nightmare; to the extent that he sees Bloom as Christ he represents salvation. The juxtaposition of art and this sense of salvation implies that Bloom has delivered a message of artistic import to Stephen. That message, it seems clear, is that art must communicate to someone other than the artist; that is, that it cannot be onanistic, that human emotions in art are the universal and satisfying revelation art offers man, that the banal and common allow communication; and that, finally, communication is a two-way, reciprocal act needing audience as well as author. Art allows a kind of community between Bloom and Stephen. As Bloom represents the "accumulation of the past," he represents not only Stephen's nightmare—something Stephen has felt is idiosyncratic, not shared—but also a hope of breaking out of the isolation that that past falsely represents for Stephen. Bloom, too, benefits from the encounter. What Bloom hears is the possibility of resolution, what he sees is the future. For Bloom, as well as for Stephen, the encounter brings some hope of a future, although the shape and meaning of that future are murky.

Community and commonness and connection with others as they are established through art are revealed, too, in the "Ballad of Little Harry Hughes."[13] In the text that surrounds the ballad, Stephen and Bloom are both "victim predestined" and the victimizer. Stephen is both the murdered child and the secret infidel. Joyce uses verbal art here to dramatize a thesis, something like "we are all one," but less sentimental than that might suggest, for we are all murderers as well as victims. Just as the comparison of the *Song of Songs* and "Suil, suil, suil arun" established shared, emotional experience, common to all peoples, so the commentary here tells us again that art shows our common, not our idiosyncratic nature. This kind of knowledge, a common denominator among men, makes Bloom a father to Stephen—to the extent that he will have a "new" one. However, Joyce's and Bloom's realism denies any literal father-son relationship—a denial that coheres with Joyce's artistic modes. Romance might make the two achieve a mystical state of paternity. In the "real" world of Dublin in 1904, strangers do not discover new fathers; nor do they discover new sons. What they discover is community, limited by the impinging facts and conditions of their society and of their own history.

Bloom's acceptance of his status—a sonless father—coheres with his social pessimism, his fears about social improvement and his own broadly political depression. In "Ithaca" the narrator relates Bloom's experience with a coin that he marked and hoped would return to him (it didn't) and with a clown "in quest of paternity" who claimed Bloom as father. That clown, "an intuitive particoloured clown," is a surrogate for Stephen who lives, like Yeats's Dubliners, where "motley is worn." Then the question, "Why would a recurrent frustration the more depress him?" elicits the answer, "Because at the critical turningpoint of human existence he desired to amend many social conditions, the product of inequality and avarice and international animosity" (*U*, 696). Bloom's frustration about his paternity leads directly to concerns political; his desire for a son is a communal, political desire as well as a personal desire. The next question asks the narrator to supply further information about Bloom's view of man.

> He believed then that human life was infinitely perfectible, eliminating these conditions [inequality, avarice, and international animosity]?
> There remained the generic conditions imposed by natural, as distinct from human law, as integral parts of the human whole: the necessity of destruction to procure alimentary sustenance: the painful character of the ultimate functions of separate existence, the agonies of birth and death: the monotonous menstruation of simian and (particularly) human females . . . inevitable accidents at sea, in mines and factories; certain very painful maladies and their resultant surgical operations, innate lunacy and congenital criminality, decimating epidemics: catastrophic cataclysms which make terror the basis of human mentality: seismic upheavals the epicentres of which are located in densely populated regions: the fact of vital growth, through convulsions of metamorphosis from infancy through maturity to decay. [*U*, 696–97]

Bloom believes that man, as distinct from nature, can be perfected; but he sees man as partly trapped in natural events, evolutionary necessities, and biological facts. The list of these "generic conditions," inevitable and irreparable, is extended so that we can see both its extent and its limitations: war, for instance, is not generic, race hatred is not generic, economic exploitation is not generic. Joyce has created a character who accepts the science of his day and many of its conclusions; "congenital criminality," a notion we might reject today, was not only accepted but unquestioned in 1900. Despite these limits, however, Bloom does, basically, believe in the perfectibility of man, a doctrine we associate with Godwin and the early nineteenth century. Godwin, a writer represented in Eltzbacher's collection, proposes other social improvements that would make sense to Bloom: nonviolent and installment plan revolution. Of course, Bloom would not need to know Godwin's works—the notions were current and the evolutionary theories of optimistic scientists lent support to the hope of evolutionary and continuing betterment of the moral and economic conditions of the race. Indeed, almost all the anarchists in Eltzbacher's book agree on the innate goodness of men, a quality overshadowed by and usurped by mercenary and selfish motives but inherent and waiting for opportunities to realize itself. Bloom, and behind him Joyce, accepts these assumptions. However much Bloom wants the perfect, he accepts less. Stephen has difficulty making that adjustment. Many of Bloom's social and political concerns provide the cultural context for an Irishman's art. And, to judge from Joyce's criticism of Shakespeare, Joyce believed knowing such conditions was critical to understanding an artist's work.

Bloom and Stephen, having established as much difference as similarity, part. Each

affirmed his significance as a conscious rational animal proceeding syllo-
gistically from the known to the unknown and a conscious rational rea-
gent between a micro-and a macrocosm ineluctably constructed upon the
incertitude of the void. [*U*, 697]

Each must go from the known (each other) to the unknown—what
waits for them ineluctably—themselves, ghosts, brothers-in-love . . . to
meet always themselves, the final unknown. As Wilde's remarks about
history suggest, one must know all about others to know himself. To
stay with Bloom would be to revert to onanism (insofar as Bloom and
Stephen are the same) or the oedipal fixation that frustrates creativity
(insofar as Molly and May are equivalent).

Their parting reinforces the Shakespeare motif by the association of
natural phenomena with the birth of Bloom, Stephen, and Shakespeare
(*U*, 700–701). As Stephen and Bloom stand urinating against the garden
wall and watching Molly, Stephen's artistic perception of the world is
parodied. As the Shakespeare motif, the Maeterlinck quotation and
theological consubstantiality have provided an intellectual portrayal of
Stephen's and Bloom's unity, here, as in the use of cocoa instead of
wine, we are presented with unity achieved through the mundane.
Crudely put, mankind is one, not simply because it shares emotion and
intellect, wit and language, but also because all men and women excrete.
We share more than Stephen has been willing to admit.

And the mirror image—the image that united Bloom and Stephen
in "Circe"—is reintroduced:

> Both then were silent?
> Silent, each contemplating the other in both mirrors of the reciprocal
> flesh of theirhisnothis fellowfaces. [*U*, 702]

The sundering is a kind of death. As Stephen departs he hears the Prayer
for the Dying, and Bloom remembers dead friends. But Stephen told us
long ago that creation means a kind of death. The son replaces his father
as soon as that son becomes a father. And in *A Portrait*, Temple informed us that "reproduction is the beginning of death" and wanted to
know if Stephen felt how "profound that is because you are a poet" (*P*,
231). Stephen knew his limitations, then, too:

> When we come to the phenomena of artistic conception, artistic gestation
> and artistic reproduction I require a new terminology and a new personal
> experience. [*P*, 209]

If this death of onanistic self-centeredness has occurred, perhaps Bloom
is the initiating factor. Bloom as Shakespeare's partial surrogate closes
Stephen's involvement in the novel; *A Portrait* ended with Stephen's
new father, Daedalus: *Ulysses* provides the third, and even less literal

father. As Stephen says, to have reconciliation there must be a sundering: the sundering takes place; the reconciliation with the Bloom figure is Stephen's necessary activity if he is to be an artist.

Pater asserted in *Marius the Epicurean* that the idealism of youth and its concomitant narrowness really need "for their correction" "the complementary influence of some greater system, in which they may find their due place" (*M*, 151). Stephen's idealism has been his artistry; the greater system, represented but not encapsulated by Bloom, is humanity and compassion: communal elements of man. For, as Pater wrote,

> that *Sturm und Drang* of the spirit, . . .that ardent and special apprehension of half-truths, in the enthusiastic and as it were "prophetic" advocacy of which, devotion to truth, in the case of the young—apprehending but one point at a time in the great circumference—most usually embodies itself, is levelled down, safely enough, afterwards, as in history so in the individual, by the weakness and mere weariness, as well as by the maturer wisdom, of our nature. [*M*, 151–52]

Stephen's literal weariness and Bloom's other wisdom conspire against the "half-truths" of Stephen's early esthetics.

Marius the Epicurean has, shortly before the end of the novel, a reconciliation with the father, dead many years. Marius returns to his father's grave:

> That hard feeling, again, which had always lingered in his mind with the thought of the father he had scarcely known, melted wholly away, as he read the precise number of his years, and reflected suddenly:—He was of my own present age; nor had [sic] old man, but with interests, as he looked round him on the world for the last time, even as mine to-day! And with that came a blinding rush of kindness, as if two alienated friends had come to understand each other at last. [*M*, 257]

Bloom and Stephen, so "alienated" from each other that much of the novel points out their antithetical qualities, finally understand each other through intellectual, emotional, and physical contact. The reconciliation between the last of the races of Bloom and Stephen is like the reconciliation of Marius and his father: Marius too *"was the last of his race!"* That reconciliation is followed in both cases by references to death; Marius dies, Stephen hears the music for the dying. Bloom sums up this chapter as "atonement" [*U*, 729]

Although it may not seem to be the case, the thoughts of an artist—Molly (Marion) Tweedy Bloom—close *Ulysses*. And those thoughts provide, among other things, Joyce's last dramatic assertion in *Ulysses* that art unites and affirms rather than isolates and denies. Molly's art, like that of an advertiser, must appeal to and communicate with an audience, for she is a performing artist. In one way the narrative of

"Penelope" seems to deny her status as artist because it purports to be an unselected, unshaped rendering of Molly's thoughts. In *A Portrait*, Stephen's mind appeared to shape and select as an artist's might; in some chapters of *Ulysses*, Stephen or Bloom appears to select, thinking about, arranging, and commenting upon the behavior of his mind. So, too, does Joyce present us in this last chapter with a mind that comments upon itself, yet Molly does not really do so consciously. We do not see the craftsman's hand; her mind wanders much more freely than Stephen's or Bloom's. In that she appears to be the least artistic of the three characters. She does, of course, rationalize some of her behavior and notions and censor others, a kind of selectivity. And she is—and knows herself to be—an artist, a performing artist, although her artistic pretensions are much different from Stephen's. For example, Molly contemplates changing the cut of her dress to "arrest" the viewer, hardly a notion of art that would be congenial to Stephen. Yet, although such an idea might lead us to dismiss Molly as as overaged sex object whose singing is merely an effort to attract attention to her, to do so is to denigrate her.

Some of her artistic judgments are, by any standards, aesthetic if low-brow. She remembers, for instance, that Simon Dedalus sang "*sweet*heart" while Bartell D'Arcy sang "sweet *tart*" (*U*, 774), and her complaint that Simon Dedalus "was always turning up half screwed singing the second verse first" (*U*, 774) has nothing to do with her age or her sexual frustrations. These are judgments of a practicing and competent performer. Even if we reject her assertion that she "could have been a prima donna only I married" (*U*, 763), she is still an active performer; whatever doubts we may have about Blazes Boylan's motives for arranging her musical tour, she is still paid for her artistry. It is not Bloom alone who thinks of Molly as a performer. Her credentials exist independent of her thoughts and those of her husband.

In one way, Molly completes an artistic triangle and so suggests something of what Joyce saw as necessary to art. While Bloom focuses on the material of art—careful observation, common decency and charity, imaginative sympathy for others—and Stephen focuses upon the artist—an isolated, traumatized individual whose mind creates private and idiosyncratic symbols—Molly Bloom dramatizes interpretive performance. She translates or mediates between artist and audience. She is a singer; she starts with the text given to her by another artist and interprets it, giving it meaning that on the sheet of music it may or may not have. She is an example of a creative reader, the reader who participates in the creation of a work of art. As she sings old and new songs, secular love songs and religious music, she acts or serves as the vehicle uniting the original artist and his audience. Perhaps calling her a vehicle limits too drastically her role as creator. The vehicle changes the original as D'Arcy's habit of singing "sweet *tart*" and Simon's drunken reversal of stanzas can attest. In a way, she changes or remakes art, shaping it to fit her needs and using all methods of communication, including the voluptuousness of her body, to entice and arrest the viewer. Molly, in that way, participates in artistic creation; she imagines, too, that she might share in Stephen's art: "they all write about some woman in their poetry well I suppose he wont find many like me" (*U*, 775).

The connection that Molly draws between herself and Stephen's art, that she might be his muse, throws light on Stephen's and Joyce's sense of the muse. Had we needed any further indication of Joyce's ambivalence about that figure, Molly provides it. To translate Stephen's original, virginal temptress/muse into Molly Bloom is to parody that conception as well as to reaffirm it in ironic ways. Molly is, in some ways, a muse. Because we as readers focus upon Stephen and Bloom throughout June 16, 1904, Molly's artistry—the ways she shapes and controls life—is perhaps the method of a muse. However shadowy she may seem for most of *Ulysses*, we feel her presence because so much of Bloom's life is focused on his wife. His vision of her "inspires" much of his activity. Imaginatively, too, Molly functions as the dramatic figure of an adultress and mother, mimicking or parodying Stephen's cogitations about his mother and Ann Hathaway Shakespeare. And she has inspired in the past one of Bloom's poetic efforts, just as she inspires Bloom's prose poem about their courtship on Howth. In these ways, she is the necessary countersign, the inspirational figure of the novel.

At the same time, Molly ironically parallels Stephen's behavior when she thinks of herself as muse. Just as Stephen has never permitted his muse figures any independent existence, or demanded from them any response, so Molly, with very little information and no contemporary experience with Stephen, and without his knowledge, transmutes herself into his muse. The irony is multiple. First, her fiction depends upon Stephen's passivity, just as his created muses must be passive in the relationship. Second, she, unlike Stephen, calculates mundane and earthy elements of the fantasy relationship; she calculates his age to see if she is too old for him. Most striking, she does not imagine a spiritual, platonic relationship filled with sexual imagery. Her fantasy affirms and manifests the latent sexuality of Stephen's visionary experiences. Third, she demonstrates that Stephen's habits of mind are not those specifically or uniquely of an artist. When Stephen has taken mundane and limited information and used it to produce images that satisfy his imagination, we have labeled him an artist. But here, at the tail end of *Ulysses*, a much more obviously "ordinary" human being does the same thing. We as readers know that Stephen hates baths and does not swim; Molly fantasizes that Stephen might be like "those fine young men I could see down in Margate strand bathing . . . standing up in the sun naked like a God" (*U*, 775). We have, again, a muse totally disconnected from the artist. All muses in Joyce's work seem to appear only in such situations of disconnection, passivity, and nonresponsiveness. And yet, these women do inspire men to kinds of creativity. Joyce's attitude is not clear-cut; the ironic parallels again suggest the limits of Stephen Dedalus.

Molly's behavior reaffirms, too, some of the values of art that Joyce dramatized in his novel. Art, in "Circe," "Eumaeus," and "Ithaca," unites all men through what they share—of psychological experience, of emotions, of identity finally; Molly's interior monologue and in consequence her mind unite all men grammatically. It is not a new point here: the pronouns *he, him,* and *his* cease to have direct and unambiguous referents on the last page of the novel as Molly's past and present men are transmuted into a single *he:*

> . . . Gibraltar as a girl where I was a Flower of the mountain yes when I put the rose in my hair like the Andalusian girls used or shall I wear a red yes and how he kissed me under the Moorish wall and I thought well as well him as another and then I asked him with my eyes to ask again yes and then he asked me would I yes to say yes my mountain flower and first I put my arms around him yes and drew him down to me so he could feel my breasts all perfume yes and his heart was going like mad and yes I said yes I will Yes. [*U, 783*]

We have seen such ambiguity before. In "Ithaca," Bloom and Stephen shared roles in "The Ballad of Little Harry Hughes"; later when they part Joyce reiterates that confusion and synthesis as each contemplates "the other in both mirrors of the reciprocal flesh of theirhisnothis fellowfaces" (*U,* 702). Molly's referents, however, move the union beyond Stephen and Bloom to all the men she has known, even if, as I would argue, the primary reference of the last *he* and *his* is Leopold Bloom. While Molly frequently distinguishes among men, she ends not doing it. There is, of course, a denigration of men in Molly's behavior, a denigration that Joyce dramatized in her: she supposes that all men are merely interested in sexuality—and their own pleasures—a supposition that inspires much of Molly's behavior. Molly, ironically, both takes men very seriously, focusing most of her emotional energies on them in this first and last direct vision of her, and mocks their pretensions, thinking of them as fools and children. Her comment about their responses to injury—"if his nose bleeds youd think it was O tragic" (*U,* 738)—is but one symptom of that pervasive attitude. She contemplates the men she has known who have ideas—"as for them saying theres no God I wouldnt give a snap of my two fingers for all their learning why dont they go and create something" (*U,* 782)—and dismisses them. Cranly, in *A Portrait,* had made much the same kind of dismissal. He claimed that "every jackass going down the road thinks he has ideas" (*P,* 242). He made the comment in the process of defending and exalting women because of their certain love of their children. As I have pointed out before, that was Joyce's position, too; it is a position that Molly seems to reassert about women: "they [men] wouldn't be in the world at all only for us they dont know what it is to be a woman and a mother how could they" (*U,* 778). Molly, the Aesthete Stephen, and Joyce seem to associate creativity with women. Molly and Joyce denigrate men and glorify them, ambivalently.

The ultimate parody, ambivalent in meaning, of Stephen's artistic credos is Molly's final affirmation, her sexual affirmation, her annunciation of the word known to all men, "yes I will Yes" (*U,* 783). Joyce claimed that " 'the book must end with yes. It must end with the most positive word in the human language.' "[14] To determine what Molly affirms with her *yes* or to whom she responds *yes* is virtually impossible. The word is not esoteric, but common; it does not announce in context or by itself divinity but rather ordinariness. *Yes,* like Molly Bloom, is quite ordinary. It affirms the past, as it responds to Molly and Bloom's courtship; it affirms the future, "I *will.*" If it affirms all of Molly's interior monologue, it affirms the contradictions, the pettiness, the sorrows of life as well as the triumphs and positive, sexual reveries. Perhaps that is the point: Molly affirms difference, contradiction. She affirms Leopold Bloom but also Stephen Dedalus.

That is part of my point about Joyce's aesthetics. He seems ambivalently to affirm modes of art and human personalities that cohere with particular modes of art that are contradictory. He seems to say "yes" to realist and to symbolist art as Molly seems to say "yes" to all of her men. She and Joyce affirm inclusively rather than exclusively. Molly, neither a traumatized, idiosyncratic, isolated artist, nor an adman, produces the word, the " 'most positive word in the human language.' " *Yes* is of a certainty Molly's—and Joyce's—final word in the novel.

Notes

1. Various critics now see some kind of dysfunction in Stephen, many describe it as oedipal. See, as instance, Mark Shechner, *Joyce in Nighttown* (Berkeley, Calif.: University of California Press, 1974) and Ruth Von Phul's essay "Circling the Square: A Study of Structure," *James Joyce Miscellany,* ed. Marvin Magalaner (Carbondale, Ill.: Southern Illinois University Press, 1962), pp. 242–44.

2. Many critics have commented upon Joyce's portrayal of women. Robert Martin Adams in *Surface and Symbol: The Consistency of James Joyce's "Ulysses"* (New York: Oxford University Press, 1962) presents one of the earliest and, I think, fairest discussions of the ways in which Joyce's own ambiguity interferes with the realistic characterization of women in his books (pp. 35–43). Stephen's tripartite woman (whore-temptress-virgin) appears in all of Joyce's work; see Zack Bowen's "Goldenhair: Joyce's Archetypal Female," *Literature and Psychology* 17 (1967): 219–28.

3. Zack Bowen, *Musical Allusions in the Works of James Joyce: Early Poetry through "Ulysses"* (Albany, N.Y.: State University of New York Press, 1974), pp. 89–91, 295.

4. See Pater passage, quoted in chapter 6.

5. Oscar Wilde, "Harlot's House," *The Complete Works,* 12 vols. (Garden City, N.Y.: Doubleday, Page & Co., 1923), 1:329–31; "The Ballad of Reading Gaol," *The Complete Works,*

1:249–83.

6. Wilde, "The Sphinx," *The Complete Works*, 1:285–306.

7. Weldon Thornton, *Allusions in "Ulysses"* (Chapel Hill, N.C.: University of North Carolina Press, 1968), p. 416.

8. See discussion, chapter 6.

9. See discussion, chapter 5.

10. Thornton, *Allusions*, suggests that Joyce may have intended to allude directly to the law under which Wilde was tried, but copied Arabic number 11 as Roman II (pp. 447–48).

11. See discussion, chapter 3.

12. See discussion, chapter 7.

13. I am indebted in this discussion to Bowen's *Musical Allusions*, pp. 323–28.

14. Richard Ellmann, *James Joyce* (New York: Oxford University Press, 1959), p. 536.

Conclusion

Through the juxtaposition of Stephen and Bloom, Joyce sketched how he differed from realists and naturalists as well as his attraction to them. When Leopold Bloom seems to suggest that Stephen should write for newspapers, or should allow himself to be hired to do occasional pieces for money, Joyce's biography indicates he parted company from Bloom. Yeats made clear efforts to get Joyce jobs reviewing and writing for periodicals; these efforts largely failed. Although Joyce did do some reviewing, he did it in such a way as to choke off any more requests. Most spectacularly, instead of praising Lady Augusta Gregory's work, he condemned it (as Mulligan taunts Stephen for doing in *Ulysses* [*U*, 216]).[1] Perhaps that was simply intellectual honesty on Joyce's part; but the effect of that review must have been to dry up further requests initiated by Yeats or his circle. We know, too, that Yeats tried to provide Joyce with entrés in London. Whether Joyce could not or would not produce the quantity of periodical writing that Yeats produced is not important; what is important is that Joyce did not—and the biographical fact counters Bloom's suggestion. At the same time, Joyce *worked* as a writer as A. Walton Litz's *The Art of James Joyce*[2] made clear long ago. He did not wait for some supernatural inspiration; he did not write as Stephen writes his villanelle in a sudden state of trance. He was willing, according to Frank Budgen, to trust to his luck.[3] But as the notebooks and his letters make clear, much of his writing was deliberate and time-consuming. When Bloom associates art with work, Joyce may applaud some of that association.

Perhaps the figure of Shem in *Finnegans Wake* can indicate as clearly as any other single piece of evidence Joyce's continued ambivalence about aesthetic modes. In that last work, Joyce both celebrated and mocked the Aesthete through Shem, who uses excrement for ink and his body for "foolscap" in an alchemical transmutation of himself into art. Shem is described as the "first till last alshemist" who reflects "from his own individual person life unlivable, transaccidentated through the slow fires of consciousness into a dividual chaos" (*FW*, 185–86). In that passage, Joyce associated Shem with Wilde through an allusion to Dorian Gray. The "alshemist" is at once an alchemist, a sham, a shaman; he is all things, ultimately good and ultimately bad. He is Shem. Certainly, the idea that the man who wrote *Finnegans Wake* was, finally, simply a naturalist is untenable. But equally, this final figure of an Aesthete artist reminds us that he was not simply an Aesthete either.

Indeed, it is well to hold in memory the ties in Joyce's portrayals that bind Stephen and Bloom, and so, indirectly, the Aesthetes and naturalists. Both characters are finally crippled sexually, finding it difficult to connect with women, although Bloom, as I have argued, is much closer to his women than Stephen. Both engage in kinds of onanistic behavior. Both wish to use the power of words to communicate with an audience; both play with words—sometimes wittily. Both believe that they must arrest the minds of their readers and that good communication operates simultaneously on several levels.

Above all, we can see in Joyce's novels the conjunction of Aestheticism and naturalism. On the one hand, Joyce's novels are intensely realistic in detail; one could reconstruct much of Dublin in 1904, as Joyce claimed, from *Ulysses*. As H. G. Wells remarked in a review of *Portrait* (reprinted in the Viking Critical edition), *Portrait* presents a "quintessential and unfailing reality. One believes in Stephen Dedalus as one believes in few characters in fiction." The novel presents a "convincing revelation . . . of the limitations of a great mass of Irishmen" (*P*, 331). Wells spends some time in that review analyzing, as a social evolutionist or naturalist would, how Stephen's environment would produce a blind and indiscriminate hatred of England. If Wells erred in seeing the novel as exclusively realistic or naturalistic, he was probably not alone in such an error. Still earlier in his career, Joyce himself pointed to the realistic nature of his work when he defended *Dubliners* to Grant Richards. In that perhaps self-serving defense, he sounded much like G. B. Shaw: he claimed that *Dubliners* might help improve the spiritual condition of his morally paralyzed land. Shaw had written of the necessity of the artist to improve "character," "conduct," "justice," and "sympathy."[4] This kind of realism came from Joyce's close observation of life in Ireland. The complaint voiced by Vivian in Oscar Wilde's dialogue that realists wrote "Blue-Books," drawing only from their own and their family's lives and from their reading, is paradoxically true of almost all of Joyce's writing; what is not true is that this drawing on his own resources produced, as Vivian claimed it would, dull or boring literature.

The plots and motives in Joyce's novels, too, provide evidence of Joyce's continued realism and naturalism. Much of the causal analysis of people's lives implicit in the plots of *Dubliners*, *Portrait*, and *Ulysses* is influenced by, as naturalism was, the relatively new field of sociology. So, for instance, not only Leopold Bloom but also Joyce seemed to believe that the ways men and women behave are caused in part by environment. As a small example, the dusty environment of Eveline causes while at the same time it is a symptom of her final entrapment; she is stuck in Dublin because Dublin has produced her. Or, as another example, Stephen chooses to be "a priest of eternal imagination" as much because of his political, familial, and religious environment as because of the aesthetic drive implied by that phrase. Joyce's attention to detail, long documented by critics, is matched by his sense of motives. Unlike the motives of the protagonists in Wilde's and Pater's novels, what causes Stephen or Bloom to behave as he does is public and discernible as well as private and hidden. Even, in an odd way, Joyce's use of interior monologue to reveal in the prose of his novels the inner workings of a character's mind and his hatred of the use of quotation marks to indicate conversation were attempts at realism.

Thematically and personally, Joyce found attractive the political and social views of Leopold Bloom although he did not share them entirely. Hugh Kenner has reminded us, in *Joyce's Voices*, that "Bloom holds very much the opinions of James Joyce on a wide range of Dublin topics: on Irish nationalism, on drunkenness, on literary pretensions, on death and resurrection, on marriage, on the hierarchy of values."⁵ Joyce entirely shared Bloom's allegiance to family, an allegiance that Stephen attempts unsuccessfully to escape (as Joyce had as a young man). Joyce's poem for his grandson and father, written late in his life, illustrates the continuing concern he had for family; so too does his at times distraught concern for his daughter, his continued attachment to Nora, and the plot and characters of *Finnegans Wake*, in some ways "simply" the story of a family. In all these and other ways, then, Joyce was and remained like his fictional naturalist, L. Bloom, adman.

On the other hand, no one can claim that Joyce ever fled utterly from the sudden insights or alchemical moments of the Aesthetes. He created and used private symbolism, esoteric and difficult of access. In truth, the entire Joyce industry runs on such a fuel. We spend hours and pages trying to understand the precise nature of his words and language, of his symbolism, and of his personal, private vision; at times Joyce announced that such an expenditure of time and effort was meet and right. While Joyce never sought to write Mallarmé's perfect poem, a blank sheet of paper, he was far from trying to write the potboilers of melodrama or dime novels, either. And, as I suggested in chapter 5, Joyce's relationship to Stephen and Stephen's ideas is not simple; we know that some of Stephen's loyalties Joyce shared.

The tentative nature of Bloom's and Stephen's rapprochement, so tentative that one can only say that Stephen *needs* to be reconciled with Bloom if he is going to be an artist rather than assert that some reconciliation has turned him into an artist—that tentativeness dramatizes Joyce's continued ambivalence and lack of resolution. To say that is not to condemn Joyce for his inability to reconcile; it is to point out the extreme difficulty he faced. The messages of advertising, for all their clarity, like the messages of Spencer's *The Study of Sociology,* are simple or, perhaps, even simplistic. The messages of alchemy are isolationist and sterile. To write at all means to forsake some magical properties, some sense of uniqueness, and to move into time and into a relationship with others. Yet to convey one's private vision, as a writer must, is to attempt to move the reader beyond himself into the unknown—and that unknown, for Joyce, was complicated, not simple, private and yet public, but not simply public.

If we turn back to one of the forefathers of English Aestheticism, we may see a radical difficulty that beset Joyce and the high moderns. Walter Pater told his disciples that "no real voice has ever pierced" its way to the individual—nor has the individual ever managed to get his voice out accurately to another. Man, in a solitary prison of his own mind, can only *attempt* communication. This view was not unique to Pater—it was confirmed by other writers and by philosophers. It explains some of the moderns' interest in narrative point of view. Nineteenth-century science believed otherwise. Naturalists, like their brethren the scientists and social scientists, believed in the publicness of proofs and investigations. Joyce's documented attraction to science may owe something to those qualities. Shaw, and the early Sean O'Casey, and other naturalists believed that they could share their ideas publicly and persuasively. Instilled with notions of the relativity of perception, Joyce may have intuitively felt that even Zola's doctor and Shaw's scribe were irreconcilably separate from their audiences: that perception of ultimate separateness contains a measure of truth.

If we believe that perception of separateness to be the whole truth, we cannot write. If we believed it wholly, we would be paralyzed as writers, for writing—at least publishing—presupposes an audience that is united to us in some ways, a group with whom we share enough that we can communicate. If we were simply separate, no one could read these words with any measure of comprehension. External and shared reality, whether it exists philosophically or not, exists as we operate in this world. Realistic, observable, verifiable detail and plausible plot help bridge that separation, even if they do not close it utterly. And words, although limited and ambiguous, and perhaps ultimately private, are approximations of those truths we can share. Joyce's allegiance to the *word,* then, is inevitable. "Words alone are certain good," wrote W. B. Yeats in "The Song of the Happy Shepherd." In that poem, the line and its value as truth are ambiguous. Realizing that ambiguity, Joyce still seemed to have something of that *credo:* "Words alone are certain good." For words alone allow the writer to communicate at all with his audience.

Notes

1. Richard Ellmann, *Eminent Domain: Yeats among Wilde, Joyce, Pound, Eliot, and Auden* (New York: Oxford University Press, 1965), pp. 41–42.

2. A. Walton Litz, *The Art of James Joyce: Method and Design in "Ulysses" and "Finnegans Wake"* (London: Oxford University Press, 1961).

3. Frank Budgen, *James Joyce and the Making of "Ulysses"* (Bloomington, Ind.: Indiana University Press, 1934), pp. 171–72.

4. G. B. Shaw, "The Sanity of Art," *Major Critical Essays* (London: Constable, 1932), p. 315.

5. Hugh Kenner, *Joyce's Voices* (Berkeley, Calif.: University of California Press, 1978), p. 23.

Works Cited

Adams, Robert Martin. *Surface and Symbol: The Consistency of James Joyce's "Ulysses."* New York: Oxford University Press, 1962.

Anderson, Chester. "On the Sublime and its Anal-Urethal Sources in Pope, Eliot, and Joyce." In *Modern Irish Literature: Essays in Honor of William York Tindall,* edited by Raymond J. Porter and James D. Brophy. New York: Iona College Press and Twayne Press, 1972.

———. "The Sacrificial Butter." *Accent* 12 (1952): 3–13.

Appleman, Philip, ed. *Darwin.* New York: W. W. Norton & Co., 1970.

Arnold, Matthew. *Selected Essays.* Edited by P. J. Keating. Suffolk: Penguin, 1970.

Beckson, Karl. "A Mythology of Aestheticism." *English Literature in Transition* 17 (1974): 233–49.

Benstock, Bernard. "The Temptation of St. Stephen: A View of the Villanelle." *James Joyce Quarterly* 14 (Fall 1976): 31–38.

Bowen, Zack. "Goldenhair: Joyce's Archetypal Female." *Literature and Psychology* 17 (1967): 219–28.

———. *Musical Allusions in the Works of James Joyce: Early Poetry through "Ulysses."* Albany, N.Y.: State University of New York Press, 1974.

Bredin, Hughes T. "Applied Aquinas: James Joyce's Aesthetics." *Éire-Ireland* 3 (1968): 61–78.

Brivic, Sheldon. "James Joyce: From Stephen to Bloom." In *Psychoanalysis and Literary Process,* edited by Frederick C. Crews. Cambridge, Mass.: Winthrop Press, 1970.

Brown, Homer Obed. *James Joyce's Early Fiction: The Biography of a Form.* Cleveland, Ohio: Case Western Press, 1972.

Budgen, Frank. *James Joyce and The Making of "Ulysses."* Bloomington, Ind.: Indiana University Press, 1934.

Chayes, Irene Hendry. "Joyce's Epiphanies." *Sewanee Review* 54 (July 1946): 449–67.

Cixous, Hélène. *The Exile of James Joyce.* Translated by Sally A. J. Purcell. New York: David Lewis, 1972.

Connolly, Thomas E. "Swinburne and the Music of Poetry." *PMLA* 72 (1957): 680–88.

DeLaura, David J. "Pater and Newman: The Road to the 'Nineties." *Victorian Studies* 10 (1966): 39–69.

Dougherty, Charles T. "Joyce and Ruskin." *Notes and Queries* 198 (1953): 76–77.

Dowson, Ernest. *The Poems of Ernest Dowson.* Edited by Mark Longaker. Philadelphia: University of Pennsylvania Press, 1962.

Dundes, Alan. "Re: Joyce—No In at the Womb." *Modern Fiction Studies* 8 (1962): 137–47.

Ellmann, Richard, ed. *Edwardians and Late Victorians.* English Institute Essays 1959. New York: Columbia University Press, 1960.

Ellmann, Richard. *Eminent Domain: Yeats among Wilde, Joyce, Pound, Eliot, and Auden.* New York: Oxford University Press, 1965.

———. *James Joyce.* New York: Oxford University Press, 1959.

———. *The Consciousness of James Joyce.* Toronto: Oxford University Press, 1977.

Eltzbacher, Paul. *Anarchism: Exponents of the Anarchist Philosophy.* Edited by James J. Martin. Translated by Stephen Byington. New York: Chips, n.d.

Epstein, Edmund L. "Cruxes in *Ulysses:* Notes Toward an Edition and Annotation." *James Joyce Review* 1 (1957): 25–36.

Feshbach, Sidney. "A Dramatic First Step: A Source of Joyce's Interest in the Idea of Daedalus." *James Joyce Quarterly* 8 (1971): 197–204.

Flaubert, Gustave. *Oeuvres Complète de Gustave Flaubert.* 21 vols. Paris: L. Conard, 1923–54.

———. *The Letters of Gustave Flaubert, 1830–1887.* Edited by Francis Steegmuller. Cambridge, Mass.: Belknap Press of Harvard University Press, 1980.

Geckle, George L. "Stephen Dedalus and W. B. Yeats: The Making of the Villanelle." *Modern Fiction Studies* 15 (1969): 87–96.

———. "Stephen Dedalus as Lapwing: A Symbolic Center of *Ulysses.*" *James Joyce Quarterly* 6 (1968): 104–14.

Grayson, Thomas. "James Joyce and Stephen Dedalus: The Theory of Aesthetics." *James Joyce Quarterly* 4 (Summer 1967): 310–19.

Hafley, James. "Walter Pater's *Marius* and the Technique of Modern Fiction." *Modern Fiction Studies* 3 (1957): 99–109.

Hagopian, John V. "Literary Criticism as a Science." *Topic: A Journal of the Liberal Arts* 12 (Fall 1966): 50–57.

Henke, Suzette. *Joyce's Moraculous Sindbook: A Study of "Ulysses."* Columbus, Ohio: Ohio State University Press, 1978.

Joyce and Modern Psychology. James Joyce Quarterly 13 (Spring 1976): 266–386.

Joyce, James. *A Portrait of the Artist as a Young Man.* New York: Viking Press, 1968.

———. *Critical Writings of James Joyce.* New York: Viking Press, 1959.

———. *Finnegans Wake.* New York: Viking Press, 1957.

———. *Letters of James Joyce.* 3 vols. Edited by Stuart Gilbert (vol. 1) and Richard Ellmann (vols. 2 & 3). New York: Viking Press, 1966.

———. *Selected Letters of James Joyce.* Edited by Richard Ellmann. New York: Viking Press, 1975.

———. *Ulysses.* New York: Random House, 1961.

Joyce, Stanislaus. *My Brother's Keeper: James Joyce's Early Years.* New York: Viking Press, 1958.

———. *The Complete Dublin Diary.* Edited by George H. Healy. Ithaca, N.Y., and London: Cornell University Press, 1971.

Jung, Carl. *The Spirit in Man, Art, and Literature,* vol. 15. *Collected Works,* edited by Sir Herbert Read et al. 20 vols. Princeton, N.J.: Bollingen Series 20, Princeton University Press, 1966.

Kenner, Hugh. *Dublin's Joyce.* Bloomington, Ind.: Indiana University Press, 1956.

———. *Joyce's Voices.* Berkeley, Calif.: University of California Press, 1978.

———. *The Pound Era.* Berkeley, Calif.: University of California Press, 1971.

Krause, David. *Sean O'Casey: The Man and His Work.* New York: The Macmillan Co., 1975.

Litz, A. Walton. *The Art of James Joyce: Method and Design in "Ulysses" and "Finnegans Wake."* London: Oxford University Press, 1961.

Loss, Archie. "The Pre-Raphaelite Woman, the Symbolist *Femme-Enfant,* and the Girl with the Flowing Hair in the Earlier Work of James Joyce." *Journal of Modern Literature* 3 (1973): 3–23.

Lukács, Georg. *The Meaning of Contemporary Realism.* Translated by John and Necke Mander. London: Merlin Press, 1962.

Mauron, Charles. "L'Inconscient dans l'oeuvre et la vie de Racine." *Annales de la Faculté des Lettres d'Aix-en-Provence.* 1957.

———. *Introduction to the Psychoanalysis of Mallarmé.* Translated by Archibald Henderson, Jr., and Will L. McLendon. Berkeley, Calif.: University of California Press, 1963.

McCarroll, David L. "Stephen's Dream—and Bloom's." *James Joyce Quarterly* 6 (1969): 174–76.

Morris, William. *Collected Works.* Edited by May Morris. 24 vols. London: Longmans, 1910–1915.

———. *William Morris, Artist, Writer, Socialist.* Edited by May Morris. London: Blackwell, 1936.

Morse, J. Mitchell. "The Unobtrusive Rhetoric of *Ulysses.*" *James Joyce Quarterly* 13 (Winter 1976): 202–7.

Naremore, James. "Style as Meaning in *A Portrait of the Artist.*" *James Joyce Quarterly* 4 (1967): 331–42.

Nelson, James G. "Aesthetic Experience and Rossetti's 'My Sister's Sleep.'" *Victorian Poetry* 7 (1969): 154–58.

Newman, John Henry. *The Idea of a University.* Edited by I. T. Ker. Oxford: Clarendon Press, 1976.

Norman, Edward. *A History of Modern Ireland.* Coral Gables, Fla.: University of Miami Press, 1971.

Pater, Walter Horatio. *Appreciations.* London: Macmillan and Co., 1910.

———. *Greek Studies: A Series of Essays.* London: Macmillan and Co., 1910.

———. *Marius the Epicurean.* London: Dent, 1934.

———. *Studies in the History of the Renaissance.* London: Macmillan and Co., 1910.

Peake, C. H. *James Joyce: The Citizen and the Artist.* London: Edward Arnold Ltd., 1977.

Quillian, William H. "Shakespeare in Trieste: Joyce's 1912 *Hamlet* Lectures." *James Joyce Quarterly* 12 (1974–75): 7–63.

Robinson, K. E. "The Stream of Consciousness Technique and the Structure of Joyce's *Portrait.*" *James Joyce Quarterly* 9 (1971): 63–84.

Rossetti, Dante Gabriel. *The Works of Dante Gabriel Rossetti.* Edited with Preface and Notes by Michael William Rossetti. London: Ellis, 1911; reprint edition, New York: Adler's Foreign Books, Inc., 1977.

Rossman, Charles. "Stephen Dedalus's Villanelle." *James Joyce Quarterly* 12 (1975): 281–293.

San Juan, Epifanio. *The Art of Oscar Wilde.* Princeton, N.J.: Princeton University Press, 1967.

Scholes, Robert, and Kain, Richard M., eds. *The Workshop of Daedalus: James Joyce and the Raw Materials for "A Portrait of the Artist as a Young Man."* Evanston, Ill.: Northwestern University Press, 1965.

Scholes, Robert. "Stephen Dedalus: Poet or Esthete?" *PMLA* 79 (1964): 484–89.

Schutte, William M. *Joyce and Shakespeare: A Study in the Meaning of "Ulysses."* New Haven, Conn.: Yale University Press, 1957.

Scotto, Robert M. " 'Visions' and 'Epiphanies': Fictional Technique in Pater's *Marius* and Joyce's *Portrait.*" *James Joyce Quarterly* 11 (1973): 41–50.

Shapiro, Harold I. "Ruskin and Joyce's *Portrait.*" *James Joyce Quarterly* 14 (1977): 92–93.

Shaw, George Bernard. *Collected Plays with their Prefaces.* London: The Bodley Head Ltd., 1972.

———. *Major Critical Essays.* London: Constable and Co., 1932.

Shechner, Mark. *Joyce in Nighttown.* Berkeley, Calif.: University of California Press, 1974.

Shields, Frederic. "Some Notes on Dante Gabriel Rossetti." *The Century Guild Hobby Horse* 1 (1886): 144.

Spencer, Herbert. *The Study of Sociology.* London: H. S. King, 1873.

Staley, Thomas, ed. *"Ulysses": Fifty Years.* Bloomington, Ind.: Indiana University Press, 1974.

Storch, R. F. "The Fugitive from the Ancestral Hearth: Tennyson's 'Ulysses.'" *Texas Studies in Language and Literature* 13 (1971): 281–97.

Swinburne, Algernon Charles. *The Complete Works of Algernon Charles Swinburne.* Edited by Sir Edmund Gosse, C. B. and Thomas James Wise. 20 vols. London: W. Heinemann Ltd., 1925–1937.

Symons, Arthur. "The Decadent Movement in Literature." *Harpers New Monthly Magazine* 87 (November 1893): 858–67.

———. *The Symbolist Movement in Literature.* London: W. Heinemann Ltd., 1899.

Temple, Ruth Zabriskie. *The Critics Alchemy: A Study of the Introduction of French Symbolism into England.* New York: Twayne, 1953.

Thompson, E. P. *William Morris: Romantic to Revolutionary.* London: W. Heinemann Ltd., 1967.

Thornton, Weldon. *Allusions in "Ulysses."* Chapel Hill, N.C.: University of North Carolina Press, 1968.

Tennyson, Alfred. *The Poems of Tennyson.* Edited by Christopher Ricks. London: Longmans, 1969.

Van Ghent, Dorothy. *The English Novel.* New York: Rhinehart, 1953.

Von Phul, Ruth. "Circling the Square: A Study of Structure." In *A James Joyce Miscellany,* edited by Mark Magalaner. Carbondale, Ill.: Southern Illinois University Press, 1962.

Wells, H. G. *Experiment in Autobiography: Discoveries and Conclusions of a Very Ordinary Brain [Since 1866].* New York: The Macmillan Co., 1934.

Wilde, Oscar. *The Complete Works.* 12 vols. Garden City, N.Y.: Doubleday, Page & Co., 1923.

Woolf, Virginia. *The Death of the Moth.* New York: Harcourt, Brace, Jovanovich, 1942.

Yeats, W. B. *Autobiography.* New York: The Macmillan Co., Collier Books, 1965.

———. *Collected Poems.* New York: The Macmillan Co., 1939.

———. *Essays and Introductions.* New York: The Macmillan Co., Collier Books, 1959.

———. *Mythologies.* New York: The Macmillan Co., Collier Books, 1969.

———. *Uncollected Prose of W. B. Yeats.* Edited by John P. Frayne and Colton Johnson. 2 vols. New York: Columbia University Press, 1970, 1976.

Zola, Émile. *The Experimental Novel and Other Essays.* Translated by Belle M. Sherman. New York: Haskell House, 1964.

Index

Aestheticism: Bloom's response to, 183; Daedalus in, 43; doctrine of experience in, 85–86, 90, 91–92; failures implicit in, 76, 79–80, 90–93; images of women in, 35, 37–38, 61–68, 116–18, 156–57; isolation of artist in, 39–40, 79–80, 82–87, 110–11, 163, 178, 184, 185; maturity of, 14, 15, 44, 59, 69; metaphors of artist in, 13, 15, 32–44, 52, 72, 98–100, 141; political consonants of, 101–3, 106–11; psychological motives of, 24, 29, 41–42, 48–49, 51–52, 56–60, 70–71, 74–75, 83–84, 89, 102, 141–42, 144, 145–47; rejection of old language systems in, 36, 54–56, 77 n.9; relationship to time and history, 14, 49, 55–56, 83–84; religion in, 33–35, 37, 51, 101; response to natural world in, 19–20, 35, 51–52, 86–87, 108; response to realism in, 11, 19; response to science in, 47–48, 49–51, 149; rhythm, theories of, 56–60, 73; separation from life of, 46, 48–49, 51; sexuality in, 150, 177, 181, 183, 190; Shakespeare in, 140–44, 148–49; transmutation, as image of the artist's work, 11, 29, 35, 36, 46–47, 48, 49–51, 69–79, 84; villanelle, as typical of, 68, 70 (see also Words)
Arnold, Matthew, 32

Beckson, Karl, 32
Benstock, Bernard, 70–71
Bloom, Leopold: and Aestheticism, 183; on art, 164, 186, 188–89, 190; as artist, 159–65, 186–87, 195; as consubstantial with Stephen, 185–86, 192; and dreams, 147–48, 175; as Gerty misperceives, 156–58; and paternity, 190–91; as patriot, 165–66, 168; as political being, 111–12, 113–14, 159, 165–69, 191; as realist, 158–59, 163, 181, 183; and science, 149, 158, 167, 183, 191; as timebound, 119, 137–38, 158–59, 191;

and women, 115, 118, 162–63. *See also* Bloom and Stephen
Bloom and Stephen: antithetical personalities of, 145, 147, 155–59; beach scenes of, 155–59; cocoa drinking, 186; compared, 170, 186–90; consubstantiality, 185–86, 192; dreams of, 147–48, 175; epiphanies of, 161; history, attitudes about, 158–59; language, discussion of, 188; literary interests of, 164, 186; "Little Harry Hughes," discussion of, 190; nationalism, attitudes about, 165–66; rapprochement between, 183–84; Shakespeare, attitudes about, 192; songs, discussion of, 188–89; writers, 159–63, 186–87
Bloom, Molly, 118, 193–97
Bowen, Zack R., 72, 190
Bredin, Hughes T., 139
Brown, Homer Obed, 104–5
Budgen, Frank, 94, 120, 123 n.30, 155
Byron, George N. Gordon, 30, 31

Connolly, Thomas E., 36

Daedalus: in Aestheticism, 43; as associated with Stephen's failure, 43–44, 79, 139, 181, 182; as displaced by Mulligan's "The Ballad of Joking Jesus," 124, 134–35; as image of the artist, 23; as image of escape and imprisonment, 42–43, 119–20; as Joyce's commentary on Stephen, 23–24, 43–44; as "new" father, 32, 42, 43–44, 82, 119–20, 175; in Pater's *Greek Studies*, 43, 45 n.19; as Stephen's creation, 23–24, 42–43
Dowson, Ernest, 65–66, 79–80
Dundes, Alan, 154 n.16

Ellmann, Richard: *The Consciousness of James Joyce*, 111, 113, 114; *Eminent Domain*, 12, 14–15; *James Joyce*, 155